SON OF THE SUN

THE SECRET OF THE SAUCERS

Original Art by Carol Ann Rodriguez

TWO BOOKS IN ONE!

THE SECRET OF THE SAUCERS
SON OF THE SUN
by Orfeo M. Angelucci
Original was Edited by Ray Palmer
This edition Copyright 2008 by Global Communications/Conspiracy Journal

Revised Edition

ISBN 1-60611-004-7
978-1-60611-004-1

Published by Global Communications/Conspiracy Journal
Box 753 · New Brunswick, NJ 08903

Staff Members
Timothy G. Beckley, Publisher
Carol Ann Rodriguez, Assistant to the Publisher
Sean Casteel, General Associate Editor
Tim R. Swartz, Graphics and Editorial COnsultant
William Kern, Editorial and Art Consultant

Sign Up On The Web For Our Free Weekly Newsletter
and Mail Order Version of Conspiracy Journal
and Bizarre Bazaar
www.ConspiracyJournal.com

Order Hot Line: 1-732-602-3407

ufo-contactee Orfeo Angelucci

ABOUT THE AUTHOR

Orfeo Angelucci was born June 25, 1912, in Trenton, New Jersey.

Science, particularly fundamental physics, has been his greatest interest and most intense study since his early school years. This preoccupation led Mr. Angelucci into work with General Motors and Lockheed Aircraft during the years of World War II and the Korean conflict.

The author's studies and practical experience in the field of airplane manufacturing have produced his unusual writings about space and its various attributes.

Mr. Angelucci believes his background was the reason for his being given the story he has told in *THE SECRET OF THE SAUCERS* and *SON OF THE SUN*.

DEDICATION

With deep affection and gratitude for their understanding and loyalty, I dedicate this book to my loving wife, Mabel and my devoted sons, Raymond and Richard.

The Secret of the Saucers

Orfeo M. Angelucci, [1955]

VOLUME ONE

Contents

INTRODUCTION TO THE NEW EDITION

FOREWORD

THE DISK FROM ANOTHER WORLD

I TRAVEL IN A FLYING SAUCER

MY MEETING WITH NEPTUNE

"WE CAN APPEAR AND FUNCTION AS EARTHMEN, ORFEO!"

THE PAST IS NEVER DEAD!

AIRPLANES DO DISAPPEAR!

FLYING SAUCER CONVENTION IN HOLLYWOOD

MY AWAKENING ON ANOTHER PLANET

THE TRIP EAST

NEPTUNE AGAIN AND PHENOMENA IN NEW JERSEY

I HAVE A VISION

HOW TO KNOW A FLYING SAUCER

STRUCTURE AND MOTIVE FORCES OF FLYING DISKS

THE TRUE NATURE OF THE SAUCER MYSTERY

THE SECRET OF THE SAUCERS

VOLUME TWO

CONTENTS

ADAM IN THE DESERT

THE DANCE IN A GLASS

THE SPEED OF LIGHT

VEGA ALERTS ADAM

VENUS, OUR SISTER

LANDING ABOARD ANDROMEDA

ADAM MEETS ANTARES

NATURE OF INFINITE ENTITIES

ADAM'S MOMENT OF ILLUMINATION

A NIGHT OUT ON VENUS

ADAM LEARNS ETERNITY

THE EASE OF FORGETTING

INTO THE SUN AND OUT AGAIN

ADAM SAYS GOODBYE

SON OF THE SUN : Secret of the Saucers

HIS ENCOUNTERS ARE SWEETNESS AND LIGHT
Introduction To The 2008 Expanded Edition

By Timothy Green Beckley

They were accused by the skeptics of being frauds and charlatans

"Out to make a quick buck off little old ladies."

You can't believe how many times I heard this slander during the period when flying saucer sightings were still pretty much a novelty. Sure I was a pre-teen, wet behind the ears in the ways of the world, and certainly a newcomer to the rapidly emerging field of UFOlogy.

My own eyes told me that there were things in the sky that just shouldn't be there. By age ten, I had undergone my first of three UFO experiences. The multiple lights that hovered over my home convinced me that the authorities were dancing on their left foot when they told the public these objects were hallucinations, balloons and reflections bouncing off of cloud lawyers. This phenomenon was nothing like that and I had to learn more.

I picked up a few books. Major Donald E. Keyhoe was convinced these UFOs were physical spaceships, craft from another world sending probes here for the purpose of surveillance. If a sighting was made by a pilot or a police officer, Keyhoe could accept the reality of the sighting at face value. But heaven forbid if a being was seen anywhere near a landed craft.

Yet, on the West Coast, many individuals were having close encounters with the occupants of these craft. There was no mistaking their mission. According to a group of individuals who became known as "contactees" because – well, because they contacted beings from space—these beings were humanoid looking (almost angelic) and here to uplift the planet's murky spirituality and bring us into a new age.

The names are still familiar (loved by some, scorned by others). George Adamski, George Van Tassel, Truman Bethrum, Howard Menger. Their stories were quite similar, though not identical. They had been invited onboard these intergalactic craft and taken

SON OF THE SUN : Secret of the Saucers

for rides to bases on the far side of the moon, or even to Venus and faraway Mars.

Were these stories true? Or were they a figment of our wildest dreams? Purely flights of our imagination? Or part of the collective unconscious, as suggested by the famed psychoanalyst Carl Jung?

For me, it was pure romance with an outer space theme. While most boys my age were interested in playing baseball and sneaking a smoke in the boys room, I wanted to find out more about flying saucers.

So I turned on the radio – one of the first transistor ones – and listened into the wee hours to a gentleman by the name of Long John Nebel. He was on seven days a week, broadcasting over radio station WOR in New York City. I should have been sleeping between the hours of midnight and 5 AM when Long John was being heard over 30 states on what in those days would have been a pretty clear channel. I just had to listen with the lights out and the blankets over my head. (It was also cold in my room, so the blanket served a purpose other than just to cut down on the sound of the radio playing in what was otherwise the stillness of the night).

My ears perked up whenever Long John would introduce his panelists. Who was going to be on the program to slam the guest, and who would side along with the "men from Mars"?

Of all the legendary UFO contactees that Long John interviewed, Orfeo Angelucci stands out in my mind. There was sincerity in his voice. He seemed charming. There was no doubt he believed in what he was saying. He wasn't a kook. He had "credentials." Long John pointed out that Orfeo actually worked for the famed Lockheed Aircraft Corporation. It was near the plant where he was employed that Angelucci had a number of his best UFO-related contacts, with some occurring as he drove across the desert at night on his way home. His experiences, no matter how wild they might seem – and they were really wild –had to be for real. They just had to be. They were so full of peace and love. Sigh.

As John C. Super explains in his book, *The Fifties In America* (Salem Press): "As humanity began to venture out into space during the late 1950s, it was only natural that curiosity about what was 'out there' would consume Americans. In many ways, the

SON OF THE SUN : Secret of the Saucers

flying saucer mythos of the decade constituted a popular, folkloric manifestation of that curiosity, but more importantly, it mirrored the fears of conquest by outriders and destruction by nuclear warfare that haunted people during this era. Moreover, in the tales of the contactees, flying saucer lore addressed Americans' hopes and dreams that perhaps their current problems might have a peaceful outcome."

The book you are now reading is confirmation of such a higher thought process. I have always felt that even if we cannot take contact experiences such as Angelucci's as the literal truth, it nevertheless behooves us not to toss out such stories from our lives. It is as if the planet itself – the Great Mother Goddess – is directing Orfeo to speak to us, and requiring us to listen in order to save ourselves from certain annihilation.

As Orfeo is told by one of his contacts: "Among the countless other worlds in the cosmos, the children of Earth are as babes. Among the other worlds of the universe are many types of spiritual and physical evolutions. Each form of intelligent life adapts itself to the physical conditions prevalent upon its home planet. Most of these evolutions exist in more highly attenuated forms of matter than upon Earth. But the majority are rather similar to man in appearance. There is a definite reason for this being so. In reality, we are Earth's older brothers and thus we will aid Earth's people insofar as they, through free will, will permit us to do so."

Orfeo confesses that he feels small in the presence of these beings: "As I listened to this gentle voice, I began to feel a warm, glowing wave of love enfold me, so powerful that it seemed as a tangible soft golden light. For a wonderful moment I felt infinitely greater, finer and stronger than I knew myself to be. It was as though momentarily I had transcended mortality and was somehow related to these super beings."

Perhaps after reading *Son Of The Sun,* we can all begin to feel the same way.

I hope the words in this book rub off on you as they have on me.

Tim Beckley

www.ConspiracyJournal.com

Artist's conception of Orfeo's original contact

FOREWORD

Many persons have asked me why the space visitors should have chosen me for contact rather than some other individual whom they considered eminently better qualified for such a contact than myself. Why, they infer, should the space visitors have picked so insignificant a nonentity as I for their revelations?

In all humility I tell you that I too have asked both the space visitors and myself that very question many times. And it is only within recent months that I have begun to understand fully just why I was chosen. But this is not the place in this book to disclose the reasons for their choice. After you have finished the book, however, you will have the answer. It is up to you then to decide whether or not you agree with the saucer beings in their choice of contact.

Thus I shall begin by telling you something of my early life and the space visitors first contact with me back in the year 1946, when I was totally unaware that I first came under their observation.

My childhood was the usual happy, carefree childhood of most American boys. I joined in the less strenuous games, attended school and was fairly good in my studies, although I was always frail and in poor health. Fortunately, my family was in fairly comfortable circumstances and they and my two indulgent uncles saw to it that I always had the best medical attention available.

My youthful trouble was diagnosed as "constitutional inadequacy" and its symptoms were great physical weakness, lassitude, lack of appetite and malnutrition. Hence I tired very easily and the slightest physical effort often left me weak and exhausted. I suffered from severe migraine headaches and as I grew older it seemed at times thaú every nerve and muscle in my body ached with excruciating pain.

When I was in the ninth grade the doctors advised that I discontinue school and continue my studies at home. This arrangement was highly satisfactory with me, for I had always been intensely interested in all branches of science. At home I was able to devote my entire time to the study of these subjects.

With plenty of rest and on a weight-building diet I gained strength and within a year the doctors believed I was well enough to return to school. But as my family had suffered some financial reverses in the meantime, it was decided that it would be best if I went to work for a while. I heartily approved. My first job was with my uncle's flooring and stucco company. He hired me as an estimator-salesman as I was not equal to any heavy work. I liked the work and enjoyed getting out and meeting people. All in all I got along pretty well even though I was considered just a kid. In my spare time I continued to study all of the books I could get hold of on scientific subjects.

In 1936 I met Mabel Borgianini, an attractive Italian girl who is a direct descendant of the famous Italian Borgias. From the first, both of us knew that we were meant for each other. Her happy, cheerful disposition helped me to keep from brooding over my health and physical inability to accomplish all of the things that I longed to do. It was the happiest day of my life when we were married. About a year later our first son, Raymond, was born and our cup of happiness was full.

A little later I suffered a complete physical breakdown and was forced to give up my job. My weight fell alarmingly from 150 to 103 pounds and I was so weak that I could scarcely sit up. After a number of medical examinations and complicated tests, the doctors decided I was suffering from a neurovascular disturbance. They prescribed complete rest and continuous medical attention.

Thus I entered a new world, a white world of doctors, nurses and hospital beds. For eighteen long months I was confined to bed. My body was wracked with excruciating pains and I was so utterly exhausted that I could not even read. Medical science was doing everything possible for me, but I knew that my doctors didn't believe that I would ever pull through. Frankly, I didn't much care whether I lived or died. Life was no longer desirable. To lie day after day on a white hospital cot with a body flayed with pain and too exhausted even to think is indeed a living hell. Death, I felt, could only mean release from pain. Especially was the confinement difficult for me to bear as I had always loved the out of doors, the sparkle of the sunshine, the whisper of the leaves in the woods, and the music of the woodland streams. Sometimes I prayed that I might die and escape the pain and awful weariness that ached in my muscles.

But weeks lengthened into months and gradually I began to improve. Finally I was able to sit up again and then to walk. It was like being reborn. I even began to take an interest in my science books once more. At last came the joyous day when I was able to leave the hospital and return home. All through those long months of confinement the faith and encouragement of my wife and family never failed. Mabel was with me through it all and if it hadn't been for her love and understanding I doubt if I ever would have made it.

My body was still wracked with pain, but I had learned to bear that. The good thing was that the terrible exhaustion and trembling weakness was gone so that I was able to be up and about. Although my family tried to dissuade me, I insisted upon going back to work on my old job almost immediately. I had been inactive

11

so long that I wanted more than anything just to be busy again.

After I returned to work, I took up courses in night school. The old insatiable hunger for knowledge was gnawing at my very soul. I realized that science had discovered much, but there were still so many things to be learned; so many of nature's secrets yet to be revealed. I was obsessed with learning the true nature of the atom; discovering a cure for the virus diseases and especially for polio, that most ghastly of all crippling diseases. I felt that a satisfactory explanation for the creation and operation of the entire universe was yet to be worked out. What was the great mystery of the creation of matter, or the actual origin of the atom? These and other similar enigmas echoed in my brain night and day.

The field of electricity and electro-magnetic phenomena interested me in particular. Probably because from earliest childhood I had an acute fear or phobia about lightning. During an electrical storm I suffered not only actual bodily pain, but mental perturbation and distress. Thus I became well versed in atmospheric static electricity.

I conducted some simple experiments on my own. I noticed that all fowl and especially chickens are nervous and apprehensive during an impending thunderstorm. It was obvious from my own reactions that they too experienced definite physical symptoms because of atmospheric conditions. Also, I discovered that chickens are subject to a "range paralysis" which in every respect parallels infantile paralysis in human beings. From my studies and experiments in this field I believed that I had discovered certain facts that might be highly significant in the treatment of polio. In my enthusiasm, I wrote a long, detailed letter on the subject to President Franklin Roosevelt, who was then in the White House.

Through the efforts of President Roosevelt my theories were heard by Dr. John L. Lavan, Jr., Director of Research, National Foundation for Infantile Paralysis. Dr. Lavan was interested and referred me to Dr. Joseph Stokes of the Children's Hospital in Philadelphia who was working along the vitamin therapy line of treatment for polio. But I never called on Dr. Stokes. From what I learned of his work I knew that his ideas were directly opposed to my own theory that a certain vitamin of the B complex group was largely responsible for the nutrition of the polio virus. (This view has since been substantiated by all research in virology.)

Returning to my studies and home experiments, I became interested in fungi and the atmospheric conditions affecting them. I studied the wild mushrooms and the particular atmospheric conditions which resulted in their sudden, erratic growth. From the mushrooms I turned to molds. It was my belief that molds are a negative form of life which leech on living matter by an illusive, subtle process of mutation.

At that time we were well into World War II. Penicillin had been discovered, but it was yet only a magic word and a deep mystery to the public. No books or reports were available on the subject. But by then I was familiar with the characteristics of fungi. In my experiments I discovered that one of the most common molds could be made to produce chemicals indefinitely if kept in proper nutrition and temperature. It was then I decided to see what structural changes would occur in the mold aspergillus clavatus in the upper atmosphere.

On August 4, 1946 I took cultures of the mold in three stages of growth: embryonic, half mature and mature. I placed the molds in baskets and attached the baskets to eighteen Navy-type balloons and prepared to send them aloft. But through an unfortunate accident the balloons broke away prematurely, carrying the baskets with the molds aloft with no means of retrieving them. My long months of strenuous effort and careful planning were hopelessly lost.

Heartsick, I sighed heavily as I watched the balloons and my precious molds ascending higher and higher into the clear blue sky. It was a perfect day, just the kind of weather I had longed for to make my test, but now everything was irreparably lost.

My family and a number of friends and neighbors were with me watching the experiment. Also on hand were a reporter and a photographer from the Trentonian, the Trenton daily newspaper. Everyone was silent staring into the heavens watching the balloons growing smaller and smaller as they gained altitude. Everyone there and especially Mabel and my father-in-law knew how keenly disappointed I was. Mabel put her arm comfortingly about my shoulders and murmured: "It's all right, Orfie. You can try again."

It was then that my father-in-law, Alfred Borgianini, noticed a craft in the sky and called out: "Look! There's an airplane, Orfeo. Maybe it will follow your balloons."

Everyone there saw the object and it was the consensus that it had been attracted to the spot by the group of ascending balloons. But as it hovered and circled overhead, we were all soon aware that it was no ordinary airplane. In the first place it maneuvered in an amazingly graceful and effortless manner. Then as we gained a clearer view of it, we were startled to see that it did not have the familiar outline of any known type of aircraft. It was definitely circular in appearance and glistened in the sunshine. We looked at each other in surprise and bewilderment and the photographer tried to get some shots of the thing. Mabel exclaimed: "Why, I never saw such an airplane before! It's round and it doesn't have any wings!"

Everyone agreed and we continued to stare as it gained altitude and appeared to follow after the balloons until it too vanished from our sight. For several clays afterward we discussed the strange object, but as in the case of most mysteries, we forgot all about it within a week or two. Today, however, any one of those persons who were with me that day will vouch for the authenticity of that strange craft.

Since then I have learned that the occasion of the launching of the balloons was the first time I came under direct observation of the extra-terrestrials. Although I never then dreamed of the significance of the event, that was their first contact with me. From that moment on for the next five years and nine months I remained under constant observation by beings from another world, although I was wholly unaware of it.

The state police force was appealed to and requested to be on the lookout for the eighteen lost balloons and their strange cargo. Also, local radio stations and newspapers publicized the loss of the balloons and requested anyone finding or sighting them to report to authorities. But nothing was ever heard about them and to all intents the eighteen balloons and the mold cultures vanished.

Several days after the loss of the balloons I stopped in at the Palmer Physics Laboratory at Princeton University to visit Dr. Dan Davis, head of the Cosmic Ray Department. Dr. Davis had always been most friendly toward me and was never too busy to take time out to help me with some of the technical problems that were always troubling me.

I told Dr. Davis and one of his aides about the experimental molds and their loss in the accident with the balloons. Dr. Davis regretted that I had not told him about my experiments beforehand, for he said that the laboratory would have been glad to supply the hydrogen gas for the experiment and otherwise help to reduce expenses. Also, he said he would have arranged to have the balloons traced by the chain of radar stations in the eastern section.

Princeton and its environs were literally heaven-on-earth to me, for it was one of the important homes of my beloved science. In the vicinity were such great institutions as Rockefeller Institute for Medical Research, the R.C.A. Laboratories, the American Telephone and Telegraph Co.; the Institute for Advance Study; the Heyden Chemical Corporation, producers of penicillin. And nearby were Rutgers University, E. R. Squibb and Co., Merck and Son and many others. Yes, I loved every inch of New Jersey with its marvelous institutions of learning and scientific research. But my love for the state was offset by my uncontrollable apprehensions of and physical anguish during the rather violent thunderstorms there. Thus when Mabel began to talk of moving to the West Coast where I'd heard there were few, if any, thunderstorms, I was easily persuaded to go along with her plans.

In November of 1947 my family, consisting of Mabel and I and my two boys, Raymond and Richard, started by automobile for Los Angeles. On the trip we stopped at Rochester, Minnesota where I had an appointment at the famous Mayo Clinic with Dr. Walter C. Alvarez, the modern Hippocrates of diagnostic medicine. I sincerely appreciated my tremendous good fortune at being granted time by this authority in the field of medicine, for many far more deserving than I have been unable to see this busy man.

Despite his fame and his importance in the medical world, I found him extremely modest and kindly. After a thorough examination he concluded that my condition was caused by an inherent constitutional inadequacy in an extreme degree. It was his opinion that the condition had been induced by a childhood attack of trichinosis from eating contaminated, under-cooked pork. He said I was fortunate to have survived the acute attack. He advised me to get as much rest as possible and never to engage in work that was not of my choice and liking in order to minimize the burden on my weakened constitution and nervous system.

At last we arrived in the Golden State on the West Coast. Southern California was a delightful new experience for both my family and myself. I decided it was paradise indeed when I discovered that it actually was practically free from electrical storms. And my boys and Mabel were thrilled with stretches of golden sand at the seashores, the mountains and the continuous semi-spring that prevails there at all seasons of the year.

We spent five months in California sight-seeing and enjoying the sunshine and the wonders of its scenery. At the end of that time we had to return to Trenton, as I had some unfinished business to attend to there. But I had purchased a lot in Los Angeles and we planned to return and make our permanent home there as soon as possible.

For some years I had been working on a thesis titled, "The Nature of Infinite Entities" which included chapters on such subjects as Atomic Evolution, Suspension, and Involution; Origin of the Cosmic Rays; Velocity of the Universe, etc. While I was in Trenton I had the thesis published entirely at my own expense and mailed copies to various universities and individual scientists working on fundamental research. Of course I realized at the time it was presumptuous of me, but I was completely carried away with my tremendous enthusiasm for ideas which I believed I understood but could not properly formulate because of lack of technical training.

It was my deep and abiding hope that some one of the scientists might understand what I was driving at and work out the technical and mathematical angles. Some of the men were interested, but none as far as I know ever exerted the effort on the theories that I had hoped they might. But at least I was satisfied that I had done my best considering the limited circumstances of my education. I was content to let the matter rest. It was obvious science had no need of me, a rank and presumptuous amateur. I must remain mute, an orphan of science!

We were all happy to return to Los Angeles and settle down in our new home. There I went into business with my father. But from the first we encountered vicissitudes on every side. For three long, difficult years we struggled along trying to make a go of it, but monopolies and stiff competition made the going so rough that we were finally forced to close down the business.

The temptation was great to return to the security of Trenton where material comfort and a small fortune awaited us if we would make our home there. But Mabel and the boys loved Southern California. As far as I am concerned, security has never been of great importance in my world of the atom, the electron and the photon. Also, there were still those electric storms to reckon with. To an electrophobe like myself, this aspect is always of primary consideration. So we decided to forget security and gamble on keeping our home and making a go of it in Los Angeles where we were all content.

This was in the year 1948 and the flying saucers were then making headlines from time to time. But I was completely disinterested in the phenomenon. Like many other persons, I thought the saucers were some new type of aircraft being secretly developed here in the United States. I figured the information would come out in good time.

For several months I worked as manager of the Los Feliz Club House. In my spare time I endeavored to write a motion picture script. It was more of a hobby than anything else. I didn't really expect the script to be accepted as I'd had no writing experience. As the idea of space travel was quite popular in the films then, I concentrated on a story about an imaginary trip to the moon. Several studios were interested in the finished manuscript, but it was never made into a motion picture.

When the club house where I was employed was finally leased to a large organization, I made application for work at the Lockheed Aircraft Corporation plant at Burbank, California. The application was approved and I went to work for Lockheed on April 2, 1952, in the metal fabrication department.

After about six weeks in Metal Fabrication I was transferred to the Plastics Unit at Lockheed. Since plastics had always interested me, I was pleased with the change. I was one of a three-man crew working on radomes, or plastic and glass housings for the radar units of the F-94C and F-94B Starfire jet aircraft. I liked my fellow workers, Dave Donnegan and Richard Butterfield. Both were honest, sincere, hardworking typical young Americans. They had their feet firmly on the ground and although interested in new ideas and scientific developments, they were strictly on the material plane and not interested in abstractions.

I was fortunate indeed to have two such men to cushion the shock of the fantastic chain of events in which I was so soon and unexpectedly to be involved. As I look back now it appears that an occult power of some sort had neatly arranged every smallest detail in advance including the particular type of job I was in as well as the two men who were to be closest to me through all of my incredible experiences. Ours was the swing shift. The unusual hours appealed to me as well as the excitement of the new work and the motley assortment of people at the plant. But I did not know then what infinitely strange destiny fate held in store for me.

SON OF THE SUN: The Secret Of The Saucers

CHAPTER I
THE DISK FROM ANOTHER WORLD

Friday, May 23, 1952, was an ordinary day in Burbank, California insofar as I was concerned. I got up at my usual time, worked around the yard for a few hours and later stopped in at the Drive-In snack bar. After several cups of coffee and an exchange of good-natured banter with some of the customers, I left and went to my job at the Lockheed Aircraft Corporation plant.

Things went along well enough during the earlier part of the evening, but about 11 o'clock, I began to feel ill. An odd prickling sensation was running through my hands and arms and up into the back of my neck. I had a slight heart palpitation and my nerves were on edge. I felt just as I always do before a bad electrical storm. As the familiar symptoms increased I went outside expecting to find heavy threatening clouds, but the night was exceptionally clear and the stars were bright.

Puzzled, I went to work wondering what was wrong with me. By 12:30 A.M., when the quitting whistle sounded, I was so exhausted I could scarcely stand; it would be a relief to get home and into bed. I took my car from the Lockheed parking lot and headed southeast on Victory Boulevard toward home.

I became increasingly conscious of nervous tension as I drove. I sensed a force of some kind about me. Never in all of my similar illnesses had I experienced such peculiar symptoms. There was no pain, yet I felt as though I might die at any moment. The prickling sensation had increased and spread to my arms, legs and up into my scalp.

Frightened, I wondered if an old illness was returning upon me. Was I going to be confined to my bed again with the terrible debility and excruciating pain of the "constitutional inadequacy" of my schoolboy days? The dread symptoms were certainly there.

At Alameda Boulevard I stopped for a traffic signal. It was then I noticed that my eyesight was glazed and the sounds of traffic were oddly muffled and far-away as though my hearing was also affected. I decided that I had better stop at one of the all-night cafes and have a cup of coffee. But at the thought all of my alarming symptoms increased. I forgot the idea of a cup of coffee. My sole and overwhelming desire was to get home as fast as I could.

I continued on Victory Boulevard toward home. I had the illusion that the night was growing brighter as though enveloped in a soft golden haze. Directly ahead and slightly above my line of vision I saw a faintly red-glowing oval-shaped object. At first it was so dim I had to stare at it to be certain it was really there. But gradually it increased in brilliance. It was about five times as large as the red portion of a traffic light. Nervously I rubbed my eyes; something was wrong with my vision! But the thing remained there; not sharp and clearly defined, but fuzzily luminous, definitely oval-shaped and deep red in color.

I continued on Riverside Drive directly toward the object, but it appeared to be receding from me so that I remained relatively the same distance from it. As it was almost one o'clock in the morning there was little traffic on the road. Apparently no one else had noticed the object as I saw no cars stopped to investigate. I wondered if I also would have missed it above the glare of the headlights if my strange symptoms had not drawn my eyes to it.

I drove across the bridge over the Los Angeles River with the object still in view. Just the other side of the bridge, to the right of the highway, is a lonely, deserted stretch of road called Forest Lawn Drive. The object stopped and hovered over the intersection. As I drew near, it gained in brilliance and its red color grew deeper and more glowing. Simultaneously, the physical symptoms I was experiencing became more acute. I was aware of a tingling sensation of pain and numbness in my arms and legs that reminded me of contact with an electrical current.

Now the disk veered sharply to the right off the highway and began moving slowly along Forest Lawn Drive. For the first time it occurred to me that the fantastic thing could be one of those flying saucers I had read about. I turned my car onto Forest Lawn Drive and followed the object.

About a mile further along the disk swerved to the right, away from the road, and hung motionless over an unfenced field some distance below the road level. I drove off the pavement about thirty feet to the edge of the declivity. From there the glowing red disk was directly in front of me and only a short distance away. As I watched it in bewilderment it pulsated violently; then shot off into the sky at a 30- or 40-degree angle and at very great speed. High in the sky to the west it decelerated abruptly, hung for a moment; then accelerated and disappeared like a meteor.

But just before the glowing red orb vanished, two smaller objects came from it. These objects were definitely circular in shape and of a soft, fluorescent green color. They streaked down directly in front of my car and hovered only a few feet away. I judged each to be about three feet in diameter. Hanging silently in the air like irridescent bubbles their green light fluctuated rhythmically in intensity.

Then, apparently coming from between those two eerie balls of green fire, I heard a masculine voice in strong, well-modulated tones and speaking perfect English.

Because of the nervous tension I was under at that moment, amounting almost to a state of shock, it is impossible for me to give a verbatim account of the conversation which followed. The invisible speaker obviously was endeavoring to choose words and phrases which I could understand, but there were several things which even now are not clear to me. I can only make a poor approximation of the gist of his words.

I do, however, remember the first words spoken which were: "Don't be afraid, Orfeo, we are friends!" Then the voice requested that I get out of my car and "Come out here." Mechanically, I pushed open the car door and got out. I didn't feel fear, but I was so weak and shaky that I could scarcely stand. I leaned against the front fender of my car and looked at the twin pulsating circular objects hovering a short distance in front of me.

The glowing disks created a soft illumination, but I could see no person anywhere. I remember vaguely that the voice spoke again calling me by my full name in words of greeting. It further stated that the small green disks were instruments of transmission and reception comparable to nothing developed on earth. Then the voice added that through the disks I was in direct communication with friends from another world.

There was a pause and I dimly remember thinking that I should say something, but I was stunned into utter silence. I could only stare in fascination at those fantastic balls of green fire and wonder if I had lost my mind.

When the voice spoke again I heard these startling words: "Do you remember your eighteen balloons and the mold cultures that you lost in the skies back in New Jersey, Orfeo?" I was astounded to hear the strange voice recalling an incident out of the past which had happened so long ago that I had almost forgotten it. "Yes . . . . yes sir, I do!"

"Do you also remember the strange, wingless craft that appeared to be observing your activities?"

Suddenly the entire scene carne back to me crystal clear in memory. I remember Mabel, my wife, my father-in-law and our friends and neighbors with me as we stared at that strange, disk-shaped object in the sky. I recalled how the object had appeared to follow the balloons bearing my precious cultures of Aspergillus Clavatus mold. I had been quite an experimenter in those days. It was then it dawned upon me that the fluorescent disks were similar in shape and behaved in the same erratic manner as had that mysterious craft back in New Jersey. The only difference was that I had seen the craft in daylight when it glistened like metal whereas the disks glowed in the darkness.

"You do remember us, Orfeo," the golden voice stated. "We were observing your efforts that day as we have watched you since then."

SON OF THE SUN: The Secret Of The Saucers

All traces of fear left me at these words, but I could not help but wonder what it all meant. Suddenly I realized that I was feeling very thirsty.

As though in response to my thought, the voice said: "Drink from the crystal cup you will find on the fender of your car, Orfeo."

Astonished at his words, I glanced down and saw a kind of goblet on the car fender. It glistened in the soft light. Hesitantly I lifted it to my lips and tasted the drink. It was the most delicious beverage I had ever tasted. I drained the cup. Even as I was drinking a feeling of strength and well-being swept over me and all of my unpleasant symptoms vanished.

"Oh thank you, sir," I said as I placed the empty cup back on the fender of my car only to see it disappear.

At that moment another incredible phenomenon began to occur. The twin disks were spaced about three feet apart. Now the area between them began to glow with a soft green light which gradually formed into a luminous three-dimensional screen as the disks themselves faded perceptibly.

Within the luminous screen there appeared images of the heads and shoulders of two persons, as though in a cinema close-up. One was the image of a man and the other of a woman. I say man and woman only because their outlines and features were generally similar to men and women. But those two figures struck me as being the ultimate of perfection. There was an impressive nobility about them; their eyes were larger and much more expressive and they emanated a seeming radiance that filled me with wonder. Even more confusing was the troubling thought somewhere in the back of my mind that they were oddly familiar. Strangely enough, the projected images of the two beings appeared to be observing me. For they looked directly at me and smiled; then their eyes looked about as though taking in the entire scene.

I had the uncomfortable feeling as they studied me that they knew every thought in my mind; everything I'd ever done and a vast amount about me that I didn't even know myself. Intuitively, I sensed that I stood in a kind of spiritual nakedness before them. Also, I seemed to be in telepathic communication with them, for thoughts, understandings and new comprehensions that would have required hours of conversation to transmit, flashed through my consciousness.

Before those two incredible Beings I felt that I was only a shadow of the shining reality I sensed them to be. It is difficult to express my feelings in words, for my understanding of them was gained primarily through intuitive perception.

After several moments the two figures faded and the luminous screen vanished. Again the two disks flamed into brilliant green fire.

Trembling violently from weakness and cold perspiration, I was on the point of blacking out when I heard the voice again. It was more kindly than ever as it said something about my being understandably confused; but it assured me I would understand everything that had happened later on. Also, I remember these words:

SON OF THE SUN: The Secret Of The Saucers

"The road will open, Orfeo."

I didn't understand. Instead the thought flashed through my mind: "Why have they contacted me; a humble aircraft worker—a nobody?"

The voice replied: "We see the individuals of Earth as each one really is, Orfeo, and not as perceived by the limited senses of man. The people of your planet have been under observation for centuries, but have only recently been re-surveyed. Every point of progress in your society is registered with us. We know you as you do not know yourselves. Every man, woman and child is recorded in vital statistics by means of our recording crystal disks. Each of you is infinitely more important to us than to your fellow Earthlings because you are not aware of the true mystery of your being.

"From among you we singled out three individuals who, from the standpoint of our higher vibrational perception, are best fitted for establishing contact. All three are simple, humble and presently unknown persons. Of the other two, one is living in Rome and the other in India. But for our first contact with the people of Earth, Orfeo, we have chosen you.

"We feel a deep sense of brotherhood toward Earth's inhabitants because of an ancient kinship of our planet with Earth. In you we can look far back in time and recreate certain aspects of our former world. With deep compassion and understanding we have watched your world going through its 'growing pains'. We ask that you look upon us simply as older brothers."

The voice continued, speaking rather rapidly. It stated that they were well aware that the flying saucers had been treated humorously by most people—as it was meant they should be. In this way they wanted the people of Earth to become only gradually aware of them and grow accustomed to the idea of space visitors. It was best that we receive them lightly at first for the sake of our own stability!

The voice stated that the disks were powered and controlled by tapping into universal magnetic forces; thus their activated molecules received and converted energy inherent in all the universe. It further explained that the complexities of the apparently simple structure of their disks were so great that to an Earthling a saucer would be considered as having "synthetic brains", although each one is to a degree under the remote control of a Mother Ship. Also, most of the saucers, as well as the space craft of other planetary evolutions, are of a circular shape and vary in size from a few inches to hundreds of feet in diameter.

A disk, the voice continued, is able not only to relay whatever is transmitted to it from a Mother Ship, but also it records precisely all visual, auditory and telepathic impressions that come within the scope of the disk. These impressions are relayed to the Mother Ship where they are permanently recorded upon what Earthlings would popularly term "synthetic crystal brains". Thus for centuries had been recorded a detailed account of Earth's civilization and the spiritual evolution of individual persons.

SON OF THE SUN: The Secret Of The Saucers

The voice also stated that in addition to the remotely controlled saucers there also existed space ships, some of which had been seen by Earthlings. It was further explained that the Etheric entities in reality had no need of space-craft of any type and when they were employed by them it was only for purposes of material manifestation to men.

I distinctly remember the voice making some such statement as this: "Interplanetary ships and saucers of various material densities can approximate the speed of light. This seems impossible to you only because of a natural principle which has not yet been discovered by your scientists. Also, the Speed of Light is the Speed of Truth. This statement is presently unintelligible to Earth's peoples, but is a basic cosmic axiom.

"Approaching the speed of light, the Time dimension, as known upon Earth, becomes non-existent; hence in this comparatively new dimension there are incredibly rapid means of space travel which are beyond man's comprehension. Also, within the Records of Light are to be found a complete history of Earth and of every entity which has incarnated upon it.

Many of the saucers—of highly attenuated densities of matter—were invisible to Earthly eyes and could only be detected by radar. Also, any of the saucers could be rendered invisible at any time, or could be disintegrated by either explosion or implosion. Thus Earthlings had seen some apparently burst in a blue or white flash while others seemed simply to vanish in the air.

I remember wondering about Captain Mantell and several others who believed they had contacted the saucers. In reply to my thought I heard these words: "Captain Mantell was not pursuing the planet Venus. He was endeavoring to overtake and capture one of the remotely controlled disks. His death was absolutely unavoidable!

"We wish to tell Earth's people that visitors from other planets occasionally visit Earth's dense, heavy, gaseous atmosphere. All are of kindly intent and none will harm man. All intelligences capable of space travel can read thoughts and see emotions. Man believes himself civilized, but often his thoughts are barbaric and his emotions lethal. We do not say this as criticism, but state it only as fact. Thus it is best to approach all planetary visitors with friendly, welcoming thoughts!"

As I listened to his words I wondered why these incredible beings hadn't landed several space ships at one of our large airports and thus convinced the world simply and quickly of their reality.

In answer, I heard these words: "That would be the way of the entities of your Earth, Orfeo, but it is not our way. Primarily because we function in dimensions unknown to man and hence interpret all things differently. Also, because there are planetary and cosmic laws as implacable as the natural laws of Earth.

"Cosmic law actively prevents one planet from interfering with the evolution of any other planet. In other words, Orfeo, Earth must work out its own destiny! We will do everything in our power to aid the people of Earth, but we are definitely and greatly limited by cosmic law. It is because the life evolution in its present stage of material advancement upon Earth is endangered that we have made our re-appearance in the atmosphere of your planet. The danger is far greater than Earth's people realize. The 'enemy' prepares in vast numbers and in secret."

For a moment the voice was still and then it said gently: "Among the countless other worlds in the cosmos, Orfeo, the children of Earth are as babes, although many of them believe they are close to the ultimate of knowledge. Among the worlds of the universe are many types of spiritual and physical evolutions. Each form of intelligent life adapts itself to the physical conditions prevalent upon its home planet. Most of these evolutions exist in more highly attenuated forms of matter than upon Earth. But the majority are rather similar to man in appearance. There is a definite reason for this being so. In reality, we are Earth's older brothers and thus we will aid Earth's people insofar as they, through free will, will permit us to do so."

As I listened to that kind, gentle voice I began to feel a warm, glowing wave of love enfold me; so powerful that it seemed as a tangible soft, golden light. For a wonderful moment I felt infinitely greater, finer and stronger than I knew myself to be. It was as though momentarily I had transcended mortality and was somehow related to these superior beings.

"We'll contact you again, Orfeo," the voice said. "But for now, friend, it is goodnight."

The two shimmering green disks faded almost out; then I heard a low hum as they flamed brilliantly into glowing green fire and shot up into the sky in the direction taken earlier by the larger red disk. In an incredibly short time they too had vanished, leaving me standing alone by my car.

Bewilderment, incredulity, shock and stark fear flooded over me—sudden conviction that I had lost my mind and gone raving mad. What I had witnessed, I felt, just couldn't have happened.

I raised my numbed hand and it was trembling violently. I saw by my watch that it was almost two o'clock in the morning. I climbed shakily into my car and kicked the starter. Panic was mounting in me. I twisted the steering wheel, gunned the engine and made a sharp, fast U turn to get back onto the road. The tires screamed and the car lurched.

I wanted to get home quickly. I wanted to get back to the world of sane reality. I wanted someone to assure me I wasn't going mad.

I drove with only a single objective in my mind—to get home! When finally I made the turn onto Glendale Boulevard and saw the lights of my apartment I breathed a heavy sigh of relief; no place had ever looked so good to me!

I left the car in the driveway and ran into the house. My wife was waiting up, worried and anxious because I was so late.

"Orfeo, what's the matter? What's wrong? You're white as a sheet!"

I stood staring at her, unable to speak.

She came to me and grasped my hand. "Orfeo, you're sick! I'm going to call a doctor."

I put my arms around her. I wanted only to feel her close to me and for the moment to try not to think of what I had been through.

She pleaded with me to tell her what had happened.

"Tomorrow—maybe tomorrow, Mae, I can tell you. . . ."

Finally we got to bed, but it was almost dawn before I drifted into a troubled half sleep.

SON OF THE SUN: The Secret Of The Saucers

CHAPTER II
I TRAVEL IN A FLYING SAUCER

I spent nearly all day Saturday in bed. The shock of my fantastic experience was so great that I found it difficult to get back to actualities. I kept having the feeling that the world I knew was a phantom world inhabited only by shadows.

It was not until Sunday that I could bring myself to tell my wife what had happened to me. I was afraid she would think I had lost my mind. Thus it was with relief I heard her say: "If you say it happened like that, Orfeo, I believe you. You've always told me the truth. But this thing is so strange and frightening—and you looked so deathly white when you came in."

I could only put my arms around her as I replied: "It scares me too, Mabel—I don't know what to think!"

Sunday afternoon I took my twelve year old son Richard and drove back to the spot on Forest Lawn Drive where I had seen the disks. There in the loose dirt I found the deep skid marks the tires of my car had made Friday night.

Richard looked at me curiously and asked what I was looking for. I pointed to the skid marks and told him that was the spot where I had seen what could only have been a flying saucer. Richard stared incredulously. "But dad, I thought you always laughed at people who believed in those things."

"You're right, son," I replied. "But that was only because I didn't know any better. Friday night I saw three of the saucers from this very spot."

Richard's eyes widened with interest. Then he began shooting questions at me so fast that I had to ask him to slow down. But I was glad he did not doubt my word.

Seeing those skid marks where I had gunned my car in panic to get away from the eerie spot assured me of the reality of my experience. I was convinced that I had been in contact with beings from another world.

Monday night I went back to my swing-shift job at Lockheed. It felt good to be back at work again! The friendly banter, laughter and jokes of my coworkers were just what I needed.

Beyond my family I told no one of that first experience, as I knew I would be ridiculed. In fact even at home very little was said about the saucers or my expe-

25

SON OF THE SUN: The Secret Of The Saucers

rience, for the subject invariably upset my wife and filled her with such apprehension that even the boys refrained from talking much about it.

But when I was alone I thought long and often about those incredible beings from that other world. The voice had promised: "We'll contact you again, Orfeo." I wondered when they would get in touch with me again and how? Had they meant soon—or would it be months or even years? These and hundreds of similar questions clamored in my mind. I wondered if I was under constant observation by them. If so, I thought that through telepathy I could signal them to return. One night I went back to that lonely spot on Forest Lawn Drive and tried to establish telepathic communication. But it was useless! No glowing red disk appeared—only the night and the empty skies that gave back no answer.

Weeks passed and still no further sign from them. Doubts began to trouble me. Time dulled the memory of that night and I began to wonder if my experience had actually been real after all.

Then early in July there began a fresh flood of well-authenticated sightings of saucers in the skies over Southern California. Local newspapers carried banner headlines announcing **FLYING SAUCERS OVER LOS ANGELES!** Some people were convinced we had interplanetary visitors and looked for mass landings at any moment.

Later in the month additional sensational sightings were reported from many other States. It seemed the skies were filled with the baffling mystery objects that defied all natural laws and behaved more like phantoms than material realities. As I avidly read each new account I became convinced anew that I knew the secret of the flying saucers. But I longed for more knowledge. I hoped and prayed for another contact with those incredible beings I had seen so briefly that Friday night.

July 23, 1952 I didn't go to work. I wasn't feeling well and believed I was coming down with the flu. I was in bed all day, but in the evening I felt a little better and thought a walk in the fresh air would be good for me.

I walked down to the snack-bar at the Los Feliz Drive-In theatre, several blocks from the eleven-unit apartment-court where we live. The small cafe has a warm, friendly atmosphere and it gave my spirits a big lift to listen to the small talk and friendly ribbing. Because of the many recent newspaper reports, the talk turned to flying saucers.

Ann, one of the waitresses, laughingly remarked that she couldn't get enough sleep as her husband insisted upon staying up most of the night watching the sky with binoculars trying to get a glimpse of a saucer. This brought on a round of flying saucer jokes and everyone was laughing, including myself. The fact that I could laugh indicates that I had pretty well gotten over the shock of my experience.

When I'd finished my coffee I left the snack-bar and started home. It was a little after ten o'clock. Beyond the theatre is a lonely stretch of vacant lots. The place is eerie and forbidding at night, for huge concrete buttresses rise from it supporting the Hyperion Avenue Freeway Bridge several hundred feet overhead. The bridge casts dense, oblique shadows down below making it a shadowed no-man's land.

As I crossed the vacant lots in the deep shadows of the bridge a peculiar feeling came over me. Instantly I remembered that sensation—the tingling in my arms and legs! I looked nervously overhead but saw nothing. The feeling became more intense and with it came the dulling of consciousness I had noted on that other occasion.

Between me and the bridge I noticed a misty obstruction. I couldn't make out what it was. It looked like an Eskimo igloo—or the phantom of an igloo. It seemed like a luminous shadow without substance. I stared hard at the object. It was absolutely incredible—like a huge, misty soap bubble squatting on the ground emitting a fuzzy, pale glow.

The object appeared to be about thirty feet high and about equally wide at the base, so it wasn't a sphere. As I watched, it seemed to gain substance and to darken perceptibly on the outside. Then I noticed it had an aperture, or entrance like the door to an igloo, and the inside was brilliantly lighted.

I walked toward the thing. I had absolutely no sense of fear; rather a pleasant feeling of well-being. At the entrance I could see a large circular room inside. Hesitating only an instant I stepped into the object.

I found myself in a circular, domed room about eighteen feet in diameter. The interior was made of an ethereal mother-of-pearl stuff, irridescent with exquisite colors that gave off light. There was no sign of life; no sound. There was a reclining chair directly across from the entrance. It was made of that same translucent, shimmering substance—a stuff so evanescent that it didn't appear to be material reality as we know it.

No voice spoke, but I received the strong impression that I was to sit in the chair. In fact, a force seemed to be impelling me directly toward it. As I sat down I marveled at the texture of the material. Seated therein, I felt suspended in air, for the substance of that chair molded itself to fit every surface or movement of my body.

As I leaned back and relaxed, that feeling of peace and well-being intensified. Then a movement drew my attention toward the entrance. I saw the walls appeared to be noiselessly moving to close the aperture to the outside. In a few seconds the door had vanished, with no indication that there had ever been an entrance.

The closing of that door cut me off entirely from the outside world. For an uncomfortable moment I felt utterly alone—lost to my family and friends. But almost immediately a pleasant warmth passed over me giving me once more that feeling of peace and security. I breathed deeply and found the air cool and fresh. Vaguely

SON OF THE SUN: The Secret Of The Saucers

I wondered what was going to happen next.

Then I thought I heard a humming sound. At first it was almost inaudible, but it grew to a steady, low-pitched rhythm that was more like a vibration than a hum.

Next I was aware that my body seemed to be sinking more deeply into the soft substance of the chair. I felt as though a gentle force was pushing against the entire surface of my body. It was a peculiarly pleasant sensation that put me into a kind of semi-dream state.

While the humming sound increased I noticed that the room was darkening as though a heavy shadow was engulfing the room in twilight. As the light I began to grow apprehensive. I had the realization of how alone and helpless I actually was. For a bad moment I was on the edge of panic in the tightly sealed, darkening room.

Then . . . I heard music! It seemed to be coming from the walls. I couldn't believe my ears when I recognized the melody as my favorite song, "Fools Rush In". The panic within me subsided for I realized how safe I was with them—they who knew my every thought, dream and cherished hope!

Reassured, I settled back to enjoy the music. In a few seconds the interior of the room began to grow light again. Soon it was more brilliantly lighted than ever. It was at that moment that I noticed a glittering piece of metal on the floor of the craft. It was the shape and about the size of a quarter. I reached down and picked it up. It was different from any kind of metal I had ever seen, for it seemed almost to be alive in my hand. It quivered and began to glow almost like a live coal; yet it remained at the same temperature as my body. Now I noticed that the piece of metal was diminishing in size. It was as though some mysterious kind of sublimation or degeneration was taking place before my eyes. Could it be that contact with my hand was causing the substance to dissipate into the air? I placed it back upon the floor of the craft. There it ceased to quiver and the odd glow was no longer apparent.

I leaned back in the chair and noticed my soiled, faded work clothes which I had worn when I went to the snack-bar. The coarse fabric appeared crude and glaringly out of place in the exquisite, shimmering mother-of-pearl room.

"Where are they taking me?" I wondered, as I half listened to the music. For I was certain that the craft I was in must be moving. Were they taking me to their world, or was I going to spend eternity lost in space in that pearly igloo?

While I was still pondering these questions I felt the push against the surface of my body lessen, then cease altogether. The music stopped playing and the humming vibration in the floor died away too. I was certain that whatever type of motive power was used was housed somewhere below the floor as the faint vibratory hum definitely came from there.

Then smoothly and noiselessly the chair made a quarter turn toward the wall. Even as much as I trusted my unseen friends I was a little frightened at this. Tensely

SON OF THE SUN: The Secret Of The Saucers

I waited, gripping the arms of the chair. Directly in front of me a circular opening appeared in the wall about six feet in diameter, but everything appeared hazy through it.

As I stared, the lights inside darkened. Then either the entire craft or the seat turned slightly more to the left and the strange window widened about three more feet. I saw a huge globe surrounded with a shimmering rainbow. I trembled as I realized I was actually looking upon a planet from somewhere out in space. The planet itself was of a deep, twilight-blue intensity and the irridescent rainbow surrounding it made it appear like a dream vision. I couldn't see it all, for a portion at the bottom of the sphere was cut off by the floor line.

Now I heard that voice I remembered so well. "Orfeo, you are looking upon Earth—your home! From here, over a thousand miles away. in space, it appears as the most beautiful planet in the heavens and a haven of peace and tranquillity. But you and your Earthly brothers know the true conditions there."

As I listened to the tender, gentle intonations of that wonderful voice an overwhelming sense of sadness came over me. I felt tears in my eyes—I who had not know the relief of tears since I was a small boy. My heart was so full of emotion that tears were the only possible expression. They flowed unheeded down my cheeks. I was not ashamed for the tears seemed somehow to cleanse and purify me and to break down the hard, unfeeling, crystalized shell of The Reasoner that I had come to pride myself upon being.

The voice said softly: "Weep, Orfeo. Let tears unblind your eyes. For at this moment we weep with you for Earth and her Children. For all of its apparent beauty Earth is a purgatorial world among the planets evolving intelligent life. Hate, selfishness and cruelty rise from many parts of it like a dark mist."

The words brought fresh tears to my eyes as I thought of conditions on Earth and how they must appear to these perfected, compassionate beings who had extra-dimensional sight.

There was silence for a moment. Then I noticed that the room was apparently revolving away from Earth. Gradually the heavens came into view—an awesome, breathtaking sight from that tiny craft. All space appeared intensely black and the stars incredibly brilliant, set like jewels against black velvet—large, small; single and clustered. I felt lost in a strangely beautiful, ethereal world of celestial wonder.

All was brooding silence, order and indescribable beauty. A deep feeling of reverence possessed me. I had never been an actively religious man, but in that moment I knew God as a tangible, immutable Force that reaches to the furthest depths of Time and Eternity. And I felt assurance that the beings in whose care I was at that moment were close to the Infinite Power.

For a moment there was deep silence. Then as I wiped away the tears I saw a fantastic object coming slowly into view through the "window". It resembled a dirigible except that it was definitely flattened at the bottom. It emerged gradually into view from the right.

I studied it closely, wondering at its composition. It did not appear to be metallic like an airplane, but was definitely crystalline and gave the illusion of transparency. Its light properties definitely suggested perfect crystal alloyed throughout. I surmised it might be some sort of crystal-metal-plastic combination. When the entire ship was in view it appeared to be at least 1000 feet long and about 90 feet thick, but it could have been a great deal larger for there was no way to judge how close I was to it.

I stared fascinated at the half-ethereal "ship", scarcely conscious that I was again hearing music. But as my ears caught a startling, unfamiliar, strain, I listened intently to music such as I had never heard or could imagine. It is beyond description, for it was not music as we know it, nor was it played to our musical scale. It was strange, haunting drifts of melody that brought visions of star galaxies and planets spinning in notes of perfect harmony.

The voice spoke again: "Brother of Earth, each entity of your planet is divinely created and immortal. Upon your world the mortal shadows of those entities are working out their salvation from the plane of darkness. Every person upon Earth and its adjoining planes of manifestation are definitely arrayed upon either the positive side of progression toward good, or on the negative side of regression toward greater evil. We know where you stand, Orfeo; but are you going to be content to drift as you have been?"

"No . . . . oh, no!" I replied impulsively. "I want to work constructively. Only grant me strong physical health and there isn't anything I shan't be able to accomplish."

The voice replied gently. "That wish we cannot grant you, Orfeo, as much as we might like to. It is only because your physical body is weakened and your spiritual perceptions thereby keener that we have been able to contact you. Had you been physically in robust health with your mortal body and mind perfectly attuned to the sluggish lowered vibrations of Earth, we could not have manifested to you.

"Sickness, ill-health and all mortal afflictions are transient and unreal. They, along with pain, sorrow, suffering and conflict make up mankind's lessons in the school of the world where wisdom and spiritual evolution are gained primarily through suffering. An explanation of this terrible enigma will be given to you later. But tonight we tell you that you can rise above the inadequacies of your physical body, Orfeo, as may all other Earthlings. Remember always that we love you and your brothers of Earth. We will do everything within our power for the children of Earth that they will permit us to do, through free will.

With these words, the huge ship I was observing began moving upward and toward the left. One large "porthole" after another opened in rapid succession as the ship ascended until what appeared to be three decks were visible and I could catch fleeting glimpses of the interior of the gigantic sky ship. The inside appeared to be of the same luminous mother-of-pearl substance as the interior of the craft I was in. But I saw nothing more, no sign of life, no furnishings or equipment such as we on Earth know.

As I watched the ship I realized that the voice as well as the ethereal music had actually originated in the great sky ship. It came to me then that this must be a mother ship and that beings in it had remote control over the movements of the saucers that skimmed and skipped through our atmosphere. It awed me to realize what a high degree of intelligence and what expert hands were behind the saucer phenomena. I felt ashamed of having pleaded for a healthy body, who had already been granted so much.

As the craft moved further out into space I noticed what appeared to be a rotor at each end of the ship. I say rotor, but actually the things appeared to be vortices of flame.

With my limited knowledge I judged these incredible disks of fire to be tremendously powerful power plants whose terrific energy could be diverted to almost any purpose. The disks I had first seen were used as radio transmitters and receivers; then as a huge three-dimensional television screen on which, through some method of telepathic contact, it was possible both to see and to hear. Now I saw those same disks apparently propelling the vast sky ship. It was my guess that just such a power plant had shot the very craft I was in a thousand miles out into space in a mere matter of minutes and without any discomfort to me. It was clearly evident that all of the bewildering and insurmountable problems of space travel that baffled our engineers and scientists had been overcome by these people to such an extent that the entire trip into outer space was as simple as a ride in an elevator.

I wondered if they had discovered the secret of resisting gravity with its counter-force; if not, then by what other means had they conquered or neutralized gravity? I remembered that Earth's scientists believed that a man in a space ship would be absolutely weightless and apt to float about. I lifted my hand and let it drop to the arm of the chair. It behaved precisely as it would have on Earth. There must be an artificial gravity induced in the floor of the craft.

I wondered too how they had overcome the menace of lethal cosmic rays, meteors, sky debris, etc. Surely my ship carried no tons of lead shielding scientists declared necessary for adequate protection from cosmic rays. Also, I wondered in what way they had mastered the terrific pressure and temperature changes so that I was never conscious at any time of variations in either? And their motive power; what was the fantastic secret of those green fireballs? Possibly they were vortices of magnetic power which operated almost silently and with astounding efficiency. What a wonder world their planet must be, I thought, as I gazed in awe at the crystalline dream-ship passing from my line of vision.

Slowly then the room turned back toward the left and the Earth appeared once more with its shimmering rainbow halo. Dimly I could make out the faint outlines of the Western Hemisphere in varying shades of misty blue. Also I could see faint puffs of light here and there which I judged to be the larger cities of the North American continent.

Two flying saucers darted into view and sped downward toward Earth. Just as abruptly they decelerated and hung suspended in space as pinpoints of light. As I was wondering about them I heard the voice say that one was over Washington, D. C. and the other over Los Angeles. Los Angeles—the word echoed in my consciousness as I gazed at the faint brush of light that was a great sprawling city. I tried to remember that Los Angeles was my home, but it seemed only vaguely familiar; a place remembered somewhere in Time.

"Tonight, Orfeo," the voice continued, "you have explored a minute distance into the limitless highways of the universe. Through your own efforts the road may later be widened for you. Tonight you, an entity of Earth, have come close to the Infinite Entities. For the present you are our emissary, Orfeo, and you must act! Even though people of Earth laugh derisively and mock you as a lunatic, tell them about us!"

"I will . . . . I will . . ." I whispered haltingly knowing that everything I said was heard by them even as all my thoughts were known to them.

"We know you will, Orfeo," the voice replied. "Thus tonight a special privilege has been yours. We love the Children of Earth and it is our desire to help them as the hour of crisis approaches. But only through such harmless ones as you can we work.

"The aggressive men of Earth want our scientific advancements. For these they would shoot our crafts from the skies—if they could. But additional scientific knowledge we cannot give to Earth except as we are now doing in a manner perfectly in accord and harmony with cosmic law. Already man's material knowledge has far outstripped the growth of brotherly love and spiritual understanding in his heart. Therein lies the present danger. To add to the destructive phase of man's scientific knowledge is not permitted. We are working now to turn that knowledge to constructive purposes upon Earth. Also we hope to give men a deeper knowledge and understanding of their own true nature and a greater awareness of the evolutionary crisis facing them. At present we are working along all constructive lines of human endeavor and especially in the fields of medicine and healing. Surely you cannot fail to see the tremendous advances which have been made in this direction within the last few years. Even greater 'discoveries' are at hand including success in the fight against cancer. Thus shall we continue to work with and through men."

I listened to the compassionate voice, trying to imprint every word on my con-

SON OF THE SUN: The Secret Of The Saucers

sciousness. But I have forgotten much and these words are only a poor attempt to recall all that I heard. The voice continued speaking:

"We know your mind is filled with questions. One question in particular troubles you and it concerns the entity the world knows as Jesus Christ. May we set your mind at rest. In allegorical language Christ is indeed the Son of God. The star that burned over Bethlehem is a cosmic fact. It announced the birth on your planet of an entity not of Earth's evolution. He is Lord of the Flame—an infinite entity of the sun. Out of compassion for mankind's suffering He became flesh and blood and entered the hell of ignorance, woe and evil. As the Sun Spirit who sacrificed Himself for the children of woe he has become a part of the oversoul of mankind and the world spirit. In this He differs from all other world teachers.

"Each person upon Earth has a spiritual, or unknown, self which transcends the material world and consciousness and dwells eternally out of the Time dimension in spiritual perfection within the unity of the oversoul.

"In the illusion of Time is written man's choice through free will whereby he set in motion the cause of error which inevitably resulted in effect, in which mankind entered mortal consciousness or the living death of his present existence. Thus was he separated from his eternal and perfect self. His one purpose upon Earth now is to attain reunion with his immortal consciousness. When this is accomplished he is resurrected from the kingdom of death and becomes his real immortal self made in the image and likeness of God. Your Teacher has told you, God is love, and in these simple words may be found the secrets of all the mysteries of Earth and the worlds beyond."

Tears coursed down my cheeks. Under the spiritual scrutiny of that great, compassionate consciousness I felt like a crawling worm—unclean, filled with error and sin. Yes, I say sin, but not in the ordinary sense men use that word. Rather sin as sin really is. And basically sin is , falsity, the living lie! It is looking at your fellow man with a friendly smile upon your face with treacherous, malicious, or mocking thoughts in your heart. Sin is any and all deviations from absolute truth, perfect love, absolute honesty and righteous motives. Thus actual sin has little to do with Earthly standards of sin.

As these realizations filled my consciousness I wanted to fling myself down upon the floor and hide my head in shame for humanity. And of all men I at that moment felt the lowliest, the least worthy to be where I was. I wondered how those great beings could love such a one as I or any of mankind. We with our bloody wars, our intense hatreds, our cheap, shoddy intolerances, our greed and avarice and our cruel inhumanity to our fellowmen. I hid my head in my hands and wept bitter tears for a creature so full of error and hypocrisy and yet so puffed up with egotistical pride over our little material knowledge.

At that moment, as in a dream, I heard the strains of the "Lord's Prayer", played as though by thousands of violins. As I crouched in the chair fresh tears poured from my eyes. My heart was filled with humility, contrition and with gratitude—gratitude that these Great Ones had even considered our miserable selfish existence.

Above the exquisite strains of melody, the voice said: "Beloved friend of Earth, we baptize you now in the true light of the worlds eternal."

A blinding white beam flashed from the dome of the craft. Momentarily I seemed partially to lose consciousness. Everything expanded into a great shimmering white light. I seemed to be projected beyond Time and Space and was conscious only of light, Light, LIGHT! Orfeo, Earth, the past were as nothing, a dark dream of a moment. And that dream unfolded before my eyes in swift panorama. Every event of my life upon Earth was crystal clear to me—and then memory of all of my previous lives upon Earth returned. *In that sublime moment I knew the mystery of life!* Also, I realized with a terrible certainty that we are all—each one of us—*trapped in Eternity* and *allotted only a brief awareness at a time!*

I am dying, I thought. I have been through this death before in other earthly lives. This is death! Only now I am in *eternity, without beginning and without end.* Then slowly everything resolved into radiant light, peace and indescribable beauty. Free of all falsity of mortality I drifted in a timeless sea of bliss.

At last, as from a vivid dream, I regained consciousness. Dazedly, I looked about the interior of the craft. Everything was the same, but it seemed ten thousand years had passed in what must have been only a few moments. I was half conscious of a burning sensation on my left side just below the heart, but I thought nothing of it then.

Ethereal drifts of music were in the air. Far away, I could feel, more than hear, a pulsing vibration beneath the floor of the craft. Also, I was again aware of the gentle push of my body against the cushioned chair. I realized I was being taken back to Earth.

In an incredibly short time the wall opened and I saw the familiar surroundings. Yes, I knew I was home again. But I also realized a little sadly that Earth could never again really be my home. In the spiritual evolution of mankind, I had been expendable in this life. Thus had I passed through death and attained infinite life.

As I got up from the comfortable chair, I reached down and picked up the strange, shining bit of metal and carried it in my hand as I left the craft. In a kind of daze I walked away from the ship; then curiously turned to look at it from the outside once more. But it was gone! I looked up and there it was high in the sky, faintly visible as a fuzzy luminous bubble. Then suddenly it was not there at all; but high in the northeastern sky I saw a red, glowing disk which changed to green and vanished.

I glanced down at the round bit of strange metal in my hand. It was glowing and livid again and appeared almost to be alive as it quivered in contact with my flesh. Also, it was rapidly diminishing in size. By the time I had reached home it had dissipated into nothingness.

As I was undressing to go to bed, I remembered again the burning sensation I had felt on my left side while I was undergoing the profound "initiation" in the saucer. I glanced down and saw what appeared to be a circular "burn" about the size of a quarter on my left side directly below my heart. The outer rim of the circle was red, inflamed and slightly raised as also was a small dot in the center of the circle—the symbol of the hydrogen atom. I realized they had impressed that mark upon my body to convince me beyond all doubt of the reality of my experiences in the cold light of the coming days.

CHAPTER III
MY MEETING WITH NEPTUNE

Following the emotional shock of that profound and bewildering trip in the saucer, I went about in a veritable daze for weeks. I continued on the job at Lockheed and resumed the routine of my daily affairs; but I was like an automaton—a dweller in two worlds and at home in neither. It is almost impossible to explain my state of mind. But the great spiritual illumination I had received in the saucer left me something of a stranger to my own planet, Earth.

I longed to tell the world, to out the truths of my discoveries; yet I knew that for the greater part I must forever remain silent. Among other glimpses of reality, I attained the realization that *time is non-existent.* What we call Time exists only in the physical worlds and is an illusion of the senses. Also, I know now that our concept of space is entirely erroneous. But who could I convince of these and other truths—who would believe me?

But because *they* had requested that I tell Earthlings of my experiences, I told many persons about my trip in the flying saucer. Nearly everyone laughed and ridiculed me. I was the butt of numerous jokes. Someone was always wise-cracking: "Are your saucer pals going to show up tonight, Orfeo?" Or: "Tell one of the saucers to land over at the Drive-In theatre, Angie, and then we'll all believe it!" Such remarks invariably brought forth gales of laughter at my expense. But I no longer cared—I *knew*, and that was enough!

As my story got around, several newspapers printed derisive accounts of "The Saucer Man". It cut deeply to see the embarrassment and humiliation it all caused my two sons. They knew people were saying their father was a "screwball". They didn't want to go to school because their companions laughed at them. I knew it all hurt Mabel too. Mabel pleaded with me to forget my experiences. I tried to explain to her why I had to tell about them, and we had some bitter misunderstandings on the subject.

I wanted so much to do something constructive, but I didn't know how to go about it. I began calling various military and defense offices. The personnel of several of the smaller ones laughed openly and passed me off, I know, as a crackpot. But it was with tremendous relief I found the really important offices referred me to men who were genuinely interested. They questioned and cross- questioned me concerning the information I gave them.

A little later I began giving weekly talks to small groups of interested people about space visitors. At first these meetings were held in private homes and then as the attendance increased we met in the Los Feliz Club House.

In what little spare time I had I began writing down my experiences and planned to publish them in a small newssheet, for I believed I could reach more people that way.

But as the days and weeks passed following my fantastic trip in the saucer and nothing more happened, I began to feel a little uncertain. The constant ridicule and laughter created even more doubts. My insistence upon the absolute truth of my experiences finally appeared to be definitely alienating my friends and even my family. My story was unbelieved upon Earth and the mysterious visitors were doing nothing to aid me. I actually began to doubt my own sanity, to wonder if the experiences had been an illusion or hallucination of some sort. And yet an inner tribunal of Truth assured me that such was not the case for *with them I had seen and known reality*—and I could never forget that.

On the night of August 2nd I and Mabel were helping out at the Los Feliz Drive-In theatre snack bar. About 11 o'clock I went outside for a breath of fresh air. Over the hills to the west I noticed a fuzzy green light apparently hanging suspended in the sky. I watched it for several moments, then went inside and called Mabel and seven or eight others to come out and see it. All of them saw the mysterious light hanging motionless in the sky over the hill. Unable to explain it, some of them declared it must be a helicopter hovering in the air. Others thought it might be a high street lamp of some sort.

But when after three or four minutes the "street lamp" climbed slowly and silently into the heavens and suddenly vanished, no one had much to say. But for some perverse reason none of them wanted to admit that it was actually a flying saucer.

As they trouped back into the cafe laughing about "Orfeo and his flying saucers", a depressing wave of discouragement passed over me. It was useless—absolutely useless—to talk to anyone about the saucers or my experiences. Feeling greatly disheartened and vey much alone, I decided to leave and walk home.

As I cut across the vacant lots the Hyperion Avenue Freeway Bridge loomed huge and dark ahead of me. The sky was overcast and the dense, oblique shadows from the vast concrete structure were heavier and more eerie than usual. Yet in the shadows of the dark archways of the bridge I had come to feel a kind of warmth and welcome, a spiritual communion with a vastly greater and more kindly world. For it was in the shadows of the huge bridge that I had come upon the saucer which had carried me out of this world.

I was thinking of these things when I suddenly became aware of someone approaching from out of the darkness. I was startled for I'd never before met anyone taking the short-cut beneath the bridge so late at night. I was about to call out a word of greeting when it dawned upon me that the stranger was coming from the dead end of the bridge. My first thought was that someone was lying in wait for me, possibly to rob me. But before I could become alarmed, I heard the stranger call: "Greetings, Orfeo!"

My heart almost stopped beating, for immediately I recognized the vibrant, beautiful voice of the being who had spoken to me in the saucer.

I stopped in my tracks, utterly speechless, and stared at the approaching figure. But then a wave of joy and gratitude flooded over me, and I finally replied falteringly: "Greetings . . . to you . . ."

He laughed pleasantly. "I know that in your mind you have given me a name— I who have remained nameless to you," he said gently. "You may call me by that name, Orfeo—it is as good as any other and has more inner significance to you than any name I might give you."

"Neptune . . ." I spoke the name slowly and reverently. For it was indeed the name I had given to this great and mysterious being. Then I added: "At last you have come to give me strength and faith."

He was near enough then for me to see that he was several inches taller than I and similar in outline to a well-built man. But the shadows were so heavy that I couldn't make out the details of his figure. But just to be in his presence once more was to sense again a tremendous uplifting wave of strength, harmony, joy and serenity.

"Come, Orfeo," he said gently, continuing on past me. "We have many things to discuss tonight."

I followed him as he strode ahead of me through the dense shadows. I could hear his solid footsteps upon the gravelled path which convinced me beyond the shadow of a doubt that he was no phantom or illusion.

He led me to a better lighted area near the bend of Glendale Boulevard where it goes up and over the bridge. I was actually trembling in anticipation of my first actual look at the mysterious visitor from another world.

When he turned I saw his face, the same wonderful, expressive countenance I had seen on the luminous screen. I again noticed especially his extremely large, dark and expressive eyes and nobility and beauty of his features which actually seemed to radiate warmth and kindliness.

Then I noticed that he was wearing a kind of uniform, bluish in color, perfectly tailored and tightly fitted to the outlines of his body. But it was apparently without seams, buttons, pockets, trimmings or design of any sort. In fact it fitted so perfectly that it was almost like a part of his body.

But as I studied him I became aware of an astonishing phenomenon: I could see his uniform and figure clearly, but it wavered occasionally, as though I were viewing it through rippling water. And the color did not remain solid and uniform, but

SON OF THE SUN: The Secret Of The Saucers

varied and changed in spots, which reminded me of an imperfectly tuned television set. Only his face and hands remained immobile and stable as though not partially obscured by a film of rippling water.

Headlights from approaching automobiles fell upon us from time to time and I remember wondering what manner of being my companion appeared to be to those in the passing cars. Did they see him at all? If so, did he appear as solid and substantial as myself?

He moved forward again, motioning for me to follow him. Without speaking he led me down the sharp concrete declivity into the bed of the dry Los Angeles River. There he sat down upon a large stone and motioned for me to do likewise.

For a time he was silent and I was acutely conscious of a tremendous vibrational field about him; a tangible emanation of serenity, brotherly love, and ineffable joy.

At last he said: "You sense and understand intuitively many things I cannot say directly to you, Orfeo. You have just fully realized that we are not like earthmen in that we function in dimensions unknown to your world. Earth is a three-dimensional world and because of this it is preponderantly false. I may tell you that to the entities of certain other worlds Earth is regarded as 'the accursed planet', the 'home of reprobate, fallen ones'. Others call your Earth 'the home of sorrows'. For Earth's evolution is evolution through pain, sorrow, sin, suffering and the illusion of physical death. Believe me, all evolutions are not similar to Earth's, despite the present beliefs of your scientists."

As I heard these strange words, my heart and mind cried out: "But why must it be so? Why should Earth's people know pain, suffering and death?"

He looked up into the heavens and in the soft light I saw deep compassion in his face as he said slowly: "The answer to that question is one of the mysteries of the illusion of Time. But I can tell you this: such conditions did not always prevail among the entities who now inhabit Earth. Once there was another planet in your solar system, the fairest and most radiant of all the planets. That planet was the original home of Earthlings. In their native home they knew no pain, sorrow, suffering, sickness or death. But in the glory and wonder of their world they grew proud and arrogant. They made war among themselves and finally turned against the Great Giver of Life. Ultimately they destroyed their own planet which today exists only as a sterile and barren ring of and debris in the solar system. In order that those entities might gain understanding, compassion and brotherly love they were born into the animalistic, material evolution of a lesser planet, Earth. Suffering, sorrow, frustration and death became their teacher. Their symbol became the Man-Beast. Each man must work out his own destiny and salvation. In the illusion of Time and through repeated births and deaths each entity slowly and painfully evolves spiritually toward its former glorified state of divinity. Eventually all the entities of Earth will again attain their lost heritage. They will have learned understanding, compassion and true love for God and their fellows."

I pondered his strange words thoughtfully, thinking as I did so that what he had said explained many apparent mysteries about man and his lot upon Earth. But soon my attention was distracted once more as I saw the figure of Neptune strangely "waver" again. Suddenly the question was in my mind: "Was he really there in the truest physical sense, or was he an immaterial projection into the physical world from another dimension? Did I see him in his true form and ordinary state of being, or merely a projected approximation of a man's appearance?" These strange thoughts frightened me a little and carried me into too deep waters.

A reassuring smile lighted his face. "Don't be alarmed, Orfeo. The answer to the troublesome question in your mind is both yes and no. On Earth form, color, individuality and the material aspect of things is all-important. In our world these illusions are of practically no importance at all. Suffice to say that for you I am an approximation of myself as I really am. I can't make it any clearer in three-dimensional terms."

I thought about my own troubled fellows of Earth. Impetuously, I asked: "What about Earth now? On the surface all seems fairly calm, but I know we are only drifting on dangerous and treacherous waters. In their hearts many people are troubled and afraid. There is the ever-constant fear of the H-bomb and of other horribly destructive weapons being developed in the laboratories. Also there is the creeping menace of Communism that is threatening the world, and so many other things. . ."

When Neptune spoke his voice was calm and dispassionate: "Communism, Earth's present fundamental enemy, masks beneath its banner the spearhead of the united forces of evil. Along with good, all men have evil in their hearts to a degree. But some are much more evil than others. Communism is a necessary evil and now exists upon Earth as do venomous creatures, famines, blights, tyrannies, cataclysms—all are negative forces which awaken the positive forces of good in man and cause them to act. Thus are they combatted, understood and ultimately their unreality becomes apparent. For evil is always eventually self-destroyed."

He paused and once more I noticed his "uniform" darkening and lightening in spots, as though it were made of restless pale bluish clouds and patches of moonlight. Then I held my breath as he continued: "Yes, war will come again to your Earth. We are powerless to prevent it. Millions in your land will fight to the end for their cherished ideals and freedom of the human mind, with only a minimum on their side for victory. The hour of travail which in future history shall be known as 'The Great Accident' is nearer than any man dreams. And already the clouds of war are on the horizon, dark and ominous; but overhead beams the rainbow, infinite and eternal. Mankind will survive Armageddon and awake to a new more glorious day of fellowship and honest brotherly love. In the dawning great New Age of Earth all will forget their bitter hurts and build constructively together upon the solid foundation of the Brotherhood of Man."

He stopped speaking and turned his radiant eyes full upon me. In the half-light his countenance was truly resplendent.

"There is not much more I can tell you now, Orfeo," he said. "Since the first publicized modern sighting of our disks in the year 1947, thousands upon Earth have come to believe in us. Many have actually seen our disks. Some have seen us clairvoyantly. Others have communicated with us clairaudiently. Still others recognize the truth of our existence and greater scope of our being, through intuitive perception. But as far as official proof of ourselves, for which so many clamor, we cannot offer that. Official proof of the existence of our disks will come. But for us to attempt physically to contact mankind through any so-called authoritative source would be only useless and possibly disastrous for them. Nearly all three-dimensional beings have no concept of, nor could they possibly understand, extra-dimensional beings. Tonight in visiting you I have broken a code—the code of 'hands off', as regards any interference in the affairs of Earth. Active cosmic law will see the necessary amends made."

He looked at me; his strange eyes suddenly saddened. For a moment I had the uncanny feeling that in his greater vision I appeared to him only as a fleeting, insubstantial shadow, utterly without reality as he knew it. In that revealing instant I knew that we of Earth are as far removed from their nature as Earth is from the Sun.

After a while he said: "I would shake your hand in token of our momentous meeting here tonight. But I cannot. I have gone too far already. For my transgression we must now recede an equal degree from you. The immutable law of cause and effect upon Earth will govern accordingly. As a result, but few will believe or even hear your account of our meeting. In the over-all picture your story will in no way change conditions upon Earth. Neither will any actual Earthly event be either hastened or retarded because of our meeting. At most your story will give only greater faith and inner conviction to the few—but it is an important few! The ways of God are immutable and apparent only to those who have spiritual discernment. In the illusion of Time all things will be fulfilled in their proper hour."

I found that I was trembling and my nerves fairly quivering. Whether from sheer emotion or actually from being within the vibratory range of Neptune, I don't know. I longed to thank him, to express the great feeling of gratitude in my heart; but I didn't know quite how. I said: "From the bottom of my heart I thank you, Neptune. I pledge my very life to you and the beings of your world, that greater understandings may come to mankind."

"We know you will not fail us, Orfeo," he replied. "No other contact may be made at this time. But have no further doubts about the reality of your experiences. The road is open now; walk it as you will. Your failure will be my own. But I smile upon you for the increased numbers who will come to know us in a truer aspect and to believe in us because of you. Strength and encouragement will be given to the millions who will rise courageously to meet the fiery trials ahead. I tell you this: the 'Great Accident' is very close and the fury of the next war will break when it is least expected; when men are talking of peace. I cannot say more."

With these prophetic words, Neptune extended his hand to me. But recalling his words, I did not grasp it.

He smiled and his face actually seemed to radiate light. "Orfeo, my brother!" he said with genuine affection. "For my sake you refused to break the code. My trust is forever in you, Orfeo. In your simple action you have cleansed me from my contact with this ground."

He paused; then added: "Soon we shall recede from Earth, Orfeo—and yet in reality we shall never be far away. Later, we shall return, but not to you, beloved friend. You will understand the meanings of these words later on."

When I made no reply, he said: "I'm thirsty, Orfeo. Perhaps you know where we might get a drink of water?"

"Oh yes . . . . yes sir," I answered eagerly, getting quickly to my feet. I remembered a small nearby store that remained open all night. "Please wait here; I'll be right back." I left him and clambered up the embankment.

As I hurried toward the store, I turned and looked back at the Hyperion Bridge. Beneath the high center arch I made out the hazy outline of a kind of ghostly "igloo" which I immediately recognized as a saucer similar to the one in which I had ridden.

At the store I bought two bottles of lemon soda and hastened back. But as I approached I was disappointed to see that the ghostly saucer was no longer beneath the arch of the bridge. Quickening my pace, I almost ran to the spot where I had left Neptune; but he was no longer there. I wasn't too surprised for I'd had a premonition he wouldn't be there when I returned.

I tossed the sodas away and sank down upon the ground. The place was appallingly desolate without him. I felt so acutely alone, so helpless and deserted—like a child left alone in a dark room when the light is suddenly extinguished. I looked upward and my eyes hopefully searched the skies. High in the western heavens I saw a soft, fuzzy green light which hung for a moment, then shot away and vanished.

"Farewell, Neptune," I said softly as I felt my eyes grow moist. "I know now Earth is not yet ready for a meeting with the beings from your world. But in the dawning of Earth's great New Age, that day will come, friend. When we have learned the meaning of true brotherly love; when we have overcome to a greater degree the evil inherent in our selfish hearts, then perhaps we will be worthy to meet the infinitely wiser and gentler brothers of your world. In those days your fellows will visit us openly and joyfully. No longer will Earth be 'the accursed planet—home of sorrows'."

CHAPTER IV
"WE CAN APPEAR AND FUNCTION AS EARTHMEN, ORFEO!"

At first I told no one of my strange meeting with Neptune, for I knew only too well that my new story would meet with even greater disbelief and ridicule. But I immediately set to work writing down my further experiences. I had already placed my first experiences with the saucers in manuscript form and planned to publish it as the first edition of a small personal newspaper, The Twentieth Century Times; but I had experienced difficulty in finding a publisher. Now I was glad the paper was not yet in print, for I could include my most recent experience with Neptune.

I worked hard on the manuscript in my spare time. But the emotional and physical strain I was under began to tell on my health and I felt the return of many of my old symptoms of extreme weakness and fatigue. In October of 1952 I applied for a leave of absence from my job at Lockheed. This was granted and by an odd coincidence the first day of my leave started on the day the first strike in the history of Lockheed was called. I had the feeling that I had been saved from additional nervous stress and strain. Fortunately, the strike ended well and work resumed at the plant within a few weeks.

With time off from work, I was soon able to complete the manuscript. Also, with the additional rest, my health rapidly improved so that I was strong enough to return to work within a month.

The fellows at the plant knew of my interest in the saucers and many of them also knew of my first two experiences. I was in for a lot of ribbing from them. But on the whole it was goodnatured, friendly ribbing so I didn't mind. Several of those with whom I worked most closely frequently asked me for some kind of proof of the reality of my experiences. I told them of the shiny piece of strange metal I had picked up on the floor of the craft and explained how within a matter of minutes it disintegrated into nothingness. Also I told them of the burn I had received during my "initiation" in the saucer which had resulted in a mark on the left side of my chest. Some of them looked at the mark in the form of the symbol of the hydrogen atom. But these things were not sufficient proof for them.

One night at work several of them had been kidding me about my experiences.

SON OF THE SUN: The Secret Of The Saucers

Al Sarradar quipped: "Just what kinda liquor you drinkin', Angie, that sends you outa this world?" Walter Seveicki chimed in: "Yeah, tell us so we can take a ride in a saucer too!"

We had just rolled out a heavy die. Al and I were removing the finished radome from it when suddenly there was a loud crackling sound as though a wooden plank had snapped. At the same instant I felt a shock in my right hand and a stinging sensation in my index finger.

The boys were startled. Al yelled: "What happened, Angie?"

I didn't reply, but held out my index finger for all of them to see. Five of them watched as a round welt appeared on my finger. The welt was not red like a burn, but appeared gray. It was about the size of a dime, a perfectly round circle with a dark dot in the center—again the symbol of the hydrogen atom.

Somebody said something about static electricity, but all of them were deeply puzzled, for nothing like that had ever happened before. Al advised me to get medical attention at the plant hospital. I told him it would not be necessary; there was no pain whatsoever. I reminded him that the same thing had happened to me in the saucer when I had received a considerably larger similar mark on my left side below the heart.

They laughed at my explanation and refused to believe that extra-terrestrials had anything to do with the sudden unaccountable phenomenon which had produced the strange mark on my finger. Yet they were mystified and today any one of them will testify to the authenticity of the experience. The odd mark remained on my index finger for some months as a constant reminder of the proximity of unseen visitors.

The latter part of October Mabel made a trip back to New Jersey to visit our folks. When she returned several weeks later my mother and father accompanied her, as they wanted to spend a month or two in California. Mabel wired me to meet them at the Greyhound bus depot.

I was eager to see Mabel again and looking forward to a reunion with my Dad and Mother. I drove downtown the night they were to arrive, as thrilled as a kid. It was around six o'clock and the streets heavy with traffic. Parking my car, I walked toward the bus terminal. It too was bustling with activity. In all of the excitement, flying saucers and space visitors were the farthest things from my mind. But as I entered the front door of the bus terminal I stopped in my tracks and stared, unable to believe my eyes. Directly in front of me and facing the was a familiar face. I knew I couldn't be mistaken—it was Neptune!

He glanced up and his dark eyes told me that he was expecting me. He was dressed in an ordinary dark business suit and carried a brief case under his arm. A dark blue felt hat with snap brim shaded his eyes. And he appeared as real as any person in the depot! After the sudden shock of surprise I started forward to greet him, but a strong telepathic command stopped me. I stood hesitant looking at him. He stood up, facing me and I could not help noticing how tall, extremely handsome and distinguished he appeared in the hurrying throngs of people. He was not smiling; in fact, his face was almost stern as though he might be angry. I wondered what I had done wrong. I completely forgot Mabel and the folks waiting for me.

His intent gaze never left me. Stalling for time I walked over to the newsstand and picked up a magazine and thumbed through it. I had received the definite telepathic impression not to approach him; thus I waited for him to speak to me. But he did not. Staring blankly at a page in the magazine I waited for further telepathic communication. It came! The gist of the message was: "The last time you saw me, Orfeo, I was in a less objectified projection in your three-dimensional world. The purpose being to give you some idea of our true aspect. But now tonight you see me fully objectified. If you did not know who I am, you could not tell me from one of your fellows. Tonight I am no half-phantom, but can move among men as an Earthman. It is not necessary for you to speak to me; you have gained the understanding. You know now that we can appear and function as human beings."

I looked gratefully into his eyes and as in my previous encounter with him, I felt again a unity of being as though I were momentarily released from the bonds of individuality.

Just then Mabel and the folks spied me. As in a dream I heard them call to me as they came rushing over to me. Like an automaton I kissed Mabel and hugged Mom and Pop. All the while they were talking and holding my hands. I was going through the motions of greeting them, but I was still so stunned that I scarcely knew what was happening.

Together we all walked toward the exit and I noticed that Neptune was following a short distance behind us. When we reached the door I was about to open it when Neptune reached out and pushed it open for us. I was more astounded than ever, for it meant that he could function in the physical world as easily as any Earthling.

Outside he walked a few paces to the left and stopped. There he opened his briefcase and removed a pack of cigarettes. He removed a cigarette from the pack and put the package back in the briefcase. Then without lighting the cigarette he tossed it into the gutter.

I was smoking a cigarette too. Following Neptune's action, I tossed my cigarette away. Mabel noticed my preoccupation and odd behavior. She looked at Neptune and then at me and asked: "Who is that man and why is he staring at us so intently?"

I didn't reply to her question as I was too confused to get involved in explanations. I said: "Come on Mae, let's get the suitcases into the car."

She knew something was wrong and I was aware of the three faces studying me with perplexity. I made fumbling excuses for my odd behavior. But on the drive home I was able to begin to snap out of it and to show them the warm welcome I felt in my heart.

CHAPTER V
THE PAST IS NEVER DEAD!

The Christmas holidays arrived with their gay, festive spirit and usual bustling excitement. By then things had settled back to normal and I had experienced no further contacts. Flying saucers seemed to have vanished from the skies; practically no accounts of sightings appeared in the newspapers. Although I had completed the manuscript for The Twentieth Century Times, I couldn't get up the courage to have it published.

Mabel kept saying: "Orfie, if you publish that, people will think you are completely crazy. Why don't you just forget it! Nothing good can ever come of it. Everything is going along so smoothly now; we're both working and the boys are happy—let's just leave it that way."

"But, Mae . . ." I'd remonstrate. "Don't you understand; these things really happened to me! It is my duty to tell what I know!"

"And just what thanks will you get for it? Do you want to be ridiculed, laughed at and considered a crackpot or a psycho? Think back! Remember how everybody talked when you first told that wild story about a trip in a flying saucer. What did it get you but ridicule! Even if it did happen, Orfie, forget it! Just forget the whole thing for your family's sake. Let's be happy and enjoy life."

Thus although I felt I was betraying Neptune, I let things drift and made no effort to get my story published. In fact on New Year's Day, 1953 our lives were going along so smoothly and pleasantly that I had decided to forget it all insofar as the world was concerned and let those incredible experiences become a part of the dead past of 1952.

But the events of 1952 would not rest. During the latter part of January, 1953 the front pages of the newspapers were carrying sensational new saucer stories. The Air Force released reports that flying disks and strange clusters of lights were numerous over Korea. F-94 Starfires had encountered several of the saucers and one of their pilots had gotten a radar magnetic lock on one of them. Northern Japan too had many sightings.

The reports made me restless. At night I frequently went outside and scanned the heavens. Frequently I saw the disks overhead as roving lights. Any casual observer would not give a second glance, but simply pass the lights off as ordinary airplane lights. And since our apartment was close to several large airports, there were usually airplanes visible at all times. I should never have been able to distinguish saucer lights from those of aircraft were it not for the peculiar sensitivity of my nervous system to the electro-magnetic effect of the saucers.

Then I began to be ashamed of myself for having failed so completely the trust that Neptune had placed in me. He had said: "The road will open, Orfeo; travel it as you will." I realized that thus far I had refused to travel the road and except for the few talks I had made to small groups I had done nothing to help people understand the strange visitors. More and more every day I realized how selfish I was in thinking first of my family and myself. Finally I knew there was no alternative for me. Come what may, I had to go ahead with publication of the facts of my experiences. It was the only constructive thing I could think of to do.

Without discussing the matter any further with Mabel, I took the manuscript for The Twentieth Century Times to several local publishers. None of them were encouraging. Far from it! The first one I approached was highly amused and a little contemptuous as he said: "You'd better send this thing to a science-fiction mag, old boy, unless you want to land in a strait-jacket."

The next publisher I tried told me how rambling and incoherently the thing was written. "You forget I'm not a writer, "I replied. "I've done the best I can and all of the facts are there."

He laughed. "You say the facts are here—but are they? You start off by saying these experiences are true and yet before the narrative is completed you have inferred several times that they could be imaginary. In fact, right here on the front page you make the statement: 'This story is either a yarn or it is real!' What kind of facts are those? And how can you expect people to accept the paper as actual fact?"

"I've thought of all that," I replied. "Frankly, it was my idea to break the news gently. In other words, to let the readers feel uncertain at first as to the absolute authenticity of the facts. To tell this entire thing at first as fact is too much of a shock for an unstable world. As you yourself say, I might be hustled off to a mental institution. Let the truth of what I have to say develop gradually."

After considerably more talk along these same lines, he agreed to publish it, but only if I would permit him to edit it and delete major portions of the story. I flatly refused and he in turn refused to have anything to do with publication of the manuscript.

And so it went. I tried publisher after publisher with the same discouraging results. At last, however, I found a small publishing house that was willing to print the piece word for word as written if I would pay all publishing costs and take all of the papers myself. I agreed to do this. But as we parted he shook his head and said: "Pardon me for saying this, Mr. Angelucci, but I honestly think you are making a grave mistake. Not only are you throwing your money away, but you are liable to make yourself a public laughing stock."

"I'll have to risk all that," I answered. "There is no alternative for me; I must publish that paper."

Thus on February 19, 1953, the one and only issue of The Twentieth Century Times came off the press, an eight-page, tabloid-type newspaper which carried word for word an account of all my experiences I felt it was wise for me to release. I breathed a huge sigh of relief when I saw the paper, for I felt that I had satisfied a debt.

When I walked into our apartment with an armful of the papers Mabel took one horrified look at one of the sheets and sank down in a chair. "Oh Orfie, you didn't do it! You didn't! This thing is dynamite. It can wreck us. Wreck your job, my job and the boys' schooling. This can finish everything we've built up here."

"I'm sorry, Mae," I replied doggedly. "Believe me, there is no other way out for me. I've got to live with myself; so I had to do it. I hope you'll try to understand."

But I knew Mae didn't understand. And as copies of the paper got around, many of her predicted reactions occurred. People began ridiculing me outright and several papers published sarcastic news items about me and my experiences, subtly inferring that I "wasn't all there". Believe me, it wasn't easy to bear, and especially did I suffer for my family. The boys were ribbed unmercifully at school and at her job at the snack bar Mabel was the constant target for the sharp barbs of wit aimed at me.

But the response was not entirely negative. Some persons became genuinely interested. About that time I resumed my weekly talks at the Club House and thus I was able to distribute the papers at the meetings. As more and more persons became interested and ceased to take my Twentieth Century Times as a joke, I began to feel that all might not be lost. And more important, I could face my reflection in the mirror again, happy in the thought that I had not entirely failed the space visitors.

CHAPTER VI
AIRPLANES DO DISAPPEAR!

Not long after my publication of the paper a new aspect of my experiences with the saucers developed. On the afternoon of March 3, 1953 I was sitting alone in the kitchen, reading. I was dully aware of the steady drone of an airplane which continued for some time. The sound apparently was coming from the west. Gradually it dawned upon me that the sound was too steady and too unwavering for an ordinary aircraft.

Curiously, I got up and looked out the door. Coming from the north I saw what appeared to be an ordinary small aluminum airplane. From where I was standing in the doorway there was nothing unusual in the sound of the craft as it assumed the normal crescendo of direct approach. I stepped out of doors and watched it fly directly overhead Until it was fairly in the face of the sun—when suddenly and astoundingly the plane was no longer there! Just as mysteriously the sound of its motor ceased abruptly too. I never saw the plane again. Confused, I went back into the house. Obviously the craft was not a flying disk, but a conventional type aircraft, for I had not experienced any of the unpleasant physical symptoms that a flying disk invariably produces in my body.

Four days later about five o'clock in the afternoon I was accompanying Jane Vanderlick, a neighbor who is employed at the Theatre cafe. We were walking to the cafe where Jane was going to open it half an hour early that day. We were laughing and talking when Jane noticed an airplane nearby in the sky, flying south. It seemed just an ordinary airplane of the most common type: "Maybe that's a flying saucer, Orfeo!"

I thought she was kidding me and replied: "Not you too, Jane!"

But her eyes were serious. "I mean it, Orfeo. There's something peculiar about that airplane."

For the first time I scrutinized the craft carefully. After a moment I had to admit there was something unusual about it. It appeared extremely dull and flat-surfaced and did not reflect any of the rays of the setting sun as it ordinarily should have done.

SON OF THE SUN: The Secret Of The Saucers

While we were both staring at it the airplane suddenly vanished right before our eyes in a clear and cloudless sky! The sound of its motor ceased just as abruptly. Both of us stood in our tracks. Jane stared at me. "What happened to that airplane, Orfeo?"

I shook my head and then replied slowly: "I wasn't going to mention it to anyone, Jane, but I saw the same thing happen four days ago. I don't know what it means!"

We stood there for some minutes our eyes vainly searching the skies for some trace of the vanished plane. I requested Jane to remember every detail of the strange incident. She promised that she would. If you ask her about it today, she will verify the experience just as I have related it to you.

Several days later I was with a group of employees sitting around the Lockheed Plant. It was about five minutes before four in the afternoon. We were waiting for the shifts to change preparatory to going on duty. My good friend, but most confirmed skeptic, Richard Butterfield, was with us. While we were talking idly, an apparently ordinary two-engine airplane came into view over the hills.

Butterfield's attention was attracted to the craft. He arose from the bench and stared up at it as though he was spellbound. His behavior reminded me immediately of Jane Vanderlick's actions a few days previously. Her eyes had been attracted to that particular plane just as Butterfield's eyes were now drawn to this one. Yet neither of the planes had any effect upon me. The crowd all noticed Butter-field's deep absorption in the small plane. Some of them started laughing and began ribbing him. I remember someone shouting: "Look! He ain't never seen an airplane before!" But Butterfield paid no attention. Finally, almost as though talking to himself, he said: "What is that?"

Several voices helpfully jibed in with wise-cracks about his being sorely in need of an optician's advice. One fellow remarked scathingly: "Any dope can see it's nothing but an ordinary two-engine airplane."

I didn't say anything, for I had noticed by then how flat-toned the craft was and how it failed to reflect the rays of the afternoon sun.

Suddenly there was an instantaneous flash that appeared to envelope the plane. When the flash was over there was no sign of a plane to be seen anywhere in the sky. The droning of its motors too had ceased. Many of the group had seen the phenomenon. They were startled and confused and everyone started talking at once trying to explain just what had happened. Others continued to stare into the skies searching for the vanished plane.

Butterfield dazedly brushed his hand across his eyes. It seemed difficult for him to come back to the norm of this world. He didn't say much, but for a long time after we had gone on the job he appeared to be in deep thought. I didn't volunteer any explanations, for the sudden disappearance of the plane in a brilliant flash was a new development for me. I kept mulling it over in my mind as well as the two previous experiences in which I had seen airplanes simply disappear into thin air. But I didn't give the incidents too much thought as I had more than enough to do to try and unscramble the puzzle of my previous experiences with the extra-terrestrials without adding more problems.

Within a week most of those who had seen the plane disappear had either forgotten the incident or had figured out some explanation that satisfied them. I saw then that the human mind does not want to believe anything it cannot understand; it will rationalize to any extent rather than face the unknown.

As the weeks passed I continued to be ribbed more and more. Some of my fellow workers were even inferring that I was lying just for cheap publicity. I would joyfully have dropped the whole thing like a red-hot coal, if I had not had the deep sense of loyalty and responsibility to those Greater Beings that neither I nor my fellows could begin to understand.

As the situation became more unpleasant at the plant, I finally decided to turn in my notice; for by then my experiences were fairly well-known throughout Southern California and thus I was in for constant ridicule. I knew I'd either have to shut up about space visitors or else quit my job. I decided on the latter.

My last three weeks at work were rather memorable. On August 14th Ernie Oxford and I were working on an airplane part outside the building. He, like all of the others when they got me alone, was harping on the space visitors and my "wild story in that Twentieth Century Times." He was contentiously declaring that neither he or his girl friend could swallow such a story.

I told him that it was his right to believe only what he wished to believe. Then I suggested that we forget the subject and concentrate on the job we had to do. But Ernie couldn't be stopped. He kept on telling me what a big mistake I was making.

While he was berating me, I looked toward the Burbank mountains and there directly over a ridge top was a flying saucer. I touched Ernie on the shoulder and pointed to the saucer. He dropped his tools and stared. Don Quinn, working nearby, saw us gazing into the sky and came running over.

While we were watching the thing it appeared suddenly to "flip" and vanished. Ernie kept asking: "Where did it go?" And after that experience he was quiet for a while. Then he began talking about the saucers and nothing else. He still didn't believe my story, but he knew he had actually seen a saucer.

Friday, August 21st, at 9:15 in the evening, the entire shift was hard at work. My mind was preoccupied and I was busy on an airplane part. Suddenly a tremor passed over me. I knew it could mean only one thing. I put down my tools and walked to the huge door, which was open only about a foot. As I looked out into the night I saw a light in the skies which appeared to be approaching the plant. While I watched, the light stopped in midair and changed from amber to red. There was no doubt in my mind about what it was.

SON OF THE SUN: The Secret Of The Saucers

I called to some of the fellows in the plant and beckoned them to join me. A number of them hurried over and we pushed open the door and went outside. All who came were rewarded. Every one of the men saw the red disk hanging over-head in the sky. While they were staring I glanced at their faces and I was deeply impressed with what I saw. Momentarily, they were like changed men. Wonder, awe, and belief were in their faces. Thus I was struck with the realization of what the mere sight of a single disk can do to the thinking of a number of persons.

While I was watching their reactions, they all turned suddenly and looked questioningly at me. I glanced up into the sky to see that the disk had vanished and only the moon and the stars were overhead. I asked where the disk had gone and all of them started to tell me.

From the many explanations I learned that the saucer had appeared to move until it was directly below the moon where it began to ascend. As it ascended it changed in color from red to amber and then to the silvery color of the moon. As it climbed higher its color became indistinguishable from the moon so that they could not tell what actually happened to it. But it had vanished. All of that had happened while I was watching their faces.

We trouped back in to work and all of the men were quiet and thoughtful. At the ten minute break I told them that on the following night at the second break I was going to ask each one of them to tell his story of what he had seen.

Every man told precisely the same story. In all there were twelve men. I failed somehow to get the names of two of the fellows but here are the names of the other nine: Dave Donegan, Al Durand, Dave Remick, Michael Gallegos, Richard Becker, Richard McGinley, Bruce Bryan, Ernie Oxford and Louis Pasko. Every one of these men will affirm the details of this sighting. The phenomenon did not happen fast; they all had plenty of time to observe and impress details on their minds.

All of them believed they had seen a flying saucer. Hence, I was enabled to leave my job with much of the stigma of untruth taken from the account of my experiences I had printed in all good faith in my Twentieth Century Times.

Among those twelve men there are two who are still deeply perplexed. They are Ernie Oxford and Michael Gallegos, for they had seen me drop my tools and go to the door as though beckoned by an unseen force. They said I behaved as though I were under a spell. Both of them started involuntarily to follow me, but on second remained on the job until I called them to come out.

Both of them insist that I must have received a message of some kind from the disk. When I told them that it was only a physical reaction and a deep intuitive feeling that space visitors were near, they believed I was holding something back from them. For they said that for a moment they too had felt something indescribable. With that I agree fully and I was happy that I was no longer alone.

Friday, August 28th was my last work night at Lockheed. I was outside working on an airplane part. That night Don Quinn was my partner. He was among those most skeptical of my saucer experiences and like the others he always insisted upon talking about them when we were together. He was telling me what a big mistake I was making in giving up my job and getting myself generally ridiculed. But I was used to such talk, and let him talk on. I glanced up into the sky and saw a silvery disk moving southeastward along the mountain rim. I immediately called Don's attention to it. He dropped his tools and stared and immediately began demanding to know what it was. "Why does it behave that way?" "How can it hang in the air like that?" I didn't reply to any of his questions.

Suddenly, it too just disappeared. Poor Don stared at me incredulous and bewildered. He admitted its flight characteristics were like nothing he had ever seen or heard of; yet he would not fully go along with the flying saucer explanation. Actually, he could not quite believe his own eyes. Thus seeing is not always believing. For I have seen other persons actually see a saucer and refuse to believe the evidence of their own sight.

It was during August that many of the strange events included in this chapter occurred. It was also in August that a revealing press release came through International News Service which recalled to my mind those cases of the airplanes which mysteriously vanished in thin air. The news item follows:

PLANES SEEN OVER ARCTIC

Washington, Aug. 1 (INS). An Air Force spokesman disclosed today that roughly twelve unidentified airplanes have penetrated the U. S. defense perimeter in the Arctic within the last year.

The spokesman said that the "invaders" were not identified as Russian so no protests could be made to Soviet authorities.

Some of the planes were tracked on radarscopes while others were seen to give off white vapor streaks. But before U. S. fighter pilots could give chase, they would mysteriously disappear out of radar range, the spokesman said.

He asserted that the "raiders" crossed the edge of the U. S. radar perimeter in Greenland and Alaska, but added they also flew elsewhere over the North American continent.

The Air Force has given pilots strict orders not to fire upon any unidentified plane unless a "hostile" act has been committed or is about to be, such as a bomber flying over U. S. territory with its bomb-bay doors open.

Could it be that those mysterious "disappearing airplanes" I had seen had penetrated the U. S. defense perimeter in the Arctic?

On the following day a counter-release came through International News Service. This counter-release negated all of the information given out in the first release.

These contradictory reports followed an already definitely established pattern. Official news releases of a mystifying nature concerning the saucers are invariably followed up by counter releases or actual retractions of previous statements.

SON OF THE SUN: The Secret Of The Saucers

As irritating and confusing as such contradictory reports are to the public, nevertheless this method of handling UFO information by the authorities is best for everyone concerned. For with a little thought, it is clear that such mystifying news stories without an official damper placed upon them immediately, might easily flare up into a nationwide conflagration of panic and hysteria. Official headquarters would be snowed under with avalanches of telegrams, letters, phone calls and personal inquiries. Thus only further confusion would result.

The story of the extra-terrestrials is one that no one can or will ever be able to finish with any degree of finality. It is my sincere personal belief that the Air Force and other responsible offices have responded to and handled the problems of space visitors precisely as those visitors have anticipated and desired them to do. As more and more thinking persons realize this significant fact, we will be prepared for greater revelations to come.

Perhaps it would be well to state here that in the cases of disappearing aircraft I do not believe the .ships dematerialize or dissolve into nothingness, as it would appear. Being composed primarily of a crystalline substance the ships may give the illusion of complete transparency or, if so controlled, they can be rendered entirely opaque. Thus, also, they can manifest any color or combination of colors, depending upon the energy employed and its control on the molecular substance of the crystal body.

It is no problem for the crystal disks to project visual images of ordinary aircraft and similarly to produce the auditory vibrations of aircraft engines. These projections may be easily picked up on a radar screen.

CHAPTER VII
FLYING SAUCER CONVENTION IN HOLLYWOOD

During those last days I was at Lockheed I thought often of Neptune's cryptic words: "The road will open, Orfeo; walk it as you will." And later when he said: "I smile upon you, Orfeo, for your greatly enhanced numbers."

Then his last prophetic words, "Strength and courage will be given to the millions who will rise and meet the great battles ahead with only a faint hope on their side for victory."

It was true, I thought; the road was beginning to open. New understandings and an ever increasing awareness were coming to me as time pissed. Also, as more and more people learned of my experiences many began to phone, write, or visit at our home, wishing to know more about the space visitors. We continued the regular weekly meetings at the Los Feliz Club House, but as the crowds increased, the Club House was no longer large enough to accommodate everyone. It was then that Max Miller, President of Flying Saucers International, an organization devoted to the study of flying saucer phenomena, and Jerome Criswell, the well-known columnist and television Man of Prophecy, suggested that we rent the music room in the famous old Hollywood Hotel for our weekly meetings. Thus we had been meeting there for several months every Sunday evening or afternoon. Opinions were exchanged and lectures on saucer phenomena were presented to enthusiastic audiences.

Paradoxically enough, as the general public's interest in the saucers increased, the press, radio, television and other news media suddenly and inexplicably dropped flying saucers from the news. Even the second-rate science fiction writers banished the word from their lexicon of horrors. Thus the public was left to grope for itself. And surprisingly enough the way was thus cleared for those individuals who had experienced actual contacts with the extraterrestrials to work freely without obstruction of erroneous "slanting" by official reporting.

Gerald Heard, Frank Scully and Donald Keyhoe were familiar names among persons interested in the saucers. These men, along with Fate magazine and Ray Palmer, had been making every effort to awaken the public to the awesome fact

SON OF THE SUN: The Secret Of The Saucers

that our world might well be under observation by beings from another planet. But now several unknown men were speaking up and declaring that they had actually had contact with the saucers and space visitors. Among these were George Van Tassel, Truman Betherum, George Adamski, George Williamson and Alfred Bailey. Those few newspapers which ran stories on these men did so with the tongue-in-cheek slant.

Sunday afternoons I was speaking to groups at the Hollywood Hotel. I knew that my audience waited patiently for clear, concise accounts of my experiences with extra-terrestrials. But they were often disappointed. Frequently when I stepped upon the platform to speak a strange transition came over me. It was as though another personality overshadowed me; someone who knew all of the answers. But the answers were not in my familiar English or Italian, but in an unfamiliar, half-remembered tongue. I would struggle to translate the ideas into English and end up by failing to be clear and direct. Thus with the understanding of the universe almost within my grasp, I was often helpless to reveal any part of it.

Nevertheless, even with my many failures to be concise and direct, the meetings gained momentum with increasing numbers in the audience.

It was then that Max Miller conceived the idea of a Flying Saucer Convention. It sounded like a tremendous idea to me. With the help of several other persons we enthusiastically began to formulate plans. It was decided that we should hold the convention at the Hollywood Hotel where there was plenty of room in the lobby to accommodate a large audience.

Various exhibits of saucer photographs, space ship models, books, magazines and pamphlets on the saucers were set up around the lobby and many circulars were mailed out announcing the event. Also invitations to speak at the convention were mailed to all persons who had been most helpful in revealing and disseminating information about the saucers and extra-terrestrials.

But response to the invitations was very poor. Less than a week before the convention was to open it appeared that none of the speakers whom we had counted upon would be present. Max was greatly worried. "It looks like we're sunk, Orfeo," he exclaimed dejectedly. "This thing is going to be the prize flop of any and all conventions." But as I looked at him, the conviction was suddenly strong in my mind that everything would come off well. I replied: "Don't worry, Max. It's going to come off much better than we ever even dreamed it would."

My prediction proved entirely correct. Every one of the speakers whom we had invited showed up for the convention, and some others besides. Among the invited speakers were Frank Scully, Arthur Luis Joquel II, George Van Tassel, George Adamski, Truman Betherum, John Otto from Chicago, Harding Walsh and a mysterious Dr. "X" who spoke long and eloquently on the saucers. He left immediately after speaking and no one ever knew who he really was or where he came from, although many inquired; for he had some startling things to say.

SON OF THE SUN: The Secret Of The Saucers

Almost to a man the speakers said they had received an irresistible urge to attend on Friday (two days before the opening of the convention). Could it be that the space visitors had been at work in their own subtle way?

At any rate the convention was a tremendous success. For three days and night the crowds overflowed the Hollywood Hotel out onto the lawns and adjacent Hollywood Boulevard. In fact the response was so tremendous that on the second morning I requested Max to stop all publicity on the convention.

Some of the larger Los Angeles newspapers covered the convention. But all news stories were of the usual tongue-in-cheek type. A few of the smaller, more rabid papers tried to "expose" it as nothing but a promotional "money-making" scheme.

The convention was a hectic one. I was busy night and day and carried on practically without sleep. When I wasn't speaking, people were surrounding me and bombarding me with endless questions. Many were skeptical and did not hesitate to be belligerent about it. But all during my ten months of speaking at the weekly meetings and the three nerve-wracking days of the convention, I never once lost my temper. A power beyond my own consciousness or control carried me through. In trying moments of heckling or confusion an upsurgence of peace and calm would pick me up and give me strength equal to the occasion.

However, on the last night of the convention, the power that was sustaining me suddenly failed and I lost my temper for the first time. A lone woman who had been especially persistent in seeking me out and cornering me to revile me and hurl quotes of scripture at me was responsible for the outburst. She knew I was wrong and she was right. And she had books, diagrams and bible verses to prove it. When at last I literally blew my top she joyfully picked up her data and departed shouting that my temper proved I was an agent of the devil. Within an hour I lost my temper several times again.

The most trying experience of the convention occurred when a large group of materialists were literally "giving me the works" in a stubborn, derisive effort to "get at the bottom of my story" and ferret out obvious flaws from a "common-sense" viewpoint.

Sincere, open-minded, honest persons who are willing to investigate the advent of space visitors never resort to such sneering interrogations. They ask honest, sincere questions on points they do not fully understand. But they have an honest desire to know, not to discredit, to sneer and to disparage.

This particular group had their minds set upon "exposing" me. Their methods, although entirely on a mental plane, would make the medieval inquisitions seem innocuous. Like little demons they parroted elementary physics and could see practical, intelligent action only behind the Iron Curtain. They knew I was a cheap publicity seeker who did not hesitate to lie about space visitors or anything else to further my own ends. No words of explanation could possibly prove anything to them they did not wish to believe.

I had undergone just as bitter and insinuating criticism before, but I was exceptionally tired that last night. I felt almost as though I were melting away before their venomous onslaught, collapsing at the seams, as it were, and suddenly I felt very, very human and down to earth. I was on the verge of exploding in anger again when a kind of veil was drawn over my conscious mind. The gesticulating figures before me faded to babbling, inconsequential shadows.

As they continued their violent attacks, my thoughts drifted calmly back to a scene of a few weeks before. I was attending a convention of science-fiction writers at the Hotel Commodore in Los Angeles. Since my experiences with the extraterrestrials, I have become interested in the field of science-fiction, for I have found that many scientific truths are adumbrated, or delineated, in science-fiction before ever they become realities of our world.

Many well known writers in the science-fiction field were present. When I came in they were holding open discussions of trends in the science-fiction field, the various new markets, etc.

One of the audience asked: "Why have all science-fiction writers suddenly stopped writing or even mentioning flying saucers?"

A speaker replied authoritatively that the subject had become taboo with them.

Another member of the audience demanded to know why this was so since the saucers had actually given such an impetus to the science-fiction field.

The speaker had no adequate answer for that one, but lamely explained that the saucers were "old stuff" now.

I was becoming impatient with the proceedings and was on the point of leaving when the guest speaker of the evening was announced. He was Mr. Gerald Heard, the well-known science-fiction writer and author of IS ANOTHER WORLD WATCHING?

Mr. Heard spoke with great eloquence and a deep, penetrating philosophy. He berated the writers for turning out material of an inferior grade and warned that the public would not continue to "stomach it", much less to buy it. Many of them squirmed uncomfortably in their seats.

As he neared the end of his stimulating and thought-provoking talk, his eyes met mine where I was seated near the back with two companions. I noticed that he seemed tired and shaken.

As our eyes met and held, a kind of mutual understanding passed between us. It was as though vortices of light opened between us in ever widening circles. Dimly, I could hear him terminating his speech with these words: "There is one in this room tonight—I do not know who he is, but he's going to upset the whole applecart." He paused, then his voice reverberated as he added: "He is the Awakener—he has not yet appeared, but he well may be here in this very room tonight. Thank you."

SON OF THE SUN: The Secret Of The Saucers

And the mystic wheels between us set in motion by the controlled magnetic vortices slowly receded and vanished.

I looked about the room at the audience, but they were no longer listening to him. Some were whispering and laughing among themselves.

As I looked about that busy room I thought that it was small wonder that the concoctors of science-fiction horror diets had declared the saucers "taboo". Far too much beautiful reality was on the side of the saucers. Harmony and beauty are much too tame for the horror boys. They have joined forces with the materialists, subversives and egoists to fight the "flying saucer sensationalists" down at every turn.

But the joke is on them, for reality has slipped quietly past them and established new frontiers of its own. The science-fictioneers were induced by subtle forces to ignore flying saucers as were many other materialistic sources of information. During the welcome lull the actual flying saucer phenomena and the extra-terrestrials were left to the inexperienced but honest handling of rank amateurs. At first these men were inept and inarticulate, but they are finding their voices and their numbers are rapidly increasing. The space visitors had actually only cleared the atmosphere for them. Had the professional spinners of horror-fiction stuck to the theme of flying saucers, the true contacts should never have been able to perform their missions.

CHAPTER VIII
MY AWAKENING ON ANOTHER PLANET

It was in the late summer of 1953 that the most beautiful and revealing of all of my experiences with the etheric beings developed. My life had been a kaleidoscope of new understandings and changing patterns since the night of my trip in the saucer, but apparently the most profound of all had to be revealed to my conscious mind in gradual steps of understanding, because the experience itself actually occurred in January of 1953 while I was still on the job at Lockheed, but it was not until six months later that I had any idea of the tremendous experience that had been mine. During those bewildering intervening six months I honestly believed that for seven days of my life in January, 1953 I had been a victim of complete amnesia. I told no one about it, not even Mabel, for so many confounding things had happened in the recent months of my life that I feared further complicating matters by relating an experience for which there seemed to be no explanation.

During those six months I experienced many very strange and disquieting hours. Vivid dreams of a hauntingly beautiful, half-familiar world troubled my sleep. Sometimes I would awaken trembling and bathed in perspiration feeling that I was close to conscious remembrance of an exquisitely beautiful experience that would explain many things. Also, frequently during the days, fleeting, tenuous memories drifted into the borderland of my consciousness.

Even more perplexing were those occasions when, while speaking to groups of persons at the Hollywood Hotel, I felt as though I were being somehow overshadowed by another greater personality; a personality who thought neither in my familiar English or Italian, but in a strange language which it seemed I once knew but now could no longer remember.

In order to clarify the experience itself, I must go back to that day in January, 1953 when it began. I did not go to work that afternoon as I was just recovering from the flu, but I was feeling so much better that I believed I could go back on the job the following day. Mabel was at work at the cafe and I was alone. About four o'clock a rather strange, detached feeling came over me. I was aware of a familiar odd prickling sensation in my arms and the back of my neck which usually announced the proximity of space craft.

I discounted the strange symptoms thinking they were only the result of my illness. Then suddenly I began to feel so drowsy that I could scarcely keep my eyes open. I remember starting toward the divan to lie down for a nap, but I later had absolutely no recollection of reaching that divan.

My next conscious perception was a peculiar "awakening" or regaining consciousness while on my job in the Plastics Department at Lockheed. Stupefied and bewildered I looked uncertainly about the factory. Dazedly, I recognized the familiar faces of my co-workers . . . and noticed the tools in my hands. I caught my breath sharply and an icy shiver quivered over my entire body as quite involuntarily I recoiled with a shudder from the entire scene. I didn't know why then, but everything seemed hopelessly wrong, primitive and crude.

In a daze I rubbed a hand across my eyes hoping to eradicate the scene. Then I was seized with a blinding vertigo and thought I was going to lose consciousness. Dave Donnegan, my working partner, looked at me sympathetically, and there was genuine concern in his eyes. He didn't say anything, but quietly took the tools from my hand and in his quiet, understanding way went ahead, carrying on alone.

An involuntary outburst of utter disgust came from my lips, disgust with everything I saw. It seemed like the Dark Ages. I remember hearing Dave say: "Are you all right, boy?"

I didn't reply; I couldn't! In panic I turned to rush out of the door. In my bland haste I bumped roughly into Richard Butterfield, the temporary lead man in my section. I must have looked acutely ill because I vaguely remember seeing the alarm in his eyes as he grasped me firmly but gently by the shoulders and exclaimed: "Angie! Angie! What's wrong with you!"

I was breathing hard. Both emotionally and mentally I was confused and uncertain. My thoughts were in turmoil. I had only one objective; to get out of that place! But the presence of Butterfield had a stabilizing, quieting effect upon me.

He smiled reassuringly while keeping his hands upon my shoulders. "Calm down, Angie, old boy," he said gently. "Go upstairs and take a break. You look beat!"

I mumbled my heartfelt thanks and stumbled up the steps, not yet aware of what actually had happened to me.

I got a cup of coffee. Never before had I needed one so badly. My hands were shaking and every nerve in my body was quivering. As I drank the hot, aromatic stuff I tried to think back, to remember why I was so shaken and upset. But my last recollection before my strange, perturbed "awakening" on the job, was walking toward the divan in my apartment. The intervening period was a total blank.

Noticing a copy of the Los Angeles Times on one of the tables, I nervously picked it up and glanced at the date. Perspiration broke out on my forehead; the date of the paper was January 19, 1953. Seven had elapsed of which I had absolutely no recollection! But even the date on the paper couldn't convince me. Trying to keep my voice casual, I asked a worker at a nearby table. He confirmed the date on the newspaper.

My body was bathed in cold perspiration. I was on the edge of panic as I sat there, my hands trembling so that I could hardly take a sip of coffee. I couldn't believe that seven days and nights had passed, leaving not a trace of memory in my mind.

Later in the afternoon when I was feeling a little better I went back downstairs on the job. But it was a real effort to behave in a normal, rational manner with my thoughts in turmoil. Cautiously and discreetly I questioned Dave and other fellow workers about those seven previous days. From their replies I gathered that I had been on the job every day and had apparently behaved in my usual manner until my strange "awakening" and violent outburst that afternoon.

At home I didn't mention my inexplicable loss of memory to Mabel. And apparently she had noticed nothing unusual in my behavior during that entire week. It seemed that in every way I had behaved in my accustomed manner. I had eaten my meals, slept, gone to and from work and helped Mabel out at the Snack Bar, as usual. It was fantastically incredible!

I told no one what had happened to me. But in my own mind I was utterly baffled and deeply troubled about those seven lost days out of my life. Imagine yourself in my place. Suppose that for an entire week your waking consciousness had been obliterated so that you could not remember a single event. Wouldn't you be deeply disturbed? Wouldn't you begin to wonder if you might not be psychopathic? In all sincerity I can tell that you would, for those were my own panic-stricken thoughts.

But as the days passed I gradually settled down into the routine of daily life. Often I tried hard to regain the memory of those seven lost days, but it seemed hopeless.

Months passed and I had about decided that for those seven days I had suffered from complete loss of memory. Except for the disquieting thoughts and vivid dreams, I had no intimation of what was coming until that memorable night in the first week in September, 1953.

I was feeling unusually restless that evening. Shortly after ten o'clock I went out for a walk. As always, my feet seemed involuntarily to carry me toward the Hyperion Avenue Freeway Bridge. In its dark, mysterious shadows I always found a kind of spiritual peace and comfort, for it was there I had met and talked with Neptune, the man from another world!

I was thinking of these things as I clambered down the concrete embankment into the almost dry bed of the Los Angeles River. Walking over to the spot where Neptune had talked with me, I sat down disconsolately upon the ground. I rested my head upon the stone where he had sat, and gazed thoughtfully up into the heavens and thought of the spiraling, endless wonders of the universe. Lost in reverie, a feeling of deep inner peace and tranquillity came over me. Noisy, clattering Earth with all of its troubles, dissensions and animosities seemed remote and relatively unimportant.

As my thoughts drifted pleasantly, I felt again the odd sensation which was always my first awareness of space visitors. But I was deeply puzzled, for Neptune had last told me: "We will return, Orfeo; but not to you."

Nevertheless the odd tingling in my arms and back of my neck was unmistakable. Hopefully, my eyes scanned the heavens. I saw nothing that in any way resembled a saucer. The intensity of the vibration increased, dimming the awareness of my conscious mind much as it had the night I had first encountered the saucer.

As in a dream my thoughts drifted back to that mysterious Monday afternoon six months before when, feeling much as I did now, I had walked toward the divan to take a nap. An astonishing thing was happening: I was beginning to remember, faintly, hazily, at first, like the sun's golden rays breaking through black clouds.

As memory flooded back I clearly recalled again that Monday afternoon. I was walking toward the divan . . . my eyes were so heavy I could scarcely keep them open. In a daze I sank down upon the divan and immediately fell into a deep sleep!

Only now I could remember waking from that sleep! My awakening was in a strange and wonderful world! I was no longer upon Earth; some fantastic transition had taken place. I awoke in a huge, fabulously beautiful room; a room the substance of which glowed ethereally with soft, exquisite colors. I was lying upon a luxurious couch, or lounge. Half awake, I glanced down at my body—but it was not familiar! My body was never so perfectly proportioned or of so fine coloring and texture.

I noticed that I was wearing only a fine white garment, closely fitted and covering my chest, torso and upper part of my thighs. A finely wrought gold belt was about my waist. Although the belt appeared to be made of heavy links of embossed gold, it was without weight. My new body felt amazingly light and ethereal and vibrant with life.

Full consciousness did not come to me at once. My first thoughts upon waking in that shining world were nebulous. Somehow the thought persisted in my mind that I was recovering from a long and serious illness. Thus I reclined there in a kind of pleasant lethargy as one does who has been very ill. Random thoughts drifted in my consciousness. Everything was so new and different and yet it was hauntingly familiar. My handsome new body was not my body, and yet it was! The exquisite room with its ethereal, softly glowing colors was like nothing ever dreamed of upon Earth, and yet somehow it was not strange and alien to me. Only one thing seemed unfamiliar: far away outside the huge, windowless room I could hear the continuous rumble of distant thunder. Oddly enough the thunder did not fill me with apprehension as had always been the case in the past. '

Gradually the dark mists began clearing from my mind. Incredible memories were coming back to me; memories of another world, a different people—another life! Lost horizons, deep-buried memories, forgotten vistas were surfacing to my consciousness.

"I remember this world!" I thought rapturously. "I remember it in the same way that a condemned prisoner remembers the sunshine, the trees, the flowers of the outside world after an eternity chained in a dark and odious prison. This is my real world, my true body. I have been lost in a dimension called Time and a captive in a forbidding land called Earth. But now, somehow, I have come home. All is serenity, peace, harmony and indescribable beauty here. The only disturbing factor is a troublesome half-memory of an unhappy shadow named Orfeo, a bondsman in a prison-world of materiality called Earth.

As the disturbing thoughts of this lost Orfeo troubled me, a portion of one wall noiselessly divided making an imposing doorway, and a woman entered. She was dazzlingly beautiful. Somehow my mind understood that she was the one in whose charge I was placed, even as I also understood that the mysterious door opened and closed automatically by means of electro-magnetic controls.

She looked down at me and smiled warmly. Her beauty was breath-taking. She was dressed simply in a kind of Grecian gown of glowing silvery-white substance; her hair was golden and fell in soft waves about her shoulders; her eyes were extremely large, expressive and deep blue. Soft shimmering colors played continuously about her, apparently varying with every slight change of her thought or mood.

Hauntingly, the thought was in my mind that I remembered her from somewhere. She seemed to sense my perplexity and reassuringly said that I was looking very well and would soon be up and about. Then she touched a control on a crystal cabinet near my bed. In response a large section of the opposite wall opened revealing a huge mirror. I looked into its crystal depths, but the man I saw was not Orfeo; nor yet was he a stranger to me. Paradoxically, I remembered and yet I didn't remember!

"I have gained weight," I remarked, not knowing just why I made such a statement, then added: "Also, I feel much better now."

She smiled and replied: "On the contrary, you have lost weight. According to all Earthly standards you are now almost weightless."

Her strange words puzzled me. I glanced down at my body which appeared to be solidly substantial in addition to being much larger and more finely proportioned.

"It's all a matter of the scale of vibration in which you are functioning," she explained. "The vibratory rate of dense matter which makes up the planet Earth is extremely low, hence Earthly bodies are sluggish, dense and cumbersome. Vibratory rates here are quite high and matter so tenuous that it would seem non-existent were you in a dense physical body. Because you are now in a body of a corresponding vibratory rate, the phenomena of this world is as real to you as your Earth world."

As I listened to her speak, I thought I remembered her name. "You are Lyra?" I said half questioningly.

She nodded her head.

I was about to ask her about herself when I was conscious again of the continuous, low rumble of thunder from outside. I became curious to go out of doors and look around. Turning to Lyra, I asked: "May I go outside now?"

She shook her head. "You are not yet strong enough, but I promise that before the seventh day you shall see all, Neptune."

Her words startled me. Why had she called me Neptune? I wondered. I was not Neptune; neither was Neptune ill! And what did she mean by the seventh day?

I was about to ask her these questions when she turned and looked expectantly toward the far wall. In a moment the mysterious door appeared and a tall, strikingly handsome man entered. It was Orion! In some confused way I recognized him at once and felt a surge of affection for him in my heart. As with Lyra, shimmering waves of translucent color played about him, seemingly reflecting his thoughts. He smiled warmly and said: "We have missed you, Neptune."

I brushed my hand across my eyes in a dazed way as I replied: "But I am not Neptune; there is some mistake."

"Are you certain?" he asked gently. "You will recall that Neptune was the name you gave to our brother who first contacted you upon Earth. That name has always held a strange, deep significance for you, perhaps because it was once your own name."

As he spoke the odd realization possessed me that he was indeed speaking the truth. In their world, I was, or had once been, Neptune! "But the other Neptune?" I asked. "Who, then, is he?"

Orion glanced at Lyra and a scintillating wave of golden light enfolded them both. Orion replied slowly: "With us names are of little significance. The brother of whom you speak was in the illusion of the past known as Astra, but in the higher octaves of light, individualized aspects such as you know upon Earth are non-existent. Even now as we manifest in this most tenuous of material states of being, you are not aware of us in our true eternal aspect. We are, you might say in terms of Earth, staging a dress-show reception for you, our lost brother. Before the Destruction our existence was much as you see it now; that it why you seem to remember all of this. In that phase of the time dimension you were known as Neptune."

Something was wrong, terribly wrong, somewhere. I thought. If only I could remember clearly . . . but everything was so confused. As I gazed at those two superbly magnificent beings standing side by side enveloped in shimmering waves of golden light, I felt intuitively that I had known them well, sometime, somewhere! I had known them on an equal level—I had been one of them! But now they were like gods to me, and I a straggler, somehow far, far behind them, my mind deluded by a loathsome illness. I pressed my hands to my eyes, trying with all of my strength to remember something important—and terrible—that I had forgotten.

Neither of them spoke. Lyra took a white wafer from the crystal cabinet while Orion poured a sparkling liquid into a lavender crystal goblet. These they handed to me. I ate the delicately flavored wafer and drank the delicious beverage. I felt renewed vitality and strength flow through my body and with it a dreamy languor of mind. Lyra and Orion smiled upon me and the scintillating waves of golden light reached out from them and enfolded me in a warm comforting glow.

"Sleep for a while, Neptune," Lyra murmured softly. Then the mysterious door appeared and they left arm in arm, leaving me alone. The light in the room dimmed and waves of soft, exquisite music flowed from the walls. I fell into a deep dreamless sleep.

When I awoke light was streaming brilliantly into the room. One entire wall had miraculously vanished revealing an outer balcony. I sat up and looked out beyond the balcony upon an incredibly wonderful and fantastic world. It was radiant with light and yet there appeared to be a heavy moving cloudbank overhead. Continuous sheet lightning flashed through the rainbow-hued clouds and the constant rumble of distant thunder was slightly louder. Also, I saw brilliant slow-moving fireballs, vari-colored flares and showers of brilliant sparks.

I was deeply puzzled, for all of this phenomena did not seem at all familiar as had so many other things in this world. I jumped up from the couch and ran out onto the broad balcony, marveling at the wonderful feeling of lightness and vibrant strength in my body.

What a glorious world I looked upon! A dream world, beyond the wildest flight of imagination. Ethereal, scintillating color everywhere. Fantastically beautiful buildings constructed of a kind of crystal-plastic substance that quivered with continuously changing color hues. As I watched, windows, doors, balconies and stairs appeared and just as miraculously disappeared in the shining facades of the buildings. The grass, trees and flowers sparkled with living colors that seemed almost to glow with a light of their own.

I caught my breath in awe. And yet, somehow, it was familiar; a world I had once known, and forgotten! A few statuesque and majestically beautiful people were walking in the pedestrian lanes. No vehicles of any type were visible. Then I saw Lyra and Orion conversing with each other near a large circular flower garden, almost directly below me. They both looked up and smiled, calling out a friendly greeting. I ran down and joined them exclaiming: "What a magnificent world!"

"Do you remember it, Neptune?" Lyra asked gently.

I hesitated, then replied: "Much is familiar, but other things are not. I can't recall the lightning and the constant thunder. And the horizon appears to be only about a mile distant and it should be—I seem to remember it was almost limitless!"

For a moment there was deep silence. Lyra glanced questioningly at Orion and a look of deep pain crossed their faces as the golden waves of irridescent light about them changed to misty purple. I realized immediately I had said the wrong thing.

Lyra touched a crystal she held in her hand and the sound of the thunder was muffled until it was barely audible. Then drifts of exquisite harmony filled the air; the same ethereal music I had heard in my trip in the saucer—only here in this incredible world each tone also manifested in the atmosphere as waves of glowing color.

I listened and watched spellbound. Lyra and Orion sat down upon the grass and motioned for me to join them. When we were seated Lyra laid her hand tenderly upon mine and Orion put an arm about my shoulders.

Then Orion spoke, saying: "Time is a dimension as your scientists now correctly surmise. But it is only a dimension when applied to the various densities of matter. In the absolute, or non-material states of consciousness, Time is non-existent. So let us say that in one of the time frames or dimensions, there was once a planet in the solar system of Earth, called Lucifer. It was of the least material density of any of the planets. Its orbit lay between the orbits of Mars and Jupiter. Among the etheric beings, or heavenly hosts, it was called the Morning Star. Among all planets it was the most radiant planet in the universe.

"The name of the prince of this shining planet was also Lucifer, a beloved Son of God." Orion paused and the sadness deepened in his eyes. Then he continued: "Earth's legends about Lucifer and his hosts are true. Pride and arrogance grew in the heart of Lucifer and in the hearts of many Luciferians. They discovered all of the secrets of matter and also the great secret of the Creative Word. Eventually they sought to turn this omnipotent force against their brothers who were less selfish. Also against the etheric beings and the Father, or Source, for it became their desire to rule the universe. You know the rest of the legend: how Lucifer and his followers were cast down from their high estate. In simpler words, the Luciferians who were embodied then in the most attenuated manifestation of matter "fell" into embodiments in one of the most dense material evolutions, which is the animalistic evolution of Earth."

I dared not look at him as his frightening words struck dark chords of memory in my heart. "Then you mean that I . . . was one of them?" Shamed tears of realiza-

SON OF THE SUN: The Secret Of The Saucers

tion blinded my eyes.

"Yes, Neptune," he said gently, as both he and Lyra put their arms around me.

Waves of bitter shame and sorrow flooded over me as I realized the terrible truth of Orion's words. At last I said haltingly: "But Orion, you and Lyra and these others walking here in the garden; who are they?"

"We were among those who did not join the Luciferians in their revolt against the etheric hosts," he explained gently. "Thus although the Luciferians shattered our radiant planet in the holocaust of their war, we entered the etheric, non-material worlds in the higher octaves of light as liberated Sons of God, while the Luciferian hosts fell into the dream of mind in matter upon the dark planet of sorrows."

"But this world?" I asked in bewilderment. "Isn't it the world I half remember?"

"Yes, Neptune," Lyra said compassionately. "This is a tiny part of what is left of that world. You mentioned that many things were unfamiliar, such as the thunder and lightning and the nearness of the horizon. These conditions are new to you. For we are on one of the larger planetoids of the shattered planet Lucifer. It is only a few hundred miles in diameter, hence the nearness of the horizon. The thunder, lightning and constant play of color phenomena in the atmosphere are the result of magnetic disturbances because of the vicinity of other asteroids. The clouds you see above are not clouds as you know them upon Earth, but they serve to obscure the debris of our wrecked planet. Only rarely do we leave our etheric state of being and enter our former time frame in individualized manifestations as you see us now."

I was stunned into utter silence and the deepest sorrow. I bowed my head as I thought of the magnificent world I had lost, the great heritage I had cast away to become a bondsman chained in a steel-like dungeon of dense matter with its erroneous manifestations of sin, sickness, corruption, evil, decay and repeated deaths. Sobs wracked my body as I of my blinded, lost fellows of Earth. At last I murmured hesitantly: "Then all of the peoples of Earth have fallen from this former high estate?"

"Orion shook his head. "No, not all, Neptune, but vast numbers of Earthlings are former Luciferians. About the others we will explain to you later. The revelation when it comes will explain many of the enigmas of your planet."

Suddenly, a terrible thought came to me, almost causing me to collapse in horror as I recoiled from it. Stark terror was in my eyes as I looked first at Lyra and then at Orion. I dared not voice what was in my mind.

Orion, discerning my thought, shook his head and his wonderful eyes radiated sympathy and understanding as he said: "No, Neptune, have no fear, you are not in reality Lucifer. In fact you are one of the Luciferians who least wanted to join the others."

Relief flooded over me leaving me weak and shaken as I heard Orion's voice

69

continuing: "Lucifer is presently incarnated upon Earth, but we may not disclose to you his present identity. He has incarnated many times upon Earth and every name is familiar even to grade school children. But some of those names would surprise you, for they are not what you might expect."

I sighed heavily, trying to comprehend all the shattering things which had been revealed to me by Lyra and Orion. Rather incongruously I remembered the phenomena of the flying saucers upon Earth, which caused me to ask: "But if we destroyed your great planet, why are your disks visiting Earth now? Why did Astra contact me? Why don't you leave us to the fate we deserve, each one of us buried in his individual grave of living death."

Lyra's hand gripped mine and Orion's arm tightened around my shoulders. "Love is stronger than life and deeper than the boundless depths of time and space," he said softly. "While our brothers are lost in the hell of unreality and turn their blinded, imploring eyes to the mute heavens, we can never forget them. We intercede unceasingly for your peoples' liberation. Thus today every bondsman upon Earth has within himself the power through the mystery of the Etheric Christ Spirit to cancel his captivity.

"Eventually all of mankind deep-drowned in Time and Matter, will surface to reality when they recognize their basic unity of being. When man is for man honestly and sincerely and not selfishly arrayed against himself, the hour of deliverance from the underworld will be close at hand. We wait now beyond the great, sad river of Time and Sorrows with open arms and hearts to receive among us our lost and prodigal brothers in that great day when they rejoin us as liberated Sons of God.

"Our disks, or saucers as Earthmen term them, are in your space-time frame as harbingers of mankind's coming resurrection from the living death. Although our disks are essentially etheric; that is, non-material, they are controlled in such a way that they can almost instantaneously attract substance to take on any degree of material density necessary. Various other types of space craft are now permitted to visit Earth for certain purposes. These are from other worlds and also space islands of various densities of matter. Some are on the borderline between materiality and non-materiality. But all are operated by intelligences highly spiritual in nature. All are on a mission of love to their brothers of the Dark World, but mankind's understanding of their ultimate intent and purpose will only become fully apparent further along in Earth's Time Dimension. We do not say that there are no negatives in the universe who have not attained primitive modes of space travel, but at present Earth is fully protected from these by both cosmic law and the etheric hosts."

When Orion finished speaking there was silence. I sat with bowed head and contrite heart as realization of the full import of his words came to me. As Neptune, fleetingly restored to my lost immortal state, I saw that we of Earth are in reality in an underworld of illusion where we mistake false shadows for reality and dream selfish dreams of separateness from our brothers.

As these thoughts were in my mind the ringing of musical chimes sounded from the sea-green building. As though this was a signal everyone arose and entered the building. Orion led us to a large dining hall. Five men and five women were already there standing at their places at a huge table. At one end of the table was a cross wing with three vacant places. Orion indicated that I should take the middle place while he and Lyra seated themselves on either side of me.

It was an exquisite room and although there appeared to be no direct source of light the room was brilliantly lighted; the substance and colors of the room and everything in it seemed to glow with a soft, radiant light of their own. Vaguely, I seemed to remember the other persons present and they spoke to me as to an old friend. It was soon apparent, however, that the conversation was for my sole benefit as it was obvious that everyone else exchanged thoughts telepathically. As they did so irridescent clouds of color about them changed swiftly in shimmering hues and patterns.

No servants waited upon the table. Yet it was laid out exquisitely with the most delicate plates and shimmering silverware. On each plate were three portions. A triangle portion of pale amber; as square portion of varying shades of green; and a round portion of . The beverage was clear and sparkling in a crystal goblet. These strange delicacies were the most delicious and delicately flavored foods I had ever tasted. And the sparkling drink seemed to give immediate renewed strength and energy.

When the splendid meal was finished and everyone was preparing to leave the table, I turned and looked at Lyra. Suddenly, I was fully aware for the first time of all her exquisite feminine beauty and loveliness. Involuntarily, a wave of desire for her swept over me. She turned away from me and all conversation in the room ceased. I glanced hastily about; all of the others were standing silently with bowed heads. On an opposite wall I saw my reflection in a huge mirror and embarrassment flooded over me as I saw an ugly mottled red and black cloud enveloping my head and shoulders.

I felt impure and unworthy to be in that shining assemblage. The others left quietly, but I had the comforting feeling of their deep sympathy for me and their understanding for my human weakness. Also, I had the strong telepathic impression that sexual desire is merely another of the erroneous manifestations of materiality. Upon Earth it is neither wrong nor sinful in any of its manifestations except when it is used for selfish, destructive and cruel purposes. If motivated by love, altruism and unselfishness the sexual appetite is no more erroneous than any of mankind's other desires. But in the higher spiritual worlds it is non-existent.

Orion touched my arm as we were leaving the hall. "We understand," he said kindly. "It is nothing, as you realize now."

SON OF THE SUN: The Secret Of The Saucers

I smiled gratefully at him. But I felt tired and very sleepy. He and Lyra accompanied me to my room where I lay down upon the couch. They sat beside me until I fell into a deep sleep.

When I awoke I was alone. I walked outside onto the terrace, but the grounds were deserted. For a long while I stood there alone on the balcony marveling at that fantastically beautiful world. Apparently it was a world of eternal youth, eternal spring and eternal day. The rainbow-hued clouds were always moving overhead shot with soft waves of sheet lightning, and the far-away echo of thunder never entirely ceased. The trees, flowers and grass were miracles of color, fire and light which in comparison made the remembered counterfeits of Earth seem like gross, dull shadows.

As I stood there marveling, I saw Lyra come out of the adjoining building. She called a warm greeting. I saw she was holding a small crystal object in her hand. When she joined me she said mysteriously: "This is the seventh Earth day and through ourselves we shall take you back."

Her strange, beautiful eyes were upon me, seeming to look through and beyond me. She did not address me either as Neptune, or Orfeo. This saddened me, for it made me realize that I was now a stranger and an imposter in their shining world.

Understanding my thought, she put her hand gently over mine and I saw a mist of tears in her eyes. Then she raised the odd crystal in her hand to her forehead. As though in magic response, a flood of beautiful melody arose from the sea-green building; not the ethereal music of their world, but a hauntingly sad and familiar strain. I recognized the sublime melody of the Bach-Gounod "Ave Maria". Tears flowed unrestrainedly down my cheeks for a half-remembered, sad people who dwelt in a strange shadowed region called Earth.

Softly she said: "You will remember this, Orfeo."

That name sounded strange upon her lips; like the name of an utter stranger. I bowed my head in bitter regret for Neptune who was, and who now was not—and for the false shadow of Orfeo who is! Confused and perturbed I turned hastily from her and hurried into my room. Somehow I had the feeling that the secret of liberation lay in the mysterious crystal panel near my couch.

But as I reached eagerly for the controls on the panel, I felt a gentle restraining hand upon my arm. I turned and looked into Lyra's wonderful eyes shining with sympathy, compassion and purest love. My own heart swiftly responded. Then suddenly, miraculously we were as one being, enfolded in an embrace of the spirit untouched by sensuality or carnality. Intuitively, I remembered that this was the embrace of spirit, shared by all of those in the light of God's infinite love throughout the entire universe. What a tragedy, I thought, that I and my lost brothers of Earth know mostly only the counterfeit embrace of sexual desire and animal passion.

SON OF THE SUN: The Secret Of The Saucers

At that moment Orion came in the door and as he stood transfixed, his vibrant love too enfolded us in its pure, golden unselfish light. All boundaries of self were lost in a unity of being. "Our lost brother is home at last," he said softly.

After a while Orion and Lyra seated themselves near the strange crystal control panel and I rested upon the lounge. Orion touched a crystal disk and immediately an entire wall of the room opened up into a huge three-dimensional void. The room darkened and I saw the void a magnificent view into outer space. But all of space was shining with light; the stars and suns glowed with a deep reddish glow and only the planets appeared of varying degrees of darkness. The scene was focussing upon an unfamiliar part of the heavens. A sun and a number of encircling planets came into view.

Then the scene centered upon a single planet in this unknown solar system. It was a smug, sleek planet and apparently as efficient as a billiard ball. But it was exceedingly dark in tone and surrounded with concentric waves of deep gray. A tangible vibration or emanation came from it; evil, unpleasant and utterly without inspiration or hope. Approaching this world I saw a glowing red dot with a long, misty tail. The fiery dot seemed irresistibly attracted to the dark world. The two collided in a spectacular fiery display. I felt Lyra's hand upon mine as she whispered. "It is an immutable law of the cosmos that too great a preponderance of evil inevitably results in self-destruction and a new beginning."

The scene shifted to a different part of the universe. Another dark, misty world came in view, although it was not as dark as the first world. About this world there was a vibrant feeling of life and hope. But again I saw a fatalistic fiery red dot approaching and it was evident that this world too was doomed. I shuddered to think of conditions upon that planet at that moment of doom. But then I held my breath as I beheld two tiny dots coming forth from that world apparently to intercept the fiery comet. Intuitively I realized that the dots were remotely controlled by intelligent beings upon the planet who were concentrating the magnetic impulses of the dots upon the comet. Suddenly the comet exploded leaving the world unscathed. I breathed a sigh of relief.

Once more the scene shifted and focused upon a third world. Obviously, this was an "in-between" world, neither as dark and hopeless as the first, nor yet as light and inspired as the second. To the left of this planet appeared another smaller body—I recognized it as our moon and the planet as Earth. From the planet several tiny space ships went out to the moon and did not return. Then a tiny fleet of space craft went out to the moon, but some of these returned to Earth.

Suddenly, terrifyingly, to the right of the planet Earth, appeared the red, fiery dot of cosmic doom. Rapidly it increased in size leaving behind it a fiery tail of flame. It was evident that the comet was being drawn irresistibly toward Earth. Neither Lyra nor Orion spoke, but a strange voice said: "In the Time Dimension of Earth it is now the year 1986."

SON OF THE SUN: The Secret Of The Saucers

I shuddered and waited anxiously, but the portentous scene slowly faded from the screen. I turned excitedly to Orion. "But what happens to Earth?"

Orion and Lyra both looked compassionately at me as Orion gently replied. "That depends entirely upon your brothers of Earth and their progress in unity, understanding and brotherly love during the time period left them between the so-called now and the year 1986. All spiritual help possible will be given them, not only by ourselves but by others from all parts of the universe. We believe that they and their world will be saved, but in no time frame, or dimension, is the future ever written irrevocably. If they bring upon themselves self-destruction of their planet through too great a preponderance of evil there, it will mean another fall for the entities of Earth into even denser meshes of materiality and unreality. As you love your brothers of Earth, Orfeo, fight to your dying breath to help them toward a world of love, light and unity."

With those awful and awesome words, he got up and slowly walked from the room, leaving me alone with Lyra.

She smiled gently into my eyes and touched the mysterious crystal panel. Immediately the incredible, huge, three-dimensional screen became active again. But no longer were we looking into the boundless depths of space and time. Instead, I saw the familiar outlines of the Lockheed plant in Burbank. There was the shop in which I worked. The scene shifted inside the plant. I saw the radomes and my working companions, Dave Donnegan and Richard Butterfield. An unpleasant sensation came over me as though I were fainting, as though I were fading into the huge screen and becoming an active part of the scene I was viewing. Terrified, I turned to call to Lyra, but she was no longer there, only a mist. Then I blacked out!

My next conscious perception was my strange "awakening" on the job at Lockheed with all of my incredible experiences of those seven days seemingly utterly obliterated from my mind.

Thus six months passed with only hazy, troublesome intimations of what had happened to me in those seven lost days. But that night as I rested my head upon the rock down in the Los Angeles River bed, it all came back to me crystal clear. Also, I remembered again my frightening, bewildered "awakening" upon Earth in the Lockheed plant, my terrible revulsion with everything I saw upon Earth as compared with the wonder world I had left, although as yet only my higher consciousness fully understood.

I remembered my fellow workers, Dave Donnegan and Richard Butterfield and their reactions to my strange behavior and apparently unreasoning outburst. In the greater scope of my new understanding I realized even more clearly how nobly they had caught me up and sustained me by their own strength through those critical moments. It was so clearly evident to me then that both Dave and Richard had the same basic inherent qualities of goodness and nobility as those godlike beings of that other world. They are both simple, humble men, average workers like myself, yet potential gods! If only they and others like them knew and could realize their divinity, their kinship with God and the greater world of true reality! If every man and woman upon Earth could but grasp the great essential basic truth that we are all one and an integral part of God, then indeed all of mankind's hard trials and bitter tribulations would be over. Yes, if only in the abstract we could momentarily attain this illumination, the heavy chains of material bondage would fall from our burdened bodies and our counterfeit world of shadows would vanish in true light.

Today, I believe with all of my heart, soul and body in my brothers of Earth. Because of the innate goodness, honesty, nobility and helpful fellowship of the countless other men and women of good will like Dave Donnegan and Richard Butterfield, my undying faith in and love for humanity is forever instilled. Even though our greater brothers of that shining, lost, wonder world should offer to take me back to my former place among them, I should have to refuse. My lot is forever with my fellows of Earth! I will fight courageously with them and for them in the undying belief that the good in our hearts will triumph over the evil. In the conviction that every human being upon Earth, trapped in eternity and granted only one small awareness of life at a time, will be liberated from our prison cells of unreality and attain again our high estate as liberated sons of God.

NOTE: The language spoken by the beings of that other world was neither my familiar English nor Italian, but another language which I fully understood and remembered while with them. But today my conscious mind recalls their language only as a meaningless jumble of strange words, although I have a full understanding in my own language of all that passed between us. I can clearly recall only a few words of that other language. Those words were spoken to me by Lyra when she first came into the room. I am certain she said, "Un doz e pez lo" (or something very similar), meaning "No, you have lost weight."

CHAPTER IX
THE TRIP EAST

Memories, fantastically beautiful memories of that other infinitely greater lost world, haunted me for days. I was like a different person. In the light of my new understanding my conception of all things was changed. I viewed everything from a new perspective. Thus I felt more than ever like a stranger here upon Earth.

One afternoon when I was in downtown Los Angeles I stood on a street corner and watched the hurrying throngs of people. All were so earnestly intent upon personal ambitions, pleasures, frivolities, worries and personal problems and so completely wrapped up in their own private worlds. Few even so much as noticed their fellow-beings on the streets. It was as though each person lived in a world apart; encased in a tomb of separateness and living death. Like shadows they hurried busily on their separate ways lost in dreams of unreality.

I realized that in truth each went his way alone; even those nearest and dearest to him never really touched the deeper core of his aloneness. This is the tragedy of mortality. Things seem pleasant enough on the surface. Earth with its flowers, trees, sunshine; the cities with their paved streets and fine buildings; the trim houses with their neat lawns—all appear fair enough. But it is like a mirage, for the material world is a prison world where each man is a bondsman locked in a prison cell. The prison cells cannot be opened from without.

Greatly saddened, I took my car from the parking lot and drove home. A storm was brewing and already a fine mist of rain was in the air. I left my car at home and walked down by the Los Angeles River where the waters were beginning to flow in the dry and dusty riverbed.

All of nature seemed waiting, quiet and tremulous, for the life-giving drops of precious water that would drench the sun-baked land and give new life to the dying trees and parched hills.

The dense clouds were dark and ominous overhead. How symbolic, I thought, of our isolation from the rest of the universe. Spiritual intelligences throughout time and space dwell in unity, communicating throughout the universe, all a part of the great harmony of the Father; but man here on his tiny planet is cut off from contact with those other worlds and fully content to vision himself grandiosely as the highest intelligence in the universe.

If only we could realize how wrong we are! We exist here on our world in a kind of solitary confinement. Our much vaunted atmosphere is one of the bars that prevents us escaping from our prison world. Also, to a great extent, it prevents contact with outside intelligences; for most of our radio and television waves are bounced back down to us by the many layers of ionized gases in our stratosphere and beyond. Hence it is much more difficult for us here on this planet to establish outer space contacts than for most other planets.

Why is this so? Why are we so completely isolated and cut off from contact with the rest of the universe?

I turned for home as the full fury of the storm broke. An onslaught of wind lashed the trees, stripping the dead leaves and branches from them. The rain came down in torrents and it was one of the rare occasions when lightning flashed in the California sky and the thunder rumbled ominously. At each flash of lightning my entire body quivered in pain. I reached home soaking wet and went to bed.

In the following weeks I continued with my weekly lectures at the Hollywood Hotel, but I was dissatisfied with my effort. I felt I was reaching comparatively few people when I should be contacting so many more.

Then in September, 1953, Paul Vest's first article about my trip in the flying saucer was published in *MYSTIC* magazine. Immediately letters began coming from all over the United States and even from Mexico and Canada. I was amazed at the public interest and the general acceptance of my story. It appeared that intuitively many persons had been prepared for the account.

Because of the article I was contacted by long-distance telephone by a man in the East who is a well-known evangelist. His broadcasts are heard over a large radio network each week. He told me in all good faith that in answer to his prayer for guidance after reading the article in *MYSTIC*, he had been shown a sign in the skies. The "sign" was the sudden appearance of a flying disk phenomenon above him while he prayed. He stated that he was so deeply impressed with what he saw that he drove immediately to the State Police barracks and notified the captain of the troop. The captain also witnessed the strange phenomenon and ordered an airplane to be sent aloft to investigate. But before the plane was off the ground the phenomenon vanished. Thus, he said, he was absolutely convinced of the authenticity of my story. He invited me to visit him in the East and make a number of appearances there.

Since I had already given up my job, we were low on funds at that time. He forwarded me one hundred dollars to cover part of our expenses on the trip East. He also enclosed a contract in which he agreed to pay me for each lecture. My purpose in going East was to reach a much greater audience, but even, the humblest of God's creatures must have sustenance for their bodies. And surely a workman, even in God's work, is worthy of his hire.

Most of the audiences in the east were enthusiastic and highly receptive to the message of the saucers. I was happy in the belief that I had sown many seeds of understanding about the space visitors. But the minister of the gospel on whose word I had made the trip, failed me completely. He has not up until the present time (one year later) paid me for my expense and time. In fact, he was content to desert me in the East far from home and relatives and leave me stranded there penniless. His name? Does it matter?

The final lecture in Buffalo was the most successful of any of the engagements. People came from as far away as Canada, completely filling the large auditorium. Thus, from a material standpoint Christianity had thrown me from the heights, but spiritually it had sustained me stronger than ever. Also, I was beginning to learn an important lesson. The hypocrites will invariably crucify, but the truly faithful will always redeem. Actually, the hypocrites far outnumber the true. But God and only one is indeed a vast majority. Similarly, space visitors and a few are also a majority. The absolute truth of these last two statements are forever settled in my own mind.

Without funds and stranded in the East, we finally got financial help from relatives, and also an invitation to visit our folks back in New Jersey. Our spirits, which had dropped to a low ebb, began to pick up. Thus we were in almost a joyful, holiday mood as the boys, Mabel and I piled the suitcases into the car and headed for Trenton. We stayed with my father-in-law, Alfred Borgianini, on Kuser Road, close to the spot where I had once sent aloft balloons with the mold cultures in personal experiments, not knowing my work was being observed.

Our reunion with family and friends was a joyful one. We were invited everywhere and were kept out almost every night until a late hour. We quickly forgot our hardships and disappointments of the past weeks and joined in the happy, pulsating life around us. But I certainly never dreamed that there, close to my old home, I should have another experience with the extra-terrestrials.

CHAPTER X
NEPTUNE AGAIN AND PHENOMENA IN NEW JERSEY

One evening in December about midnight I was returning to "Pop's" place alone. Pop Borgianini lives on the outskirts of town in a pleasant suburban area of average homes and small acreage farms. Clouds were overhead, but it was not a particularly dark night as there was considerable reflected light from the city.

I drove into the yard and parked my car in my usual spot. As I sat in the car for a moment breathing the clean, fresh air and looking out over the twinkling lights of the countryside, I heard a familiar voice call my name. Surprised, I glanced around to see a tall, well-built figure approaching from a shadowed corner of the yard. Because I was so completely unprepared for such a meeting, it took me a moment to collect my thoughts and realize that the familiar voice could be none other than that of Neptune. As he came nearer to the car I could see him fairly well in the soft light. He appeared just as he had that night down by the Los Angeles River. His closely-fitted "uniform" wavered like restless clouds of light and shadow.

But somehow I felt altogether different meeting him now; there was none of the eerie feeling I had experienced upon the occasion of our first meeting.

He seemed to feel much as I did, for he said cheerfully: "A merry Christmas to you, Orfeo." His warm, radiant smile was still the same, as was his noble bearing and everything else about him; yet I was able to comprehend and understand him so much more easily now. I wondered, had he descended closer to my level, or had I, since my strange "awakening" in that other world, risen nearer to his?

He answered the question for me. "You are indeed a dweller in two worlds now, Orfeo. Sometimes it is difficult for you to determine which world is substance and which is shadow, or if both are not merely differing degrees of substance. But you have done well, considering all that you have been through in these last two years. In reality you are now liberated from your planet, Earth and are a citizen of the cosmos. For seven Earth days you were conscious in our world as it existed in Time, while I kept watch over your physical body as it performed it normal duties here on Earth. Thus in a way I am a part of you even as you are a part of me. There now exist eternal bonds of understanding between us.

SON OF THE SUN: The Secret Of The Saucers

As he spoke, I thought of a puzzling statement he had made to me during our first meeting. It was that memorable night down by the Los Angeles River. I distinctly remembered that he'd said: "We shall return, dear friend, but not to you." I remembered the words so well because I had been so saddened to hear them. Thus as I looked at him now I was thinking that his very presence there seemed to belie those words.

He smiled again and said gently: "In reality we have not returned to you, Orfeo. You came to us. When you awakened as one of us, you had come home. Don't you understand? We are not returning to the shadow, Orfeo; our lost brother has returned to us. And from our first contact with you we never in reality ever left you."

I grasped the meaning of his words, for I well knew I was no longer the same person who, confused and bewildered, had stepped half-fearfully into the saucer that night under the Hyperion Avenue Bridge. "Yes," I replied thoughtfully. "What you say is true. Earth to me now often seems like a strange land where I have been a prisoner who has forgotten his native home."

"But you are no longer a prisoner, Orfeo. You have broken the chains of matter. Thus can you realize that you were a prisoner—and that realization is all important. The vast majority of Earth's people never dream of their true status."

He paused, and after a moment I said: "You know, of course, about the lecture tour . . ."

"We were with you through it all," he replied. "Several times you had a definite awareness of our presence. But even so, it was all a bitter disappointment to you. On more than one occasion you thought it was the end of all your hopes and plans. But there is no end to anything, Orfeo . . . ever! Nor should you let the material aspects of any situation perturb you, such as the Reverend "X's" failure in your hour of need. Upon Earth there are wheels within wheels. When one wheel fails, another is forced to bear a heavier load. But the wheel that fails will be required to carry a double load further along in Time. That is a law of Earth. Thus accept all with courage and equanimity."

After a moment, while I pondered his words, he continued: "On the West Coast all is comparatively quiet now. But the road is opening. Many have attained tenuous, new understandings. The governments of the world could say much more to the people about the saucer situation, but they will not until the zero hour is at hand. Are not those your thoughts?"

I did not reply, but smiled at him, for I knew that for a period of time I could have revealed many things about the saucer situation that were believed to be well hidden—and thus have stolen the thunder from many. Instead it was given to them as their very own even as the rains and the sunshine, but they failed the trust.

He continued slowly and thoughtfully: "The days that are to come upon Earth are known to me, but they are as yet mercifully veiled from you and from your

SON OF THE SUN: The Secret Of The Saucers

fellows. This I can tell you: the hour of tragedy is close on Earth. In history it will be known as 'The Great Accident'. Wide devastation, suffering and the death of many will result from it. Perhaps you can guess how Man himself will be the direct cause of 'The Great Accident'.

"It is permitted only as a last hope of waking mankind to the terrible realization of the ghastly price he will pay if he enters the bloody holocaust of Armageddon. There is still a slight chance to avert the War of Desolation for in the Time dimension nothing is absolute. But if the horror of the War of the End of an Age shall come, cur multitudes are at hand to aid all of those not spiritually arrayed against us."

I bowed my head and as afar off I heard echoes of the hauntingly beautiful music of that Lost World; sad music as though thousands of angelic voices were joined in a hymn of sorrow.

At last Neptune said softly: "My brother of the universe, be not dismayed. Remember it is always darkest before the dawn. And the dawn is close for Earth. So close that the first glorious rays are already breaking for many in your world. Already we can behold the shining reality of your great world of tomorrow—a world of brotherly love and fellowship when Man is for Man and bound in unity through the love of the Father. The clouds on the horizon will pass quickly and tomorrow the sorrows seem only as dreams of darkness. We of the universe wait for the dawning of Earth's great tomorrow when we can welcome the children of Earth into our midst. Let our love and our faith sustain you and your fellows. And now, goodnight, Orfeo."

With those words, a silvery mist obscured the outlines of his figure. He faded away into almost complete transparency, although I could hear the echo of his footsteps as he walked away. It was obvious that his figure could definitely gain in density at will and also gather and resolve light.

As in a daze I got slowly out of the car and went inside the house surprised to hear so much noise and commotion in the dining room and kitchen. When I entered I saw that the room was full of people. Many of our relatives were there as well as some of the neighbors. Everyone seemed to be excited and was talking and gesticulating. No sooner was I inside than Mabel and several of the others rushed up and started telling me what they had seen off to the northeast a few miles away.

From the explanations I gathered that they had seen what appeared to be two round, large lights apparently playing tag with each other below the cloud bank. The phenomenon had continued for about fifteen minutes. They were still so excited that they interrupted each other to describe the capering antics of the two strange lights.

But having just come inside from my profound experience with Neptune, I was not in the least excited by their reports. They could not understand why I was so

81

calm and disinterested. It irritated them slightly. My sister-in-law, Alice, asked, a little peevishly, if I didn't believe what they told me. All of them were obviously let down because the news appeared to have no effect upon me.

Of course I believed every word they said. Why shouldn't I? One of my brothers-in-law had nearly broken a leg jumping out of a high kitchen window to get a better look at the strange lights. I believed them all right, but I could not permit them to project their interpretations and reactions upon me. When they finally quieted down some I said: "Look how excited and close to hysteria you all are tonight. Suppose the Air Force should release the full impact of certain saucer news straight from the shoulder? Millions of people everywhere would begin reacting just as you are, only to a greater degree. Yet none of you are quite certain of what you saw. If the Air Force released certain definite information, there would be no uncertainty. It could be the beginning of national panic that no amount of sane reasoning could quell. Thus the public gets news releases of flying saucer activity, but immediately a retraction or an explanation in terms of known phenomena follows. A dampener of some sort is always placed upon such news. Never in the history of our country has any office, individual or branch of the government handled news items in such a manner. The whole picture actually, is clearly before our eyes. And yet where does it get us? Still no flying saucers landing cozily in our back yards. Small wonder the present policy is not to publicize saucer stories."

Finally, almost at dawn, the excitement quieted down sufficiently for us to get to bed and get a few hours sleep. The following day the newspapers carried reports of the sighting of strange "lights" by many people throughout the countryside. No one had "hallucinations". No one saw just the usual type of lights. After all, masses of people don't today excitedly report street lamps, searchlight beams, etc. How stupid can we get?

But the news was far too sensational! It had to have a damper put upon it quickly in one way or another. Fortunately for the flying saucer experts, it was about time for Earth to pass through a meteor stream.

Three days later, an old friend of mine, the local weatherman, made an official pronunciamento, blithely explaining away the lights in a simple and perfectly reasonable manner. They were, of course, meteors, he announced in the papers. We were expecting a shower of meteors, weren't we? Well, what else could those lights be but meteors? Official sources never fail!

Good, old Mr. White, the weatherman, God bless him. I like him. I have always liked him. Even though he always lost in his guesses with me, with the local farmers, and with most other prognosticators concerning the condition of the weather on the following day. I have seen him lose for weeks in succession and never guess the weather correctly in one instance. This delightful game has been going on for years. The weather perversely remains pretty unpredictable even for the experts.

But coming out so badly in his rounds with the weather, the weatherman had no compunctions in tackling the flying saucers.

Thus Mr. White, or his press secretary, is still attempting to explain away those confounded "meteors" to a number of stubborn individuals. For it just so happened there was an overcast of clouds and mist that night. Two of the mysterious lights played around with each other below the clouds for nearly fifteen minutes. They were round, large, white lights without the fiery tails respectable meteors are supposed to flaunt. Now, Mr. White, these people, dozen of them, are either , or else they saw something out of this world which cannot be neatly explained away by your pat little explanation.

What quality within you caused you to offer the explanation in the first place? Did you see and study the phenomenon as did those others? Could it possibly be that you were prompted by disturbing feelings of uncertainty, insecurity and fear of the unknown? You just wanted someone to say those lights weren't there, so badly that you finally up and said it yourself!

But enough for our good friend, the weatherman. Like the weather, he's always with us.

Elsewhere the overall saucer picture was improving. It appeared the road was being opened from new angles. By the end of December, 1953 hundreds of new reports of saucer activity were coming in. Also there was the significant news of Canada's construction of a flying saucer observatory. It was located near Ottawa and known as Project Magnet. Essentially a UFO detection station, it was being equipped with complex and expensive electronic equipment which were designed to detect gamma rays, magnetic fluctuations and gravity or mass changes in the atmosphere. Thus the instruments could detect immediately any magnetically controlled disks in the vicinity. The engineer in charge of the project, Wilbert B. Smith, stated that he believes there is a 95% probability that the UFOs do exist. He based his report upon the massive files of data on well-authenticated sightings on hand.

Also, Canada was actually building a jet-propelled flying saucer. Another step in the right direction. There were many new developments in the United States, but most of it was hush-hush stuff. But the flood of reports from all over the world could not be ignored. Great Britain officially recognized the phenomena. Other countries heard from were Australia, New Zealand, Sweden, Norway, France, Germany, Brazil, Japan, Denmark and many more.

But of course there were still the "die-hards", those who flatly refused to recognize the realities of this century. Of this last subversive element I met a number on my tour of the East. Failing in their desperate attempts to convert me to Communism and slant my talks along the Party Line, they invariably defiantly demanded: "Well then, just what do you think is wrong with Communism?"

My reply was invariably the same: "Absolutely everything is wrong with it! There is not one iota of right in it. Its only possible good is its ability to awaken to action the positive forces of good which are often sleeping. Communism is the negation of all that is honest and good in the world and in humanity. They would enslave the human mind. Their obstructiveness is willful and planned. We must eventually meet this murderous element at Armageddon; when it will be victory for one side or the other. Good will triumph, or evil! Every entity in this world and the adjoining planes is now aligned definitely upon one side or the other. No matter what the outcome of the conflict, the positive element of good will ultimately attain a greater life and progression; whereas the negative will meet death, destruction and a new beginning in a more hostile environment. As you have made your choice, so be it!

Shortly before the New Year we left New Jersey and set out on the long journey home to Los Angeles. We drove leisurely and enjoyed the scenery, so different from our perpetual springtime of Southern California. The boys especially got a kick out of it. Between Carlsbad Caverns and El Paso our car stalled on the desert. It was late at night and we were many miles from a town. I remember Mabel remarking dejectedly as she shivered in the cold night air: "Well, Orfie, we could certainly use some help from those flying saucers right now."

I smiled at her attempt at humor in our unfortunate situation. But the boys hopefully scanned the heavens as though aid might be imminent. As for myself, I had learned that the space visitors never in any way interfere in mundane affairs. Thus, of course, no glowing disk obligingly appeared to succor us. A very much down-to-earth truck did, however, and we eventually made it to the next town where I discovered that a tiny wire had become disconnected and short circuited the electrical system.

I felt rather foolish as I thought of how grandiosely I had been expounding the principle of infinite electro-magnetic power in flying saucers, but was utterly helpless in handling a simple problem in the electrical generation of my own car. The experience caused me to remind myself sharply that I could actually get lost between worlds, unless I kept my feet firmly upon terra firma, my home as of now.

Back home in Los Angeles I had the unpleasant feeling of being definitely let down. And I didn't know where to begin to start picking up the threads of my previous activities. The entire situation appeared as being rather futile and much too big for me, to have any effect. But several days after our return I received a phone call from Mrs. Dorothy Russell of Manhattan Beach asking if I would give a talk before the prominent Neptunian Club in her city. She didn't know it, but she was responsible for picking me up out of the depths and launching me once more upon my mission. "Neptunian Club," I thought as I hung up the receiver. "Could the name be just a coincidence?"

At Manhattan Beach I spoke before a packed clubhouse. The meeting was a tremendous success and everyone in the audience was receptive and enthusiastic. Additional lectures in other Western cities followed. Also, I resumed my regular weekly meetings at the Hollywood Hotel. All in all I felt things were progressing as well as I could hope. At times Mabel still urged me to "forget it all", and go back to work at Lockheed again. But I knew I couldn't ever do that. Come what may, I would tell all who would listen about the space visitors.

CHAPTER XI
I HAVE A VISION

Hundreds of volumes could never put into words all that has transpired in my life and states of consciousness within the last two years. The enthrallment, the divine ecstacy and the joyous rhapsody of breaking the chains of matter and mortal mind cannot be even dimly imagined. Yet in our sad world of pain and woe one must pay with anguish in equal degree for each upward step. Hence, I tell you in all truth that the vast majority would cringe from facing the bitter sufferings and trials that have been my lot in this and previous lives before I attained the revelation of the infinite majesty of reality.

Today I can see in the higher octaves of light and hence understand the unreality of all my sufferings. All that I endured was the illusion of pain superinduced by the limited vision of my material mind in those periods when the supposed suffering occurred. It is perfectly clear to me now that physical pain, mental anguish, material obstructions, defeats, disease, adversaries and adversities exist only within limited material consciousness. My sufferings seem to be real in the erroneous three-dimensional physical plane of existence and within the time dimension. But in the light of the truth of my eternal self, the supposed suffering is in reality non-existent.

To many people what I have just said may sound like an absurd paradox, but thousands of others will understand my meaning, for they themselves have been through this evolutionary process in varying degrees. As one emerges into the truth of spirit from false material consciousness an entire new concept of materiality is attained. Increasing numbers of persons will go through some stages of this understanding within the next few years, for material adversity in all of its many aspects will be stepped up to a considerable degree. We are at the beginning of the Days of Sorrow!

Today it rained again in Los Angeles. Water is flowing in the bed of the Los Angeles River. In the late afternoon the sky began clearing. As evening was coming on I walked down to the river, stood on the bridge and looked over the concrete guard rail.

SON OF THE SUN: The Secret Of The Saucers

I looked down upon the spot where I had sat at Neptune's feet. A great wave of emotion swept over me shaking me to the innermost depths of my being. "Ah, Neptune," I thought, "do you, too, feel the poignant tragedy of Earth when you set foot upon this ground?"

As in a dream then I heard a gentle voice saying: "Consider Earth's solar system and the many other solar systems throughout the universe. Are not the planetary units of these solar systems the true archetypes of the flying disks? The disks, like the planets, are round, suspended in ether, propelled by ether waves and magnetic light from system to system.

"Many of the entities of the various worlds throughout the cosmos have discovered the basic principles of the universe and hence have been enabled to travel in the various solar systems. Their actions and thoughts are in perfect harmony and full accord with the laws of the cosmos. They respect the rights of all worlds and of all individuals everywhere. But most of all do they respect and act in perfect harmony with the infinite mind in which they live and move and have their being.

"Speak to all you see, Orfeo. Tell them of the undiscovered wonders of the material universe and of the infinitely greater wonders beyond. You will speak with the truth of harmonious love, which is the only real authority. In reality, all is light; eternal light throughout space, the reverse of the testimony of the material mind. Within the spiritual universe only the points behind the planets give the illusion of darkness where a mere trifle of light is occulted by the body of the planet. But in reality darkness is only an illusion created by the false thoughts of material consciousness. All who come out of the illusion of darkness into the light will never again be lost in the illusion. Throughout the universe entities wait eagerly to aid your brothers of Earth, but the choice is up to each individual, for every mortal being has been equally endowed with free will. You, Orfeo, have walked through the valley of the shadow of death and emerged into eternal light. Help others to do likewise."

For a while then there was silence as inexpressible thoughts and emotions flooded my consciousness. At last the voice continued: "Behold, two thousand years are rolled back tonight before your eyes."

As I listened to the incredibly beautiful voice, my eyes were upon a revolving aircraft beacon light on a nearby hill. While I watched, the red and green of the beacon light resolved into a soft amber color and the amber flame in turn became a shining sword. Slowly the sword was transfigured into a cross and upon it I saw the figure of a Man in death.

While I watched spellbound, He awakened and looked down from the cross upon me. His face broke into a radiant smile, and with no effort at all He stepped down from the cross and walked toward me in shining beauty. I looked again at the cross and it was only a shadow that splintered into nothingness.

SON OF THE SUN: The Secret Of The Saucers

As He walked toward me I heard a tremendous chorus of voices singing joyous music, and floods of happiness overflowed my heart.

I looked again and He was standing just beyond the wall of the bridge. I beheld Him more clearly than the light of day, yet in no detail, as when one looks upon the sun and beholds only radiance.

I heard His voice inquiring gently: "What is your name?"

I replied: "Matthew." But even as I spoke I corrected myself mentally. Matthew was my middle name.

He said: "You chose that name yourself when you were a small child. You wanted no other name but that one. Do you remember?"

I nodded my head, for I did indeed remember.

And then I heard him say: "But Matthew was a publican. And were you not as a publican before May 23, 1952?"

I bowed my head in shame before Him, for I realized that I was indeed as a publican and perhaps even worse.

In a voice filled with infinite tenderness then, He said: "Do not be ashamed, Orfeo. Don't you remember I always chose the publicans and harlots over self-righteous hypocrites?"

Veils were dropping from my eyes and I was remembering details of a life lived many lives ago back in Time. I hid my face from His sight and tears of shame and remorse blinded my sight.

"Do not weep, Orfeo," He said gently. "That is all in the past now. But I am with you today even as I was with you then. Tell mankind that I live and love them today even as I did two thousand years ago when I walked the shores of . But tell men that to know me today when soon I shall again appear publicly upon Earth they must find me first within their own hearts."

He paused and my eyes could no longer bear to look upon the radiance of His beauty. And then he said: "Remember, Orfeo, wherein it was revealed to you not long ago that beings from other worlds now walk upon the Earth. Each is a double of the other and they have of their own free will entered the valley of sorrows that is Earth, to help mankind. One moderates another when too little is accomplished or when certain limits are exceeded. No man upon Earth shall know them except the ones to whom they reveal themselves. And who publicly claims to be one, is not at all. Only by their fruits may they be known. This is the beginning of the mysteries of the New Age."

Slowly then, the shining vision before me faded until He was no longer there. Only a soft shining green light remained pervading the atmosphere. I stood for a long while in silence as the heart of creation enfolded me in infinite peace.

At last, I was just turning to go home when I heard a familiar voice call to me: "Orfeo, what are you thinking?"

I turned and saw Neptune standing on the banks of the river, close to the spot where we had sat some eighteen months before.

As I tried to collect my thoughts, I replied: "Don't you know what I'm thinking, Neptune? Or am I lost to you now?"

"No, Orfeo, you shall never be lost to me," he answered. "But there are sublime moments when no one may penetrate another's world of thought. Or perhaps I should say that those who would do so are not able, and those who could would under no circumstances do so."

"I understand, Neptune," I said. "The ultimates are for all, but in moments of realization one becomes a universe within himself and hence is protected by the powers of the cosmos. You then are as we and we are as you, children together in the Father's infinite worlds of manifestation." When I had finished speaking, I was surprised at my own words. It did not seem possible that I could be saying such things to Neptune. And yet I had said them and he was smiling at me as though my thoughts were his very own.

But as I looked at him he vanished from my sight. And suddenly I felt alone and very small and insignificant. I ran along the bridge to the pathway leading down to the spot where Neptune had been standing. He was nowhere to be seen; but in the archway of the bridge I saw again the softly glowing outlines of a flying disk.

The door of the saucer was open and while I was wondering whether or not to enter, a woman appeared in the entrance. It was Lyra, more exquisitely beautiful than I had remembered her. Smiling at me she stepped from the craft and it seemed that the blades of grass trembled mysteriously and the wind stirred, vibrant with strange music that was barely audible. All of nature seemed to stir as though touched by a caressing hand. She walked slowly toward me and her shining white gown fairly scintillated as though in protest to the dense, irrational atmosphere of Earth. All of the infinite love for man in his Christly potential which I was feeling at that moment, was blissfully culminated in the wonder of her presence. She who encompassed all love, all compassion and all understanding and whose radiant eyes were a benediction.

When she was closer to me I saw that her gown shimmered like restlessly drifting moonbeams, just as had Neptune's darker uniform here in our dense atmosphere. In her hand she was holding a glass which she held out to me saying: "Drink from this glass, Orfeo, and your normal consciousness shall return. You will then be an equal with your own fellows and able to show them the way."

Uncertainly, I took the crystal goblet from her, but I dreaded to drink from it, for I feared that she and Neptune and all the world might recede forever from me.

She smiled again and a soft golden light enfolded her just as in her world. "Everything we have done with you both in your world and in ours has been adequately moderated. Hence all that you experienced in the higher worlds has been compensated to a similar degree in the lower. Thus be neither glad nor sorry for all that has thus far been granted to you. Remember, love is understanding and understanding is love throughout the universe. Hence love is the constant of all worlds. By love I mean only selfless love and not the carnality which is often mistaken here on Earth for love. Love is infinite freedom. Drink from this glass and know peace again within yourself."

Slowly I raised the glass to my lips and drank. When I had finished, I let the glass fall to the ground, but heard no sound of it. The drink seemed to clear my head and to give me a feeling of strength and normalcy. Lyra had not faded as I feared she might. Rather she appeared to be more real than ever before.

"We must go now, Orfeo," she said gently.

Her words greatly saddened me for I dreaded to think of her leaving me. But only for a moment, for I immediately realized none of them would ever in reality leave me again. Slowly, I said: "I understand what you meant about the drink, Lyra. For now I feel that I am at home again upon Earth as I used to be. I shall never forget you, Lyra, for I am a part of you and Neptune and Orion and your world, even as you are a part of me. I know now there is no death other than that which men upon Earth call life. Also, I know there is no evil act in the world which cannot be atoned. Lyra, you shall be with me always."

With those words I bowed my head and when I looked again she was gone as though she had simply faded into nothingness. Only an exquisite fragrance was left permeating the air as if bowers of invisible flowers were everywhere.

When I thought to look for the outline of the saucer under the arch of the bridge, it was no longer there. I stood for a time in the soft reflected light of the evening, at peace with myself and all things. Although they were gone, I no longer felt alone, for in reality I knew I could never be alone again in this life or any life to come.

I turned and walked home. When I opened the front door I felt a tremendous wave of warmth and peace that awaited me in my own house. The boys were busy with some magazines and Mabel was sitting in a rocker sewing buttons on one of my shirts. When I came in she looked up and smiled and for the first time in months I seemed to see her clearly for the wonderful person she is. With the light from a floor lamp falling on her hair and in her simple dress she looked like a Botticelli madonna. Within her I beheld all the mystery and wonder of womanhood: she was like a reflection of Lyra, the highest potential of feminine evolution.

"We've missed you, Orfie," Mabel said. "Where have you been?"

"Oh, just down by the river, Mae," I replied as I kissed her more tenderly than I had in months.

She rewarded me with a smile as she said: "It's so good to have you home again."

Her words increasing my feeling of peace and serenity, for I was home again. Lyra and Neptune had indeed given me back to my family.

I walked over and turned on the radio for news. Busy, eager voices were enthusiastically staccatoing the latest horrors of the terrible devastation of the recent H-Bomb test. News of the tremendous discovery of a hideous nerve gas, a pint of which would kill an entire city of people. Earthquakes. The rumble of war in Indo-China and other danger spots. Unrest. Anxiety. Murders. Suicides. Fear. More reports of the subtle evil forces insidiously at work here among us weaving their own devious webs of deception and obstruction. Man against man to the bitter end! Oh God, how long, I thought. How long before the compassionate Earth shudders in revulsion—shaking the stars!

As I switched off the radio I realized more than ever how much work there is to be done. In reality this age of discord and stark materialism is already in the past and we have entered into the New Age. Many spiritually awakened persons today are well aware of the true state of affairs. To all of these men and women of honest heart and sincerity of purpose and to all of those in past ages who have worked against fearful and bitter odds for the good of man and the betterment of his lot upon Earth I have dedicated my life.

Now is the hour! The great promise of the golden dawn is breaking. The light of its revelations is imminent in religion, medicine, scientific research and all other fields of human endeavor. Fulfillment of the great promise of the ages is at hand. Space visitors are the harbingers of dawn upon Earth.

Mistakes shall occur, but we shall correct them. When war, tribulation and cataclysm come, even these shall quickly pass. For the rainbow of eternal promise is now in the heavens. The shining hosts of the great brotherhood of the spiritual federation of the universe are waiting to receive us into their midst and to let us know them as they really are. The highest flights of our imagination and air wildest dreams cannot compare with the wonderful world of reality that lies ahead in Time for us.

The universe is you—and you are the universe. The infinite numbers of entities in God's mansions in the cosmos are essentially as you and I as we are and have ever been in true spiritual reality. If we will but waken from our dark dreams of death they will lavish life and beauty upon us. Thus choose for yourself. There is no in-between road today. We have come to the dividing of the way and it is now one path or the other for every entity upon Earth and its adjoining planes of manifestation.

CHAPTER XII
HOW TO KNOW A FLYING SAUCER

A flying saucer can manifest its presence in many ways. A few persons whose neurological sensitivity is similar to mine may detect a saucer's presence by physical symptoms such as I have described earlier in this book.

Only recently Mr. Vernon Tyler, Director of the Santa Monica Municipal Airport, had such an experience. He relates that on Wednesday evening March 24, 1954, he retired early. About ten o'clock he was almost asleep when he felt an odd prickling sensation along the back of his neck and down his arms and spine. He said the hair on the back of his neck felt as though it were standing up which reminded him of some sort of electrical phenomenon. He was wide awake immediately and filled with a peculiar sense of urgency as though he were in contact with something or someone. He jumped out of bed and went to the window and looked outside, but saw nothing.

He walked around the room restlessly for some time with the distinct feeling that someone wanted to contact him. At last he went to bed again and finally fell asleep. The next morning a friend, Fred Carlyle, phoned him and wanted to know what was going on over Tyler's house about ten o'clock the night before. Startled, Tyler questioned him. Carlyle said that he and his family had watched four strange objects, or lights, directly over Tyler's house maneuvering in an incredible manner and without sound for some time.

That same day similar reports were given to the Santa Monica Outlook newspaper by Mrs. Genevieve Downer and her husband, Steven; Lillian Colbary and her daughter, Marilyn, and Mr. and Mrs. Arthur Swalge, all of whom saw the mysterious objects over Tyler's house. It later developed that many other persons in the neighborhood had witnessed the phenomenon, although they hadn't phoned the newspaper.

But of all the persons in that residential area, Tyler was the only one known to have experienced the unusual physical symptoms. Later on, when he read the article I had written about my physical symptoms in saucer contacts, he stated that his sensations were identical.

SON OF THE SUN: The Secret Of The Saucers

Thus physical reaction to the electro-magnetic qualities of a saucer are unusual. If you experience them, you may be certain your body is attuned to extra-sensory perceptions.

Since a crystal disk may be as small as two inches in diameter and can penetrate material densities, a disk may be present in a hall or room at any time and may or may not be visible to the eye. In the darkness they sometimes appear as softly glowing floating lights which appear and vanish suddenly.

Many persons have seen a flying saucer and have failed to recognize it as such. Hence we are going to list here the most common manifestations in order that you may better judge a UFO should you see one:

THE ROVING STAR: One of the most common appearances of the disks and the least reported are those which merely rove around in the night sky. Often they are mistaken for airplane lights or a star. But if you hear no sound of an airplane motor and the "star" appears to move, then you well may be observing a disk.

THE METEOR: If you see a "meteor" that leaves no fiery trail behind it, or one that changes color peculiarly, watch it closely. Also any "meteor" that appears to "hover", or one that changes its course suddenly to an upward sweep, or to an angled turn, is probably a saucer. Also any large round fireball that follows a definite horizontal path and then bursts in a brilliant shower of sparks, either with or without noise, is definitely a particular type of saucer phenomenon. Similar to the latter is a huge "meteor" that appears to explode in a blinding flash lighting up an entire area, but without sound. These are all manifestations of UFOs.

THE SILVERY DISK: This one cannot be mistaken. At first glance it appears as an airplane, but something causes you to give it a second glance. Then you see it can't possibly be an airplane for it is round and spherelike. Or it may appear oval-shaped or in the form of a half sphere. It may appear to pulsate or if you cannot actually see the pulsation you have the definite impression that it is pulsating, for the effect is registered more upon your nerves than upon your retina.

Often there appears to be a darker center to this silvery, metallic-appearing disk. Also, the disk may seem to wobble through the air or weave along like a seasick man. The darker center may appear to move off-center. Sometimes it continues to move all over the surface of the disk as though in rhythm with the odd wobbling motion of the disk.

What is this dark area in the silvery disk? It is the control beam focus, the beam connecting the disk to the one in control. This extra-terrestrial type of "radar" beam has the disk so strongly gripped that the very motion of the disk is vectored by the beam. The same mechanism holds for the incredible right angle turns. It is like a yo-yo which is held firmly by the string.

WHEEL WITHIN WHEEL: This type also has been frequently sighted. The strange effect of rotation of wheels-within-wheels is manifested for different purposes. As in the case of many other types of manifestation, it has been used by

93

extraterrestrials to impress a certain individual or group of individuals. If you see a saucer of any type, you may rest assured you have been "chosen" for the sighting for some specific reason.

The multi-rotation effect in this type of UFO is caused by actual disk-within-disk rotation. The peculiar visual effects result from the conversion of magnetic force into energy focused in the disk.

The energy must be converted and dissipated, so it is discharged at the outer edges of the saucer. When those in control wish to make a display for the benefit of an individual or group of persons, they merely "gun-it-up" and the static electric discharge then shows as flames, darting streaks, fireballs, or similar phenomena. They can also direct this force behind the object, giving the impression that the disk is jet-propelled.

Magnetic propulsion was scoffed at just a year ago and some still scoff even though model disks in our laboratories have been made to respond to this force to a limited degree. In reality, this field has become one of the most vital and secret research projects in the United States, Canada and certain other nations, one of which has advanced further than we like to think.

Incidentally, the magnetic principle explains any behavior of flying saucers ever reported. Proceeding from the magnetic principle of propulsion and its dynamics, we would ultimately discover the secrets of constructing a flying saucer of a primitive type. This very fact has proven the existence of the saucers beyond any and all doubt.

Yet insofar as the extra-terrestrials are concerned, final proof of the saucers had to come to us from the actual testimony of sightings and experiences. This was finally accomplished. Work was immediately commenced in laboratories of various governmental agencies on the magnetic principles of propulsion. And then what happened? All official mention of saucers vanished on all fronts. Insofar as the public is concerned, the saucers just aren't any more, although hundreds of reports continue to come in. Only Frank Edwards, the ex-A. F. of L. newscaster from Washington, D. C. and a few other courageous souls mention the true facts.

All official statements are now made along academic and conservative lines mentioning our own researches and "discoveries" in the fields of projected missiles, magnetic researches etc.

What a strange paradox indeed. The very ones who fought valiantly for recognition of the saucers are literally given the final coup-de-grace; whereas those who fought it tooth and nail are busily engaged upon electro-magnetic researches.

The space visitors have revealed much, enough to give us ideas to go ahead scientifically in new and heretofore unknown directions and potentials, but unless we learn the ethics that go hand-in-hand with mechanics, all of our knowledge will be taken from us. The space visitors are trying to teach us as we would teach little children, but smart little boys that we are we just won't learn.

SON OF THE SUN: The Secret Of The Saucers

THE TRIANGULAR FLAME: Many have seen this type of UFO manifestation. The triangular flame is no more than a total configuration of a number of disks in formation. These are made to discharge electric energy in that shape, and the disks become invisible while the entire configuration shows up. Or, it can also be a semi-material object with the powerplant of the disk incorporated within it. Any of these are very simple to produce for those in the remote control station which, of course, is the mother ship. Within laboratories here on Earth some of this phenomena can now be produced in limited degrees. But no one is talking and certainly not behind the iron curtain.

DISAPPEARING AIRPLANE: This type is a projection both visual and auditory, but the mechanics are too complex to go into here. All we can say is that if an airplane attracts your attention irresistibly and seems to hold you by a strange, intangible force, it may be a disk-projection. You may be absolutely certain of this if it has a dull, flat surface that does not reflect sunlight and, of course, when you see it suddenly vanish before your eyes.

THE TORPEDO: The torpedo, or cigar shaped craft is rare. You probably would be first attracted by its seemingly swift, silent flight. It is shaped something like a dirigible but is much more graceful in appearance. Portholes may be visible in this type, or they may not, depending upon whether they were opened at the time of the sighting. It may hover motionless in the air, or suddenly disappear into nothingness. But of this much you can be certain if ever you are lucky enough to see such a craft: you were meant to see it for a definite reason that will either be clear to you at the time, or later on. These are the master ships of space and are often hundreds of feet in length, although some of the smaller ones may be no larger than a large airplane's hull.

THE FLYING SAUCER: This object is spherical, hemispherical, or just disk shaped. It is the motive shape and is a utility craft of many uses. Its size can vary from less than two inches to miles in diameter. The larger ones out in space usually have plastic canopies and serve sometimes as passenger ships.

Thus we have listed all of the types of extraterrestrial craft which have thus far manifested in our atmosphere. Any of them may be flatly opaque, or may instantaneously be rendered so transparent that the best mortal vision cannot see them. In reality, they are most active when they are invisible. It is thus that they photograph and record words, thoughts and deeds, check births and deaths and reincarnating egos, record undercurrent trends in governments, etc. They are the silent observers and recorders of all.

Although one may contact you in absolute silence and be invisible to your physical sight, some moment in the future you may have a "spiritual awakening", when you will remember the saucer's vigil. The awakening may be years after the actual contact was in effect. It seems the extra-terrestrials really "favor" such persons by keeping them entirely undisturbed by visual experiences. Today these millions of persons are those who know space visitors are here. They do not know how they know it, but they accept it anyway. Most have never seen a saucer knowingly or have caught only an uncertain glimpse of one. But for them the day is coming when through extra-dimensional perception, they will "remember" and their eyes will be opened. Several of the finest contacts to date are of this nature.

On the other extreme are those who have seen spectacular displays of UFOs and go their way skeptical and unimpressed. These are the persons the space visitors can never touch. They live in a dark world of their own.

Because of the seemingly harsh planetary laws prevailing upon Earth, any type of spiritual growth involves pain. Thus both God and nature appear to hurt most those they love. So it is and must inevitably be with space visitors. The ascent from Hell is not easy! So as God tries with suffering those who are dearest to Him, so must the extra-terrestrials to a degree. In the over-all picture no one is ignored except those who wish to be ignored. The choice is up to the individual.

CHAPTER XIII
STRUCTURE AND MOTIVE FORCES OF FLYING DISKS

Contrary to present concepts, we do not conquer space, we cooperate with it. A good dancer does not force steps and movements into a rhythm. He feels the music and cooperates with it. A good pilot does not rip through the air. He cooperates with its dynamic forces. Birds accomplish this naturally.

Notice fish in a bowl or tank of water. They glide and dive in streamlined beauty as they feel every slightest movement and vibration of the water. Their motions are in perfect harmony with their environment. Throughout all of nature there is no conquest of the elements. There is only harmony and cooperation with the laws of the elements. The creature who defies these laws must inevitably suffer.

Space is today the most challenging frontier. It is also one of the most dangerous. Any wrong interpretation or calculation of space will result in immediate and violent reaction.

Space ships do not carry walls of lead many feet thick. The cosmic rays in outer space could easily penetrate these. In reality space ship hulls are not much more than many layers of skins something like plywood but made of plastic-crystal substance. Some layers are positive ionized, and some negative. These are insulated from each other with neutral layers between them.

The approaching cosmic rays are rendered unstable by the field of magnetism constantly maintained around the ship. Upon reaching the hull of the ship they are completely shattered. Then the positive and negative charges are absorbed by the many-phased charges of the various skins of the hull. Thus, not one cosmic ray should penetrate inside. This is harmonic cooperation with nature's forces.

Harmony and cooperation are positive in effect. Man's first space ships may evolve from his present limited knowledge and still navigate space to some extent, following many of nature's laws. But many of those first experimental craft will meet with destruction and failure because only the highest degree of harmony and the finest perception can survive space navigation.

First, it is well to understand that atoms are not in reality whirling particles of energy. They are simply "bubbles" in the ether. Also, light rays are merely portions of these bubbles, but in elongations; thus in reality appearing as darting fissures, or splits in the ether.

There are endless variations of magnetic fields, or fluxes in the entire universe. From the bubbles (atoms) they bounce away in all directions, producing magnetic spheres. From the light rays they proceed away at right angles to the rays so that magnetic vortices accompany the rays. Cosmic rays produce their own magnetic wakes in their paths. Thus the ether is in constant motion at all times in all places.

The flying saucers utilize all these forms of energy. They direct in precise control the conversions of the energies, and use the same forces as means of attraction and/or repulsion in the endless sea of the ether. Thus, their directors can use magnetic and gravitational forces far beyond our wildest imagination.

They do not require our Earth's fields. Indeed, Earth's field and ether slip-stream are in their way. In outer space the flying disks flow and seem to dance in gracious beauty.

Many of the flying saucers that we have seen in our skies are actually crystal disks, grown in chemical baths. Like the stem and capillaries of a leaf or flower, all the functioning systems are grown into it. Therefore these systems could be utterly invisible. These systems would include the conducting wires spiralled from the center to the extreme outer edge, the spirals becoming narrower in cone shape. At the extreme edge they come to less than pinpoint, and the excess electrons are forced into "ground" from these points. This function can be stepped up until the very disk seems to give off flames. Usually, however, we see it only as a fuzzy halo fringe around the object.

The crystal property of the flying disks refines all the electro-magnetic and corpuscular energies into varying frequencies and wave lengths. Among the etheric beings, however, it is possible to create a saucer of any degree of materiality merely from a projected thought form which attracts material substance to it.

Since, however, the majority of saucers thus far sighted have been of the crystal disk type, we shall confine explanations to these alone. (Although the thought-form projections behave in a very similar manner).

CHANGING OF COLORS IN DISKS

As the crystal is stepped up by electro-magnetic energy its lattice structure undergoes definite changes which cause the disk to emit light of various colors. That we might observe this phenomenon is one of their reasons for revealing it in the skies.

The lattice of the crystal can be arrested at any attitude. When it is suspended in an attitude of transmitting, all light will pass through, and the disk becomes completely invisible.

When electric force is discharged under normal conditions, a flame, or darting lightning is visible all around the disk. Thus we see flames of all colors; also darts and streaks of fire, and in some cases, even an exhaust trail when the entire effect is directed backward or forward of the flying object.

By directing a sudden impulse of energy and resistance to the energy simultaneously into the disk, it can be made to explode into a shower of spark fragments.

RIGHT ANGLE TURNS

A flying disk is not just guided. It is completely controlled. The master beam from the mother ship holds like a vise. This is always the case when they perform right angle and sudden turns. Thus they can assume incredible speed, and suddenly veer sharply without any damage to the disk. Every atom and molecule is vectored in the same direction at the same time. Any gravitational effects from inertia are neutralized, or non-existent.

During my trip into space in one of these crystal crafts, you will recall that I picked up a strange coin-shaped piece of metal from the floor. This piece of metal appeared to be quivering and livid in the palm of my hand: and as I held it the metal became almost glowing, as a piece of live coal, and yet it was the same temperature as my hand. Within forty minutes the metallic disk had disappeared. Apparently its elements were sublimated by some type of evaporation process. Thus, it is apparent they can explode them at any rate of speed they wish; and in a limited frequency of energy they would explode with not the least sound. Such remote control by complete vector is an accomplished fact with our space neighbors.

It should be clear now to see that they can appear to the human eye and yet never register on camera film. Or, on the other hand, they can be made to show up on film when they were not visible to the human eye.

Presented with the true, simple explanation of the flying saucers, some people find it harder than ever to accept. They prefer to cling to the ideas of impossible tons of lead shielding and all the other ponderous aspects of space ships as conform to our limited sciences, most of which will have to be discarded before we even put a ship into outer space.

FLYING DISKS—EXTRA DIMENSIONAL CAMERAS

A flying disk is maneuvering over a city, or some area of the Earth. Every living thing and all their vibrations, seen and unseen by the naked eye, are picked up by the transmitting disk, which in turn relays these impressions back to the mother ship. There it is all permanently recorded on crystal instruments in detail.

Most of these scanning and recording operations are conducted when the disks are entirely invisible to us. When we do see them, they are usually just capering for us, or for some particular individual, to whom the display reveals a message, or an awakening. Both, spiritual and physical evolution upon Earth is timed, and is in gradual steps. Space visitors are in no hurry, and they enter in the evolution gradually, in the timing permitted them by cosmic rhythm and law.

Yes, indeed, the flying disks are both receiving and sending units. They are three-dimensional camera, television, radio, and motive entities, all in one. In fact, they are practically a synthetic brain, lacking only consciousness itself. Their manipulation is intrinsic and seemingly boundless. We on Earth are close to arriving at this technology in the realm of hypothesis, at least.

CHAPTER XIV
THE TRUE NATURE OF THE SAUCER MYSTERY

Only a short time ago we should have been obliged to go to great lengths to convince most people of the actual existence of flying saucers. Today, fortunately, we are spared the indignity of such futile efforts. The saucers definitely are here, and the majority of persons now are willing to admit this awesome fact. But the interpretation of flying saucer phenomena is an entirely different matter. As strange as it seems, the mystery of the unidentified flying objects is little nearer a solution than it was in 1947 when several flyers first made reports of sighting nine of the disks near Seattle.

Since then impressive files of new data have been amassed, but much of this evidence is so contradictory and bewildering that instead of offering a solution to the problem, the new facts have only rendered it more complex. Significantly enough, the most erroneous conceptions have been ponderously expounded by those whose every thought and utterance is in slavish conformity with the known laws of physics and the analytical laboratory method of approach. Insofar as the saucers are concerned, the "I know it all because I can prove it" attitude, whether uttered or insinuated, has only indicated with absolute certainty that no infinitesimal part of the true answer is known.

Today it is almost impossible to ignore the saucers, and those who attempt to do so are motivated in no small degree by egoistic personal prejudices. Yet to accept them unreservedly as coming from outer space is still considered by many to be somehow laughable. Thus have the saucers become a ready target for jokes and laughter. It is well that this is so, for a measure of humor is always a safety factor in any human struggle to new heights of understanding. The coming of the saucers will ultimately prove one of the most tremendous struggles of the ages in the evolving consciousness of mankind.

The story of generic man and his history upon Earth presents a ponderously slow, painful and often bloody pageant of evolution out of evils inherent in himself. No animal is as cruel as man. The pages of history are stained with records of deeds motivated by violent intolerances, vicious hatreds, arrogant lustings for power and wealth, sadistic cruelties, connivings, treacheries and mass slaughtering of fellowmen. Thus have we evolved to our present questionable status.

Yet as in the days of the building of the ancient tower of Babel many of us arrogantly feel that we have attained dizzy pinnacles of wisdom and scientific "know-how". Whereas, from a cosmic viewpoint, we are but an innately selfish, warlike species of earthbound grubs who have only within the last few years become conscious of the boundless universe. Only during the last fifty years have we learned to build ponderous vehicles that will fly and explore a tiny way above the surface of our planet. And our first thoughts are of conquest: conquest of new planets, conquest of the moon for a space station to police the world. Even as our agile minds are busy with these thoughts, we continue to plot mutual slaughter of our own kind.

Even the dulled wings of our imaginations will not permit us to imagine that intelligent beings who inhabit other planets in the universe may not have evolved as we did through cruel animalistic natural laws of survival of the fittest, the cruelest and the most insidiously clever. Thus with the first reports of the saucers people everywhere considered with alarm a possible intrusion of space craft from other worlds. We, by our own standards, expected them to have predatory ideas of conquest and enslavement of mankind. As a result the flood of horror films of monstrous extra-terrestrial invaders has not yet ceased.

As a matter of fact, the coming of the saucers is not an intrusion of a new order on our Earth; neither was it omitted from the original plan of nature on this planet. The saucer phenomena we have thus far witnessed is an integral part of a vastly greater plan for us than our finite minds can begin to comprehend. Thus, the saucers definitely are not to be feared!

But it would be a terrifying thought to think that we are drifting aimlessly all alone in boundless time and space upon an insignificant speck of matter we call Earth. In reality, we are not alone either during our sojourn upon this planet or in the universe. Our conscious minds, however, are so limited that we base practically all of our conclusions upon a strictly material foundation. Hence most of our conclusions are erroneous. But the secret of life we have been unable to fathom from any material viewpoint. In the final analysis even science must revert to the abstract idea of a vastly greater intelligence as the source of life. But having admitted so much, can we believe that this intelligence has long ago abandoned us here upon our ball of clay? To many it has seemed so, but only because the erroneous nature of our conscious minds is incapable of realizing mankind's true condition and state of being.

It is the will of the Creator that we perfect both our planetary home and the microcosm of our individual selves. As long as man progresses in the right direction, no matter how slowly or precariously, he shall continue to receive greater spiritual insight and a gradual broadening of material horizons in the fields of science. But each revelation of the hitherto unknown comes to us bounded by its own mystic shroud. Slowly these mystic shrouds of matter are expanding as concerns the macrocosm and ever closing in upon the atom. But as advanced as we like to think we are, in our present state of consciousness, a revelation of the true beauty behind all things would shatter our conscious minds. The eternal enigma "inside" even a humble bacterium enthralls the researcher and holds him spellbound. Yet, even he cannot behold its true reality!

Thus it is my sincere hope that the factual story I have told you about my contacts with extra-terrestrial visitors will prove not only a discovery of the true nature of the beings from out of space and time, but perhaps the infinitely greater discovery of your own true self and from whence you came, why you are here, and whither you are bound.

Although my story is given in good faith, some are bound to doubt me. For man does not trust man because the evil inherent in the human heart so often betrays him. Yet to many my words will bring greater understanding and release from the bonds of a prison. My experiences are interwoven with the truth of man's being as inextricably as strands of thread are a part of the fabric.

If this very day my story could be proved to every skeptical person, the mystery of our space visitors would be ended. And we should be ready and eager to greet them as brothers in the infinite federation of the universe. But ideas preponderantly spiritual cannot now and have never been capable of proof by material methods. Hence no material proof of the reality of my experiences may be given to satisfy skeptics.

First, to remove all possible fear from the idea of space invaders, I wish to state that in the vast majority of cases those who have conquered the problems of space travel have progressed to, or have always existed in, a state of spiritual consciousness which we today can conceive only in the abstract. For one of the immutable laws of the cosmos is that evil projected to its limits is self-destroyed; hence too great a preponderance of evil invariably results in self-destruction and a new beginning in greater densities of matter. Evolving toward good or evil, life and brotherhood, all go forth in majesty akin to the glory of the gods of the ancients. The evolved spiritual intelligences of the planets communicate only with the graduates of other planets; none others are or may be aware of their true natures.

Today the evolution of Earth both material and spiritual has reached its most critical point. Thus chronologically speaking the hour has struck upon our planet which has not only permitted, but demanded the influx of outer space entities and their material manifestation in our sphere of consciousness. They have come as harbingers of light to do everything possible to turn the tide of destruction which threatens to engulf Earth and terminate in a new fall for man into greater darkness and bondage in heavier chains of matter.

In the space being's contacts with me there has actually been some factual evidence—almost enough to serve as proof, even to materialists. But not quite enough! The evidence has been minus that same enigmatical fraction of verification necessary in nearly every instance of saucer manifestation throughout the world—whether in case of personal experiences or with official branches of certain governments (except in a few specific cases involving spacecraft of a most primitive type from which factual and technical data have been obtained, as intended by them). And herein we find pinpointed a significant clue to the true nature and mission of space visitors. They have ingeniously enshrouded their presence in mystery; certainly not because they have any desire to be mysterious, but only because we are not sufficiently mature to bear the impact of the full revelation of even the least of our extraterrestrial visitors. Understanding of them will come eventually, but only through our own interpretations. Thus will we begin to understand in terms of our own finite and immature intelligence some of the mysteries of beings who live in worlds less erroneous than our three-dimensional, pain-pleasure, suffering-and-death sphere.

In any research, in any revelation, in any miracle when so many individuals and groups of individuals have witnessed a certain phenomenon, or some phase of that phenomenon, it is usually sufficient proof to accept as true the existence of that phenomenon. When this point is reached the boundaries of understanding usually advance further. Insofar as the saucers are concerned, we have now reached that point. Hence, I am now telling my story more completely. Parts of my story have previously appeared in the single issue of my own newspaper, The Twentieth Century Times, and parts have been published in MYSTIC magazine, but never before has the entire account appeared in print. Only now has the mystery of the saucer phenomena come to an apparent dead-end which requires elucidation before anything further may be gained from extra-terrestrials. In other words, this book is Earth's answer to their signals to us. I hope it will produce results.

VOLUME TWO
SON OF THE SUN
by Orfeo Angelucci
Original Copyright, 1959
by Orfeo Angelucci

SON OF THE SUN

DEDICATION

This book is dedicated to those people with that soul which ever projects a little further than the senses, which perceive only things of the present that come, pass on, and are no more the things we knew. To the marvelous souls who, in the early spring, work to sow what others reap in the late fall.

Such a one was Adam, whose story it is my privilege to pass along in these pages.

Therefore, in dedicating this book to these souls; it follows that it is dedicated also to Adam, the physician from Seattle. Very much so.

ACKNOWLEDGMENT

Special acknowledgment is gratefully made to the following:

First of all, to my beloved wife, Mabel, whose unfailing devotion has been the cornerstone of my life at all times, whether the path was sunny or shaded. This includes, of course, my sons, Ramon and Richard, and my daughter-in-law, Pat.

To the Truehart family: Marcile, Bill and Gloria; Marcile, for her untiring assistance and inspiring interest which helped so much to produce this book; Bill and Gloria, for their gentle patience during the long months this work was in preparation.

To Earl Brewer, whose friendship and hospitality set the essential spawning ground for the events herein contained and recorded.

To Lillian Meyer, whose sympathetic insight constituted a vital contribution to the work.

To all my wonderful friends and relatives who have graciously kept me in the warmth of their esteem no matter where I have ventured, or what I have seen.

To Ray Palmer, whose latitude and respect for the thoughts and opinions of others have helped and inspired me for years.

To Henry George, economist-philosopher, who to me is Thomas Payne, Benjamin Franklin, Thomas Jefferson and Arthur Brisbane all embodied in one personality; Henry George, who cared so much for all humanity.

And to the living, boundless Universe.

Orfeo Angelucci

CONTENTS

SON OF THE SUN: The Secret Of The Saucers

Chapter 1
ADAM IN THE DESERT

"In the final analysis, Orfeo, there is only one virtue—the love of pure learning."

For a moment he paused; and he saw that moment, and felt that moment in its depth of meaning. He was looking at me, or rather far beyond me, as he did not look again during the next three days of our close association. He was seeing things in this moment that could not be spoken. As he came slowly back to the reality of our being here together in this little restaurant, he added, with an air of secondary importance:

"And all else is but procrastination and dissipation in the eyes of the One who awaits our evolutionary awakenings."

Adam and I had talked of many things, and his words had been as silvery threads spun on a scroll of eternal knowledge. But the words just spoken stood out like golden threads among the silver. Even as he spoke them to me he seemed to be living in another world, and looking alone into the universe in one cosmic swoop. I felt sure he was looking into the very core of effects, causes, aberrations, corrections; into the Cause behind all causes.

In those simple words, and his searching, burning, brown eyes, there was such an all-engulfing vision that I was swept into its depth with him in harmonious understanding. I saw what he saw, felt what he felt; a feeling of oneness with all that is. It was the flash of many ages in one swelling burst; yet it was the eternity of the split second. I was so devoid of self-awareness that I felt more like formless thought than a being of flesh and blood.

Material things flashed before me in a comprehension that was almost tangible, and the pulsating quiet of the universe became a rhythmic thunder. It was as if all things had been frozen and were now suddenly melting into a vaporous essence that further confirmed his words.

I had to agree with Adam; that in the final analysis there is only one virtue—the love of pure learning. Paradoxically, I could see the reverse of that axiom. The ultimate sin must be sustained ignorance.

SON OF THE SUN: The Secret Of The Saucers

Adam did not speak as a man having a complex of any kind. He felt neither inferior nor superior. Yet he had just come through an experience of learning and romance that was not one which mortals of earth usually know. It was one to be compared with cosmic grandeurs, like huge meteors, comets, and supernovae. It included a love that must soon be relegated to a nebulous memory, for its exquisiteness was too ethereal for undeveloped earth people. Of course, Adam had been guided through the experience by experts who would not put any person through it at random just for fun.

According to Adam, these people were not of earth but were visitors from another world. I believed him from the very start, believing him even more after he had told me all there was to tell. In the course of three evenings he narrated his fantastic story to me.

Sitting in the little desert restaurant in the heart of Twentynine Palms, Adam told me he had read my book, "The Secret of the Saucers," but that he had never expected to meet me in person. And as for me, I certainly had never expected to meet one like Adam, for he had recently gone into the sun and out again. He did not flinch when he told me this. Indeed, there was a mystical look on his face which as much as said that his trip into the sun was not quite his top experience-that other events more extraordinary had recently occurred. And I believe each one on earth is destined, in time, to have similar experiences.

Adam's whimsical grin told me of his faith in confiding his story to me. As he related detail by detail, I listened as a jurist might listen to a defendant or a plaintiff, returning him smile for smile and comprehension for comprehension. What man or woman wouldn't have been totally intrigued by his words, enthralled by the truths of their essence, and completely swept away by his sincerity? If a man hands you the secret of the universe so you see the universe respond as if in confirmation, would you ask who his parents were? If the words he speaks are living symbols of light, would you stop to inspect his credentials and thereby miss the essence of the words?

This I know. If one thousand people on earth were to understand what Adam told me in toto we may rest assured that earth's redemption is more than hypothetical; it is certain.

How did I meet Adam? Why was it essential that I meet him? Let us begin at the beginning.

Adam had gone into the sun and had emerged out of it without a burn. Other than normal perspiring, he had suffered nothing physically. I was trying to absorb this whole idea while gazing unrelentingly at his handsome, inscrutable, honest face. At the same time, the idea that he had only seven months to live, as he had told me, needed to be digested. The weight of these two thoughts made me oblivious to everything else around me.

I had come to this desert valley for one reason: to work here, and in time bring my family to reside here permanently. In fact, the day I arrived I found work with a furniture store laying floor tiles. It was November 1, 1954.

It was a wonderful feeling to be in my own line of work and situated in a community that I more than just "liked." Behind me were my recent years of lecturing on "flying saucers" and their impact on our future space age.

These lectures and magazine articles had brought me in contact with many people by mail and in person. Among them was a young man named Earl Brewer, of Seattle, Washington, who had met me through driving a friend to my home. Somewhat frail-looking, of Scandinavian descent, he possessed gleaming, child-like, blue eyes which were completely disarming. Although he had only a casual interest in my space visitor contacts, we liked each other from the start and became fast friends.

In September of 1954, Brewer again came to my home in Los Angeles. This time he came south to stay, as doctors advised a dry climate for his health, and he inquired if I knew of a place meeting this requirement where it would be possible to make a living. I suggested Twentynine Palms, California, and he decided to locate there.

Thus, when I looked him up several weeks later, informing him I intended to be here for quite some time (having already found work), he was beside himself with joy. He insisted that I share his small place, which though hardly larger than a cabin, had a tiny living room, kitchen and bathroom. It would be good to have a level-headed companion like Earl, so without ado I brought in my scant luggage and this spot became my week-day home for about six months. On week ends I commuted to Los Angeles to be with my family.

The cottage was situated on the road to the Twentynine Palms Marine Base north of the small village, at a point where the road makes an eastward bend and merges with an un-paved road. The intersection is known locally as "Indian Corners." Here only the passing traffic and the occasional barking of a dog break the desert quiet.

The town of Twentynine Palms itself lies near the gateway to the Joshua Tree National Monument. It nestles in the Great Morongo Basin in which are cradled also the communities of Joshua Tree, Yucca Valley, Pioneertown, and Morongo Valley. Earl began to feel better here in the High Desert and he agreed with many others that it is one of the most healthful spots in the country.

Earl was working also, and was fast becoming a desert native. In the middle of December, 1954, however, he decided to take a plane to his native Seattle for a stay of three days. Those three days were to catapult me into new horizons. They were not only to renew my lagging spirits, with respect to the subject of outer space, but to unfold things which were heretofore completely beyond my credulence. In retrospect, I feel certain that my stay of six months in Twentynine Palms and Earl's unexpected three-day visit to Seattle coincided with a prearranged plan of visitors from space.

When I came home that Friday evening after Earl had embarked for Seattle, I washed, changed clothes, and decided to have dinner in town. For some reason I did not feel lonely.

Driving the short mile and a half to town seemed more pleasant, somehow, than usual. In fact I began to feel more exuberant by the moment as I drove. I decided the cafe I would select would be the one where Earl and I had dined several times.

"Tiny," the proprietor, was fond of his monicker, which mocked his weight of over 300 pounds. "Tiny" did things in a big way. He wanted lots of room, and lots to eat, so he felt everyone else wanted the same, and gave his patrons generous portions. His waitresses did not merely bring glasses of water to the tables, but glasses plus a large pitcher for refilling. It was not a big cafe, but "Tiny" made you feel big in it. He and his place embraced one in an atmosphere of "welcome, friend." The front window filled nearly all of one wall. As you entered, the counter was to the right and a few tables spread here and there to the left.

As I neared town, I felt strongly that "Tiny's" was just the place for me. Though it was the middle of December, the evening was mild. I parked the car, and as I walked toward "Tiny's" I felt a strangeness in the air. There is a cosmic spell over the desert most of the time, but tonight the mystery was less distant and intangible; it was close and pulsating. The sand, the streets, the very buildings seemed to have a softness about them, and the stars were gently glowing lights in the warm, velvet heavens. It was a clue, I suppose, to what the evening held in store for me, but I didn't recognize it. Just beyond that door I would be swept from normal living into a state not of earth, yet not quite of another world. An exciting, new, nameless sensation.

I opened the door, and my eyes fell at once upon a young man sitting alone at a center table. He looked at me, smiling as though he was waiting to see me. We had never met before, for having once seen this face, it was not likely to be forgotten. So strikingly handsome was he that if beheld but once for only a few seconds in a crowd, an indelible impression of his countenance would be imbedded in the memory.

Instead of walking to the counter, where I normally would eat when alone, I walked to his table, drawn there as if under a spell. His smile did not waver. Our eyes met in an intense gaze as we made a brief appraisal of one another, and an inner communication passed between us, as though we had always known one another. I approached his table and said casually:

"Hello—friend."

"Hello, Orfeo," he replied immediately, his smile never wavering.

"You know me?" I asked, as I pulled back a chair and sat down.

"I know you only as well as you now know me. Please, just call me Adam, and do not ask my real name. In seven months I shall be gone, and you have enough wounds of the spirit without adding my memory to your future."

The way he said it left no doubt that he meant seven months left to live, and I felt a loneliness and sadness at his words. Adam had expected me to feel this way upon first hearing about his short future, but he donned an air of indifference to my reaction, and his spirited demeanor had a steadying effect. He made me feel that we had more important things to talk about than his physical welfare and his length of life.

The waitress came to the table and asked if she could help us. Adam smiled at her and replied, "One of your sizzling steak dinners, please."

He had ordered it for me, and I nodded in approval. Then I noticed the pitcher of water on the table. There were two glasses besides Adam's own glass.

"Adam," I asked. "Are you expecting someone else? Am I intruding on you and whoever you may be waiting for?"

"No, Orfeo. Why do you ask?" He said it with such assurance that I felt I was just seeing things.

"But there is a third glass on the table, Adam. Are you expecting someone besides me?"

He looked at the glass. Then he looked at me with puzzlement. "No," he said thoughtfully. "I must have said two glasses to the waitress, and she may have understood it to mean two more besides my own."

But Adam doubted his own explanation of it, for he looked several times at the third glass, and I could detect by his expression that he was asking himself if a third guest were to appear, after all.

As for myself, I decided to drop the thought for a while. Adam himself was enough of an enigma to me until the third person should arrive, if at all. Then he broke the silence.

"Would you like a bottle of beer, Orfeo?"

I looked at the pitcher of water. His own glass contained a sparkling liquid the color of pale ginger ale, fizzing and bubbling continuously, though he had already drunk half of it. The lively bubbles arose from the remains of a tiny tablet at the bottom of the glass. My answer to his offer was a hurried, "No, Adam. No beer for me. I will take the water," and I poured some from the pitcher into my glass.

Adam smiled even more broadly as his hand went into his coat pocket. He brought out an oyster-white pellet and held it before me as he remarked: "O.K., Orfeo. Then how about a very rare champagne?"

Returning his reassuring smile with my own, I took the pellet and dropped it into my glass. Immediately the water bubbled, turning slowly into the clear, pale amber contained in his own glass. I lifted the glass a few inches from the table, looking into it with a feeling that this might be the drink I dared not hope for. The exhilarating aroma rising from it could not be mistaken. I had tasted and smelled the same liquid before. I put my lips to the glass and merely let the liquid touch my lips. That was enough.

"Adam—Adam, I can't believe it! Please don't fool me." My sudden excitement had taken me from earth number one to earth number two. I could feel my whole being swirling into another domain from the mere recognition of the nectar. I could not control my spiral ascent, nor did I want to. Adam's eyes had continued smiling into my own.

"Yes, Orfeo," he assured me. "It is nectar. A mild, diluted form, but the real nectar, just the same."

I wanted to take a few sips, but just then the waitress brought servings of soup and salad to me. Up to this moment, in spite of my sudden exhilaration, everything had appeared normal to me. But I knew that very soon everything would appear differently. So I tried to evaluate the objects about me as they truly were so I would not lose my sense of orientation when the environment took on an enhanced aspect.

Ah, yes. No wonder Adam had expected me. No wonder he seemed so alive and alert. To him all the surroundings were of a different pace and appearance. Before I opened the door, he had already come under the pleasant spell of the nectar.

What was more important, he was in the protective care of others somewhere, perhaps nearby, perhaps far off—unseen, and not of earth, nor of our solar system. Soon I, too, would be engulfed with him.

I thrilled from head to foot as I took the glass, lifted it to my lips, and swallowed twice from it. At that instant I entered, with Adam, into a more exalted state and everything around me took on a different semblance. No longer was I in Tiny's cafe in Twentynine Palms. It had been transformed into a cozy retreat on some radiant star system. Though everything remained in its same position, added beauty and meaning were given to the things and people present there.

Among the patrons dining that evening were two marines from the nearby base. They were sitting at the front end of the counter. Sometimes they glanced our way as they talked and drank beer following their meal. There was a trace of disdain in their expressions, especially in the younger one's. This was not directed at us, but rather was part of their general outlook, colored by a grueling military life. Yet now, since taking a little of the nectar, I saw them as two vibrant humans in the pageantry of life—not only my life, but all life. If they could see themselves in the same broad scope, their lives would not seem to them so desolate or remote.

The waitress brought the rest of my order. Adam nodded a pleasant thank you to her, then looked at the bubbling nectar in my glass. He glanced at the empty glass, that third glass at the place on the table where no other person was expected to sit. His puzzled look betrayed the fact that he was asking himself constantly why it was there. It did not disturb him, but merely seemed to puzzle him.

I decided to wait awhile before drinking any more of the beverage. I wanted to take in more of the situation before going under its complete influence. It was then that Adam spoke abruptly.

"In the final analysis, Orfeo, there is only one virtue; the love of pure learning."

In the short pause that followed his words, the whole life cycle of a galaxy must have gone past Adam's vision. Then he added: "And all else is procrastination and dissipation in the eyes of the One who but awaits our evolutionary awakenings."

I was, in spirit, suspended in a tenuous world by now. When he uttered these words I felt it was time to take some of the sparkling drink. The additional nectar made no difference in my feeling. The first two sips had done all that a river of the nectar could do.

Adam had spoken these words as if they were the end of a long conversation between us instead of the beginning. I turned toward the two young marines and noticed that one of them was now smiling. They must have heard Adam. We continued to eat, slowly. Food had never before tasted better to me, for the beverage made me feel splendid. Adam began to speak again, this time in subdued and well controlled tones.

"I am a medical doctor, Orfeo, from Seattle. On my next birthday I shall be 38. A little more than a month ago it became necessary to close out my practice."

He paused as we took a few more bites of our food. In the same subdued voice he then resumed, maintaining a calm, pleasant poise.

"To me, the profession is steeped in the Hippocratic Oath, as it is with so many others. It was my hope to some day devote my time and means to biological research. I gave much thought and some study to the fundamentals of biochemistry, and even to physics.

"Then this condition came upon me. For a time I was seized by the same fear, despair and sense of futility that, as a doctor, I had seen fall upon so many others. There were the same futile hopes patients had displayed so many times that perhaps some error might be present in the diagnosis. I could not believe it was now my turn, and I looked desperately here and there for some new discovery by science, an announcement that such conditions were now curable. After all, such news could come any day. I called the Mayo Clinic, the Johns-Hopkins Institute, Cornell and others. There was not even a flicker of hope in cases such as mine.

"Under the strain and despair, my capacity to serve as a good doctor ended. Rapidly I became resigned to the inevitable. Somehow, after one becomes resigned there is an inner rebirth, when whole lifetimes seem to be lived within short days."

I took in every word in silence as we ate. It was hard for me to believe that this gentle, light-brown-haired man who looked so healthy and handsome was not long for this world. There was a quality that gave to his eyes the appearance of changing from light brown to light blue, and back to brown. His mind, alert and quick, was resilient and tolerant about all things. He seemed to be truly happy, not for the present time, but for a glory he could foresee for mankind. I had the feeling I was in the presence of the most civilized person on earth.

I did not say a word, confining myself to listening. Under expanded awareness, produced by the nectar, I needed neither to confirm his words nor submit any opinion, for our minds were in rapport. He continued.

"As soon as I became resigned to the inescapable, there was a sudden surge within me; a light, almost visible, flashed all about me, and I was no longer afraid. There was ethereal music at the same time, and I have not yet ceased to hear it."

I drank a little of the nectar. Even this had no more effect to add to that of the first two swallows. My eyes met Adam's, and there was an at-one-ment of mutual understanding, such that a few well-chosen words could tell the history of an entire solar system. I nodded for him to go on—I was eager to hear more of his story.

"Well, Orfeo," he resumed, "I had only nine months to live, and as I closed my practice, I flailed out, trying to grasp as much life as could be packed into each day. It was a mixture of desperation and rapture within me—fear and courage and ecstasy, all alloyed into one tangled cocktail of livingness."

He paused a moment, trying to recapture the acute power of that tornado of consciousness. But for the nectar we drank, neither he nor I could have remained so placid at the assault of his words. His aspect rendered him overwhelmingly handsome as he continued to tell his story.

"That is how I came to be interested in even such things as flying saucers, and all pertaining to the universe. Before, I had considered such things as silly and of interest only to simple and peculiar mentalities.

"I went to hear a talk on flying saucers, sponsored by a small group in Seattle. At this gathering I obtained your book, The Secret Of The Saucers, among other books and articles.

"In your book I found a kindred spirit. I felt it was trying to say something to humanity, pointing clearly to something which goes mainly unseen. Then, also having read your essay, I found the two wrapping up the whole concept from alpha to omega.

"Well, in a short time I had closed out my practice. I did not even know where I was going, nor to whom I could turn for that final assurance and courage. Suddenly it dawned on me that through all the years of my practice I had missed out on warm friendships such as most people enjoy, and there was not even a woman I could call my beloved. Within me there was one inclination, crying out silently, but ever so strongly. It was the call of the desert.

"In your own writings you had mentioned Twentynine Palms, and this place rang within my consciousness with a tone of 'must'. So, here I am, Orfeo; or rather, here we are."

It was hard to discern any worry in Adam's face as he smilingly ended this part of his story.

What was it that was seething up inside me? Why did I like this man more than any other man I had ever met, and yet, felt on guard against him more than against any other man? Was it the utter magnetism of his way and attractiveness? Did my own experience and learning and philosophy not hold up under his challenging presence? Could I not admit within me that he was utterly handsome, and that in his company I stood out as almost nothing? Yet I liked him, and I liked him to such a degree I would give my life in his behalf. He was noble, he was gentle, he was as sincere as a child, and he had an elastic understanding of nearly everything. What was more, I felt within me he had a story to tell that was far beyond even him.

Our glasses were empty, so I poured water into both of them. As if I expected it of him, he responded by taking a pellet from his pocket, breaking it in half, and dropping a piece into each glass. Again he looked at the third glass, trying hard to figure out why it was there, but try as he would, it was just an extra glass. If he could not figure it out, it would certainly be no use for me to try. Soon, it proved to be the most important glass on the table. He took a drink from his fresh glassful, and I followed suit. Then he resumed his story.

"While dining here in Twentynine Palms recently, I got into a conversation with two men who were going back to Los Angeles that same day. I learned that one of them owned a homestead cabin not far from here. Soon I had paid him fifty dollars for the rent of it for two weeks. He gave me one of three keys to it, and told me it was mine for even three weeks if I wanted it.

"Suddenly I felt free. I mean really free. A rustic home in the desert was mine. I had means and a medical man's knowledge of man and woman, yet I had nothing in the past. Life is short at best, and my knowledge was only theory and protected license. People in general seemed to be living in a knowledge beyond my knowledge and they took nothing seriously, not even life, not even death. At least, that is the way I felt for a couple of days, and then my entire attitude on everything changed. I started from the very beginning. Now I find myself asking me what, when, how and why? That last is the one beyond approach—Why?

"I entered the labyrinth of questions, and I have found that only the doomed have an answer, only the doomed have been able to fathom the depths. I want so much to leave the wisdom of the dying, which has before this evaporated into the ether. Instead, I find and truly believe I have learned the glorious promise for the living. After all, what can I depend upon to think of or to remember me except the living? Whatever we leave behind us is exactly what we inherit, no matter where or when. So, permit me to tell you everything, and then may you carry on the blazing torch.

At this point he stopped and looked at me inquisitively. Then, almost cautiously, he asked me, "Say—I wonder if that is not, after all, the wisdom of the dying?"

He had caught the meaning in my own smile, though I had not said a word.

SON OF THE SUN: The Secret Of The Saucers

Quickly and anxiously he shot another question at me.

"How is it you seem to be so easy to tell all this to? Why is it you seem to understand all that I say?"

I paused a moment before answering. This man puzzled me now. My instinct had told me from the moment of our meeting that he knew the answers to all of life, had the wisdom of the cosmos, yet here he was, asking me to tell him something as if he did not already have the answer.

It was not until later I realized Adam had absorbed wisdom and understanding during his experiences, but had not as yet become conscious of his great knowledge. It was to return to his memory gradually, while he told me his story and we discussed the truths.

"Because, Adam," I finally answered him, "I once felt doomed for long months. It eventually dawned on me that we are all doomed in this short and single existence. Don't you think that young marine who finally smiled, and is trying to overhear what we say, feels the same way? Most of us intuitively sense that same logic, regardless of how joyful or how tragic a situation may be. We always know that 'this, too, shall pass'. Only life and eternity do not pass away. A person is either intelligently aware of some infinite purpose, or a person is a mere animated volume of nothing. We are so concerned about eternity, which must be spent somewhere, either on earth or elsewhere. And does not eternity concern the final truth of all things, material or spiritual?"

Adam leaned forward toward me, his brow wrinkling. Something I had said had an impact upon him.

"What," he asked, "do you mean, that life does not pass away?"

I replied with an ease which surprised both him and me. "Well, I mean that life never passes away. Because of the very prevalence of life you and I are here. It passes from individual bodies, true enough, and it may even vanish from an entire solar system. But there will still be life throughout the universe.

"Oblivion has only one condition, Adam. It is the same state that prevails with absolute zero, and in probing oblivion we find that it does not exist, just as absolute zero does not exist. By the same line of reasoning we find that life also has only one condition, and that is consciousness. In the physical world we find nothing but that which we call matter and motion. Nothing is at absolute rest.

"Absolute zero, Adam, does not exist. Oblivion can neither be felt nor described, and certainly not imagined. Therefore oblivion does not exist, any more than does absolute zero. But consciousness is felt by all creatures in the same frame of description. All life could be whittled down to one entity, or distributed to an infinite number, but there would be no addition or subtraction of consciousness."

Adam smiled. His lips tightened a little as he rolled his eyes upward, straining hard to get the picture clear in his mind. Before he should lose whatever grasp he had of what I had just said, I offered another approach.

SON OF THE SUN: The Secret Of The Saucers

"Let's start from the beginning, Adam, as all things start. Let us suppose the Supreme Fatherhead willed to remove all creatures from the Universe. All right, it is now devoid of mortal life.

"Now, then—we suppose the Fatherhead willed just one being to appear, created in life. Every creature that ever existed before would feel he was that life in its consciousness."

Adam's smile became radiant. But he had one more question.

"O.K., Orfeo. Now, suppose the Supreme Fatherhead created another being? There would now be two. The one cannot feel the life of the other. They would be experiencing different feelings in the same frame of mind. How do you reconcile that with your concept?"

Of course, he already knew the answer, but he wanted to hear it in words. Truth and fact appear to all or us in the same clear perspective. By the gleam in his eyes I could feel that he and I were again "at one". I replied at once.

"It would make no difference, Adam. There would be the consciousness that you and I are alive. And it would be as though all the universe were alive. Even now you and I think alike, and feel alike. The nectar caused our faculties to be brought to a certain level, so we feel exactly alike and think exactly alike. You could suddenly feel something that had not touched me, and I would feel exactly the same way as you if the something touched me also.

"I may touch a flame and feel the burning, while you feel nothing. But if the flame touched you in the same place you would feel what I feel. If I stub my toe my nose feels nothing of it. Yet both are part of the same life of me. A drop of ocean water is the very consciousness of the entire seven seas, though they be separated.

"In the deepest coma, in the deepest sleep of anaesthesia, there is yet some consciousness, and that is the reason we feel unconscious. But when we really pass away, and true oblivion would seem to engulf us, there is a sudden transpiration, and in an instant we are alive again, somewhere, in a new life just emerging. Oblivion is just impossible, Adam."

Adam forgot to keep his voice low. He burst out joyously. "Now I am sure I am not afraid to die! There is eternity. None of us, not even the amoeba, truly dies. Every living thing is just a continuation of some unit of life, living all over again. The number of souls that can exist is infinite, and even varies. And therein is the beauty of fact. It makes the requirement of the propagation of an individual spirit unnecessary, and even unfounded. More than that, Orfeo; I believe no one truly accepts that a formless consciousness propagates our existence. Yet, no one can deny his present state of being. We occurred once, so why can't we occur again? It is that simple," he concluded.

Remembering that we had not finished eating, we resumed our meal. Receiving another enlightening flash, Adam added, "And we inherit the very same world we leave. Whatever it is when we leave it, that is what we are born into again. It can be a stage set with the means for working out our atonement if we are aware, or it can remain a perplexing theater of some bizarre existence."

I added only two words. "Precisely, Adam."

The effect of the nectar did not wane, and we were both in a delightful mood. We looked again at the empty third glass. At least it had been empty. Now it was nearly half filled, and with the same amber bubbling liquid we were drinking! Adam and I exchanged looks, each thinking the other had poured something from his own glass. This idea we dispelled at once, for within my memory I recalled a similar phenomenon in the past, and something within Adam made him see the light also.

"Do you think what I think?" he asked.

"Yes," I replied, "I believe I do."

"Then let me be the one to say it, Orfeo. Your book already states that you know of such things. I have a story to tell you, and if I can explain this phenomenon you will find it easier to accept what I relate."

"Yes," I agreed. "Tell me how you think the nectar got into that glass."

With childlike glee, yet with deliberation for the sake of accuracy, he lowered his voice again and carefully gave me his explanation of what had occurred.

"We are directly observed by the Space Visitors. From their ship, wherever it is, they were able to confuse my words, so that without knowing it, I asked the waitress to bring three glasses instead of two. Yet I remember only that I asked for two."

I nodded in comprehension. "Go ahead; I follow you."

"They directed water vapor, unseen by anyone here, into the glass, and condensed it back to water. At the same time they directed an invisible, fine stream of the nectar powder to mix with the water. They cannot be too far away."

"Well spoken, Adam," I interjected, "but wait. It does not matter where they are. The powder may not have come from their own supply. Count the pellets in your pocket."

"Good," said Adam. "I should have four pellets, without doubt."

His hand went into his coat pocket and came out with only three pellets. Try as he would to find the fourth, he could not. We said no more. We knew that the Space Visitors, by remote control, had sublimated one of his pellets into vapor and directed it into the glass.

Adam looked appraisingly at the pitcher of water. He put his finger on a spot on the outside and turned it around for me to see.

"The water was up to this dark spot, exactly. There is just about half a glass now missing." He paused pensively a moment, and then spoke a little somberly.

"Yes, Orfeo, I have a story to tell you. I am certainly glad you have seen these things happen here. Now you should have no trouble believing my story."

"Adam," I assured him, "you do not need to convince me. One thing alone was enough. When I saw the pellets that produced the nectar, what other evidence did I need? No one of earth could have given them to you."

The waitress came and asked us for our choice of dessert, and only then did we notice that we had finished our meal. We ate our dessert slowly and silently, for we were both in a galaxy of mental reflections. Still under the prolonged influence of the nectar, we were transcended from reality. Even the usual softness of Twentynine Palms would sound loud to our heightened senses, were we to be conscious of the reality around us.

SON OF THE SUN: The Secret Of The Saucers

Chapter 2
THE DANCE IN A GLASS

As we lingered over our dessert, Adam persisted in staring at the glass which seemed to have filled itself with the strange liquid. I could feel that his almost mesmerized interest in the glass was fraught with expectancy.

Were my ears deceiving me? Was that music I heard coming from the direction of the glass? It must be music. No sound could be so enchanting unless played by some skilled musician. To describe it in words would be disfiguring its mystic flow. The ear had to be highly receptive to hear it, yet every haunting note came through clearly. Indeed, the fluid in the glass was being used as a radio, converting waves beamed at it back into the original broadcast. It was so faint that only ears made sensitive by a substance such as Adam and I had drunk could hear it.

Adam's eyes became moist. He absently ate his dessert, his eyes remaining steadfastly fixed upon the glass. The world around him must have ceased to exist for him. I saw his expression change from its normally deep one to another that became fathomless, taking on the aesthetic demeanor of a mystic god. The music became even more beautiful, until it was impossible to discern whether the mood preceded the music or the music preceded the mood, so perfect was the timing. I was held spellbound, looking upon this face which had become more intensely handsome in Adam's preoccupation. I was, in fact, more intrigued by his countenance for a time than by the glass with its ethereal music.

Then slowly I too looked again at the glass and was held in amazement. A miniature young woman was dancing in the nectar! Her golden-blond beauty was as arresting as the miracle of her projection in the glass. Not only was some intelligence using the liquid as a radio, but it was also being used as a television unit.

Her arms moved in rhythmic motion with the graceful thrusts of her dancing body. Her feet were so light and responsive that the music itself seemed to emanate from them. The expression on her face was that of a maid who had found bliss and eternity among the angels. I had not seen her eyes, for they had not once shifted their gaze from Adam's eyes, all the while she danced.

Why, I thought, would she not cast just a passing glance my way?

I heard a sigh come from Adam, from deep within him. As I forced my eyes from the glass to his face, I could see tears pouring down his cheeks. Except for these, his face seemed frozen into a handsome mask. He was not ashamed of his emotion. Indeed, he seemed oblivious to everything around him as he surrendered to the fullness of a bittersweet joy.

The girl danced on in the glass, the fervor of her movements mounting in proportion to Adam's swelling emotions, apparently drawing out all of his passions, all of his tenderness with her dancing. There must have been an experience between Adam and this beauty which she wanted him to remember, and she seemed to be accomplishing her purpose very well, even as a miniature in a glass. His feeling was so apparent even I, a bystander, could decipher it.

So perfect was the projected figure that it seemed to be a flesh and blood girl submerged in the nectar. Her graceful rhythm was matched by the soft folds of her white silken robe, which swirled and swung about her as though it had an awareness and a life all its own.

Without a word spoken or sung, the theme of the dance was self-revealing. In all its movements the very soul of universal womankind was being expressed. In the flowing glides and abrupt leaps all the caprices of woman spoke. The figure's hair danced about with a delight all its own, as though full freedom was in each strand, yet each was under perfect control of the sprightly head containing its roots. All things of her, about her and around her reflected the spirit of her dance.

Even our table had taken on life from deep inside, although it remained motionless. The livingness of everything seemed to be torn asunder by the deep but quiet sobs coming intermittently from Adam.

I was aware that he saw and felt more than I could see or feel, and I did not look at him. The music, the dance and the sheer loveliness of the girl held me captivated.

In the climaxing moment of her dance, one thing remained apparent: The over-all effect was rejuvenating and wholesome. I became one in love with her, with everyone and everything, including motion itself.

While Adam was in the grip of anguished memory, I was experiencing an opposite reaction. I heard the music I most longed to hear, I watched a near-angel dancing to it, I saw a face and form which left nothing to be desired. Seeing her, I saw heaven all around.

Two wet spots on the table were the visible evidence of Adam's soul-purging. Unmindful of my presence, he wept on profusely, yet in a strange rapture.

The music became a crescendo, apparently heedless of the fact that others in the cafe might hear it. The girl's dancing accelerated to a living tornado. Then came a crash of cymbals and drums, a steady roll of musical thunder, and she whirled in my direction, looking for the first time squarely into my eyes as she fell gracefully to her knees.

Hers was a stern, accusing look. I would have wilted under the impact of it, except for her beauty. Anything would be a pleasure, coming from her. She was the personification of the etheric hosts, and she told me by her intense look and her graceful finale that she condemned me, not only on her own behalf, but by the bidding of all life in the cosmos. She was clearly conveying the message that I would yet come down a few notches in my arrogant self-esteem. (I mistakenly thought I had long ago shed false pride and arrogance, but evidently the higher civilizations did not think so.) Because she was so delicately beautiful, so gentle, so incapable of giving harm to body or spirit, I accepted her stern, silent pronouncement at once.

Then she grew smaller and smaller, until she had disappeared entirely. The bubbles rose steadily in the glass as if nothing had happened. My eyes turned slowly to Adam's, even as his turned searchingly toward mine. Softly, almost wanly, he asked, "Did you see her?"

I nodded slowly, and I saw he understood that his own feelings were not strange to me.

Soon the liquid in the glass lowered to the halfway point. It was being drained away as mysteriously as it had been brought in. The two young marines were looking toward our table very intently.

We could not know whether they had heard the music or had pieced together any comprehensive story from what they must have overheard. We did not care, because they had become to us just what they were—two average, intelligent human beings. True enough, life was all one thing, no matter what the individual experience might be at the time.

We remained silent for a while. In the silence I gathered some insight into the person Adam, this Adam who sat before me. He had had an experience of the heart which seasoned his person and his soul, yet seemed to be gone from his hold forevermore. The greater part of him—his life, his emotions, his motives—all these must have gone with her passing out of his life, whoever she was.

In such experiences, the one that hurts the most is usually the most recent. Yet, according to Adam's own story, this must have been his first love, and certainly it would be his last. Again, I reflected, one who has had a hundred love affairs gets no more impact from all of them combined than one who experiences only one. More than that, the one has more impact than the one hundred. Like life itself, love remains one thing. Any coloring of it remains for the disposition of the individuals. Any abuse of it comes from the inferior nature of the individuals. Any miscomprehension of it is due to the ignorance of the individuals.

Adam exuded in his every aspect the fact that he had once hit the zenith in love. He made me feel as if I had not yet come upon its first note. At the same time, it was clear that his interest in all fundamental things was of parallel intensity. His preoccupation with the memory of his recent love did not erase his interests in other things. The scope of his love did not detract from the scope of his capacity for all things. It seemed his horizon was equal in all directions, with no dead ends. This, then, was the type of man with whom I had the privilege of communication.

As these thoughts ran through my mind, Adam reached toward the third glass, which was now less than half filled with the nectar, and poured half the contents into my glass and half into his own. It was then we heard a summoning whistle come from the direction where the young marines were sitting at the counter. The younger one was hailing us, and when we looked toward him he waved as his companion and he arose to leave. The other one waved also, and we returned their "goodnights." Suddenly, the four of us had become friends for no apparent reason. They could have been our sons insofar as age was concerned. Surely in the scope that Adam saw things, we were brothers.

"You see, Orfeo?" he asked. "Why could not the whole world be at one in friendship, in consideration, and in all things? People dream of such a day; religions are built entirely on that objective. There is a constant evolutionary trend towatd that one end. The final truth always was—and shall be in the future—that all will be just One. All matter, all spirit, all motion, will be found to be ONE thing. The Great Will knows it, and patiently waits for us to come upon it through our own efforts. Only when we have overcome all the obstacles clouding our eyes and senses shall we see it, and in that moment we shall know Eternity."

As he finished, we drank the remainder of our nectar. The cafe was being readied to close for the night. Tiny came to our table. "You're welcome to stay, gents. We are closing early tonight, but you can watch the place for me," he smiled from his bulky, warm self. We took the hint, bid him goodnight, and stepped outside.

There we lingered for a while. Adam still had his wallet in his hand. Pulling out some bills, he said, "As long as you are with me, I'll pay all the way. I have more money than I can spend in seven months. Now, here's a hundred dollars for you. Take it and don't give me any apologies. That's all you're going to get, anyhow. I could easily give you thirty thousand and have a few thousand left over, but it is going to charity and research, Orfeo. I'm sure that is where it belongs, and you would do the same. I have the money and the experience, yet I cannot write it down. You are not as well off as I am, but when you are even worse off you will write about me."

It was hard to tell whether Adam coldly knew the future for me, or whether he was hard pressed for time and was doing things at a fast pace. He was sure of himself, and I had to admire his methods. But his abundant means accentuated my scant ones and I found myself imploring, "Adam, I don't want thirty thousand dollars. Just give me enough to write the material and get it published on my own. I will start Monday morning. I promise you."

"All right," he agreed, "you will get it. But only after I have told you everything. Then you can remind me of my offer, and ten thousand dollars will be yours."

I was ready now for anything. I felt rich, powerful, warm, and secure. Adam, too, appeared especially exuberant.

SON OF THE SUN: The Secret Of The Saucers

"Well, shall we go to your place, Orfeo?" Adam asked.

"Yes," I answered. "We have electric lights, water, gas, two radios, and books. Earl has gone to Seattle, but he would be more than happy for us to use his little domicile."

As I finished speaking, a rap sounded from inside the glass door of the cafe. It was Tiny waving a last goodnight to us. We bid him the same, and we looked into the cafe. We saw something odd was happening. All the tables had been cleared except ours, where the third glass still stood in its place. Now. before our eyes, it grew smaller and smaller, until it disappeared completely. Adam and I faced each other without speaking, and nodded in comprehension. Smiling, Adam spoke, half to me and half to himself.

"The waitress never brought that glass in the first place and no one but we two could see it. We were conditioned by the nectar to see a projected mirage. Come on, Orfeo, let's go. I'll meet you at your place. I have a real story to tell you."

"Do you know where my place is?" I asked.

"Sure," he replied. "Indian Corners, about one and one-half miles out Utah Trail in the direction of the Marine Base. It's that little house off the road, on the left side."

Within five minutes, we both arrived at the house and parked our cars side by side. I did not know then how far Adam was to project me into the life of other worlds. I unlocked the door of the house and turned on the light. When I attempted to apologize for the smallness of the house, Adam said, "Never mind that. Let's turn on some music and feel in contact with the rest of the world." With that remark, he walked over and adjusted the radio's dials until he had found something he liked.

It was 10 o'clock in the evening. I was ready now to hear his story, but to give more hospitality to the atmosphere I put a pot of fresh coffee on the stove to brew.

"Orfeo," Adam began, "you will write all this down some day. But remember, you will not write it until you feel the time has come that the world can see the verity of it all. Also, I would rather you wrote it in the second person than quote me directly. However, I won't hold you to that. Write it the best way you can, write it without holding back anything. You know me only as Adam, and no other name will ever matter. As I live again and again I will feel more that this was part of me than if you mentioned my present identity, for we remember nothing in our separate lifetimes except the beginning of our creation. The rest will be remembered only on that final day of perfection. You know, Orfeo, we all feel as if we were Adam and Eve. What other names in history do any of us feel so close to? You were right, life is but one consciousness. All that counts is the beginning and the end, a man and a woman. In their perfect state that is all the life there is in the infinite universe."

"O. K., Adam, I promise it will be as you say. That is, if I ever do write it."

SON OF THE SUN: The Secret Of The Saucers

We sat down at a small table in a corner. Adam crossed his legs and began to speak. He referred briefly to the two marines in the cafe. In deep reflection, he said that the problem of the younger fellow, whatever it might be, was to that one and to earth itself as ponderous as the problem of world destiny. He smiled as he told me that the lad would evaluate his problems differently after tonight.

"Yes," I agreed. "Especially after your abandonment to the flood of tears which poured from you."

"Was I crying, Orfeo? Funny, but I don't remember it. I felt wonderful, in spite of what I saw."

"Yes, Adam, you were crying. I would not have disturbed you for anything. Your feeling was beyond any help I could give, anyway. To a certain extent I even shared part of it, knowing neither why nor what. I somehow felt the emotions of an etheric romance, and I breathed in the aroma of its outer aura. No doubt those two marines felt it also, to some extent."

I paused a second or so. Then I had to say these few words, which poured from me almost involuntarily.

"Adam, that young woman in the glass. She ended her dance by turning suddenly toward me, and fell to her knees, bowing. Yet her eyes remained fixed upon me, as if accusing me of something, as if saying to me, 'You, too, shall go through trials. And no one but yourself shall feel concern.' I believe there was profound meaning in her gesture, but I cannot imagine what it is. I would feel anxiety over it, but her beauty and gentleness had a softening effect. I keep seeing her, and to be truthful, I do not want to let her vision leave my mind."

Adam rested his head in his hands, closed his eyes, and assured me. "She meant no harm, Orfeo. As for hate, she does not know the meaning of the word. You may not know her, but she knows you. You will come to know her through my story.

"In her world she is one of the hindmost. But she is learning. At times, learning is like bliss, at other times, it is a strain. Learning of things subordinate to man comes easy, but learning about man, about life and the truths, comes hard. Even the initiate finds himself, or, as in her case, herself, always in the midst of a struggle. It is as if one were always on the second rung of the ladder of wisdom, never on the last. The more we know, the lonelier we become, until that last rung is reached. Only then do we lose the sensation of loneliness. What man on earth would not be painfully lonely if he paused long enough to do some truly profound thinking? But in the glory of the final ascension, thinking becomes life itself, and then loneliness becomes an erased fantasy."

(As I listened to him I realized it was going to be very difficult to relate his story in the second person, as he suggested. In the months that followed I had to decide to tell it as it could be told, to adhere to the facts, and swing from first person to second person when and however required. After all, he did say to disregard anything he advised, if necessary.)

SON OF THE SUN: The Secret Of The Saucers

At intervals we could hear the traffic passing by about thirty yards away. The aroma of the brewing coffee was pleasant. Now and then an airplane droned past, going eastward or westward. There was nothing outwardly different about this night, but Adam and I felt different. In a sense, we were different. We were still enhanced by the effect of the nectar.

Then Adam began his long story. The telling of it took up most of three nights.

* * * *

"It may sound strange, Orfeo, but after the first shock of realization of my incurable condition leveled off to a resignation and acceptance of it, all things seemed to change in my perspective. It was as though my whole being did a flip-over, like pulling the cord of a Venetian blind. What had been to me the big things of life became insignificant, and the little things took on great significance. I had been seeing life and the world in a distorted way, as a trained seal might see it. But the reality of my condition, and the sudden and urgent awakening within me, brought everything into proper scope. There was now more meaning to everything, even to a spider's web. There was less meaning to the artifices of man-made things; they became mere fads, coming and going.

"In the blindness of the masses, I began to perceive a vaporous thread of essence, a small essence distilled from the gigantic world of turbulence. This essence became the paramount thing in my new-found existence. This thread, I sensed, is interwoven in all that goes on about us. It is what you might call the mass record etched on the ether. At any rate, it is all that matters on this planet and on all worlds, in the ultimate sense. It is all the basic truths distilled by man himself from his own mass follies. On each side of this thread lies a vast wasteland of regrets, willful mistakes, obstinate and vain blindness.

"Almost everything you can perceive going on in earth's affairs at this moment, Orfeo, shall be added to the bulk of that vast wasteland. Only truth is filtered out, perhaps slowly and painfully, but filtered out, nevertheless, to be added to the thread of essence, becoming finally a vast sea of substance which will engulf and purify all the wasteland around it. That will be the day of Oneness, of Redemption, and only then can the vision of perfection and eternity become a reality.

"I can now see more of this essence in the natural smile of a child than in the words of all the sages of history. No, we do not die. We simply are born, wilt, and come back to inherit the jungle of hypocrisy we leave.

"Being a doctor, I tended to regard health as an unnatural state, while sickness was the normal. My patients were of utmost importance, and other people were meaningless entities who would eventually become ill, and thereby gain true stature as human beings. In the perverted values of man at this uncivilized stage on earth, there may be some truth in this view. But I know now that health is the virtue, and sickness the sin. Learning is life, and ignorance is death. The only oblivion that can be felt is ignorance. The only pain is sickness, be it of the body or of the soul. The only rapture is perfect health, be it also of the body or of the soul.

"Why, then, Orfeo, why, I humbly ask in my ignorance, did I receive the first flicker of a spiritual dawn when I became afflicted and doomed?"

His words, his fervent sincerity, had tapped a small reservoir of wisdom within me which I had not known existed. I got up from the table, turned off the stove and brought cups, spoons and sugar to the table for our coffee. I answered him while doing this.

"Because, Adam, the real value of yourself is that thread of essence within you, like the thread that weaves through all society. The bulk of you, in personality and aspect, was conditioned by society. You accepted things as those around you molded them. You had to make a success of yourself in that society, so you conformed. You forgot your childhood intuitions and instincts, almost giving your very soul to others around you. You even insulated yourself against the call of love from your other half, which can be filled only by a woman. You were capable, so success came easily to you. You are handsome, and except for your present illness, you are very healthy by earth standards in our present stage of civilization. You felt that others might be sick and infirm, but you, never; you felt like one privileged.

"It was as though God had set a special stage to serve you in your string of successes, the end object of which you could neither see nor care about. You felt that God would give you a heaven after you had become totally successful. But you could not see that God does not expend one creature for the mere gratification of another. It is all a brew in the caldron of progress, Adam. You today, me tomorrow. Ignorance of the truth makes it so. We were put here from the beginning in a primitive state of mere survival, and all the elements and substances of attaining to perfection were provided us at the same time. From that nearly impossible condition, and purely by our own efforts through learning and intuition, we must attain to perfection. It is either that or its utter opposite, the destruction that ultimate arrogance brings. Now, let's drink some of this nice, fresh coffee."

We sipped a little coffee, pausing a few moments, then I finished my reply to his question.

"You see, Adam, what happened to you happens to a good many. It happened to me, and that is why I understand your plight. The sudden impact of realizing what you had made you shed the blanket of barnacles from the real you. The one important thing now was the fact that there was to be an end to you. Spiritually you came face to face with a great truth. You wondered, how could it all end? After all, you were created. And that is your big perplexity—why must a creation end? Your saving grace, Adam, is the beauty of the real you which you now know. That does not die. It will be added to the weaving threads until they fill all space as far as the eye can see. That is life. That is what never dies. Beauty always is. And you are beautiful, Adam, if you will pardon my inept words. You are beautiful physically and spiritually.

"You are more successful now than ever. Knowing you have not long to remain in your present being, you find a rapture, a rapture that comes from the grand horizon your eyes and your soul see. You do not see death, you see life. You do not see hellions, you see angels. You hear their song swell into all space accompanied by the music of the ether, the flow of the spheres. Yes, I know, your last few days will know agony once more. But your eyes will never show what your physical form feels, for they will show only what your soul knows. So many men and women and children have passed over with that same light in their fading eyes.

"Adam, listen to me. It is not only you who must go. Thousands will have passed on before your seven months are up, and soon after, the rest of us. Yet there will be more people on earth than ever before. You and I will be one of them. We must inherit everything unto the Great Day; remember?"

Before I had finished, Adam held his head between his clenched hands and was swaying slightly from side to side as tears squeezed forcefully throug his tightly closed eyelids. They were not tears of sadness, but tears of insuperable joy. I could not help but feel that one of the mild sins of this man was that he had never given himself to the joy of a woman's love. I wondered for a moment what the meeting of Adam and a woman his equal would be like.

The radio changed to rock and roll music. Adam jumped up and changed it immediately.

"It's a crime," he said, "to rape the beauty of the night with such demoniac noise."

He managed to find a faint station with tolerable music, and then came back to the table. I could feel that his emotional control was being strained, perhaps in anticipation of something he was to tell me in the story. It was only momentary, for he soon became his calm self again and resumed his story.

"I closed out my practice. Books, records, and things that I valued I packed away. The balance I gave to a fellow physician who was younger, and of whom I was fond. I went to see a few of my clients, more to ease the hurt and loneliness that was soon to come over me than to take care of them. I could not have treated them anyhow, as they were all under the care of other physicians now. I never saw my office after it was cleared out. I knew it would be more than I could stand.

"But that is gone into the past. As I said to you this evening, I searched and groped for straws to cling to, for some hope, for some finding of science that might cure my affliction. I found myself reaching through the limits of my familiar medical world into other fields of thought—I was putting myself in touch with a larger universe, which, though it had always beckoned to me, I had felt I did not have the time to explore. All my pursuits and interests had been confined to my own profession.

"In the last few weeks, I have found what so few find. Believe me, my cup does run over."

I interrupted him for a moment.

"Hold it, Adam, just for a moment. I told you that you had that fine thread of essence in you, all the time. No matter what your course in life, you were never really coarse or ugly within. You were never insensitive to the sea of higher verities around you. You merely chose to be oblivious to it in an objective degree. Now suddenly you have jumped, or fallen, into it. That's all. Go ahead with your story."

"Orfeo," he began again, "you seem to paint me as pure white. Please know that there are many spots on and around me. But enough of that.

"After I rented the cabin where I am now staying, the entire desert valley around me seemed to become a place of mellow things. There was such a honey-like character about everything that it seemed like the halfway place between our earth and Paradise. Perhaps the people here are like people anywhere else, but you feel that nothing could mar the mystic promise that hovers over this valley perpetually. Even the most blase and indifferent person seems to feel a soft spell of some kind here. I cannot name it. You don't know of anyone who has found a name for such a spell. You feel momentarily the very square yard of sandy ground under your feet can carry you away to the stars— even into the sun."

At the last words he paused, gazed deeply into space and, his voice dropping to a whisper as though reliving a divine moment, he repeated slowly, deliberately, "Yes, indeed. Into the sun . . . and out again."

I poured a little more coffee into our cups, letting him keep to himself whatever he saw or felt. Then, hoping to draw him out more, I interrupted him again.

"Earl and you are likeable fellows, Adam. Odd that you are both from Seattle. You seem to know about him too. You knew where he was staying, for you came here tonight by your own guidance."

Adam looked at me in surprise. He groped mentally for an answer to my question.

"That is strange," he said. "I seem to have known him all the time. Yet I have never seen him. I don't know how or when the fact that this was his place occurred to me."

He leaned over his cup as he put his fingers to his forehead, narrowed his eyes, and probed deeply into the vault of memory. Then he cautiously suggested, "Maybe . . . and only maybe . . . I might have been given the facts about him and you during the closing part of my recent experiences. But I can't remember clearly."

"Fine! Good!" I exclaimed. "I myself think that is how you got it. It strikes an identical note in my own such experiences, where the memory closed on the events of recent things, to re-open on them months later. Somehow, in some way, I am more associated with your experiences than I had thought before now. Go ahead,

SON OF THE SUN: The Secret Of The Saucers

Adam, tell your story."

My fervor gave him the spark. Too much spark. He was transfixed on an image in his mind. Though he could not remember how he knew of Earl, he was remembering something that was dear, yet gone. I left the radio on, as he seemed to enjoy the soft music.

"Adam," I said softly, "what is it that makes you feel so? Could it be she who danced in the glass?"

He smiled gently, took one deep sighing breath, and finally began his story. The stars must have twinkled a little brighter that moment when he started, and as his words were etched in eternal record on the sentient cosmos.

"This cabin where I am staying has no electricity, no water, and no gas. There are several trees scattered here and there. One of them is what I call a desert willow.

"On my third night, I was standing near one of these willows. The very firmament seemed strangely different. I felt as though it were centering its complete attention upon me. There was not a breeze, and the air was very pleasant. The ground seemed to have become conscious, pulsating its harmonic communion with every part of Creation unto infinity. I could hear the crickets and the howl of coyotes, sharply blazoned in this design. Honestly, I could have spoken with them all if they had been close by. That was how I felt."

We sipped our coffee. I was "all ears." This was the story I wanted to hear, especially from one such as Adam. He continued.

"I was sweeping into me all the cosmos, or else it was enfolding me. I don't know what happens in such awakenings. Perhaps it is both; perhaps it is Creation caressing itself.

"Then there was music. Had my mind created a music to go with all this? Was I capable of creating such an ensemble? Yes, I was sure that only my ears could be hearing it, that it surely must exist only in my imagination.

"Ah, what a relief! At last something was moving. Besides myself, it was the only thing that I could see or feel moving. A star had decided to roam the heavens. It must be a wayward star, I thought at first. Of course I should have known better, but in such instances as this, logic is absent momentarily. Soon, this star was describing a complete circle. When the circle was completed, the light went out, but I kept on looking for it.

"It appeared again at the point where it had just gone out. This time it was much larger. It then described a smaller circle, changing from its previous amber to a yellowish green. The light grew steadily larger. This time, without stopping or disappearing, it continued to circle, getting bigger all the while, and the circle becoming smaller. It was spiraling down, obviously, and this thought startled me for the first time since I had started to watch its maneuvers.

"This was no star. It was no meteor. The circles became very small, while the object was growing larger. Its light pulsated from green to orange-yellow, getting faint, and flickering as though its glow was dying out. I could still hear the faint music.

"Suddenly I realized the music was not imagination, nor was it a creation of my own. And the object! It was a space ship of some sort spiraling down close to earth.

"At that instant the light went out completely. Had I at last seen one of those so-called flying saucers? Were there really such things, I asked myself?"

He paused to sip a little coffee. How wonderful, I thought, that the nectar still had the strength to keep us awake and alert. Adam resumed his story.

"I was thrilled, Orfeo, to put it mildly. There was no doubt in my mind that I had seen a real space ship. I wanted to shout out to the world about it, but only the creatures of the desert would haveheard me. Tonight there must be angels all around, I thought, and I could shout it to them, but they knew it better than I. I could not remain suspended like this. Perhaps I should rush back to town, and ask if anyone else saw it.

"Before I could do anything, the music increased in volume. This could not last. In all my rapture there seemed to be a depthless emptiness, almost unendurable. I was in some way being swept emotionally into this emptiness. Then a voice filled it completely, and the emptiness vanished. It was a feminine voice, sweet, musical. It strummed my taut nerves gently back to quiet and comfort.

"The reason," he interrupted himself, "I have asked you to call me Adam, Orfeo, is because that is what she herself called me."

He looked at me a little accusingly, and asked, "Orfeo . . . are you believing me? You have a little grin."

"Well, is it a 'must' that I believe you? If I said I did not believe you, would you stop telling me the story?" I asked him.

"No. No, I would go on just the same, so long as you listened."

"All right, then, Adam. Now I should like to ask you: As far as you know, is it all just as you experienced it? You are making none of it up?"

"As heaven is my witness, it is all true. If anything, I may need to leave out some things which are of little consequence," he said, with conviction.

"Then what difference does it make, Adam, who believes you or who does not? Naturally, I myself believe you. Do you forget? You are talking to a veteran, not a recruit."

"That's right, Orfeo. I forgot for a moment," he smiled, and eagerly went back to his story.

"The voice said, 'Adam, may I speak with you?'

"I did not answer by word, but in amazement just nodded my consent. Almost at the same time, the air a few yards in front of me shimmered into a congealing form. It became a dome-shaped craft, sitting there on the sand. A lovely woman stood near it, facing me. Her smile was enough to tell me that it was this ship I had seen gracefully spiraling to earth. She simply stood there by the ship of ethereal beauty, and she beside it, of living beauty.

"I tell you now, Orfeo, before you ask me. She was not Lyra, of whom you wrote in your book. And it was not the one who danced in the glass this evening.

"The lady asked me, simply and directly, 'Having nothing to lose and nothing to gain, Adam, would you like a trip into the new estate which to you, until now, has existed only as a dream, or hope?' "

"Even now I did not speak. I could only nod my consent. She thereupon walked straight up to me. She extended her hand toward the softly glistening ship, turned about and we walked together toward it. A sliding door silently provided an opening. What I could see of the inside of the craft glistened more intensely than the exterior. It was indeed identical to the one you described in the little paper containing your story. I could not help but recall your description as I entered. And then we sat. . ."

"Hold it at minute, Adam . . . hold it!" I exclaimed. "I knew something was out of place. The light struck me suddenly when you mentioned the little paper that carried my story. I can understand that. But several times this evening you mentioned my book. It isn't even published yet. How did you know about the book?"

"I'm sorry, Orfeo, I meant your newspaper story, I guess."

"Oh, no, Adam. You said you purchased the book at a lecture, and you even know its title, 'The Secret of the Saucers.' Also, you know of a few things that are only in its manuscript, nowhere else. Has Earl told you about it?— Still, even he would not know as much of it as you have told me."

"I don't remember, really," he pleaded. "Perhaps it was shown to me in my recent experiences, just as I knew you would meet me tonight, and as I knew about Earl and his house here," he stated very sincerely.

"Yes, Adam," I assured him. "That is just it. I am of the opinion that you were shown, or had read to you, a copy of the manuscript by the visitors from space, themselves,"

"That must be the answer," countered Adam. "Another example is the fact that I recognized you as you walked in the door at the cafe. I even called you by name, so sure was I that it was you, yet I can't recall how I had come to know you. Let's let it go at that for the time being; it may all come out later on. As in your own experiences, at the moment I seem to remember clearly only the things I have yet to say, and as I tell them they fall back, lost to me for the time being. So, let me continue to tell my story.

"As I was saying, we sat down on the two seats that were firmly fastened to the floor. She took the seat on the left and I the one on the right. She was not a phantom, but very real, for we were sitting close enough that our arms touched. The door slid closed as we sat down, and I could no longer discern the door area from the rest of the hull.

"The seats were soft, and were of the same tone as the ship itself. The floor was so identical to the hull it was hard to distinguish it as a floor except that it was flat and under foot. The ship became completely opaque, so we could see nothing through it. The glittering colors of its crystal-plastic material faded to more subdued tones, and it became a little darker.

"We sat back comfortably, and soon I could feel a slight push of the seat against my back, legs, and head. We were in motion. Then the interior darkened, and all the diamondlike glitter disappeared. But soon it lighted up again. Yes, Orfeo, I recall having read the same in your account, but you did not know why the ship had darkened, then became radiant again. This I was anxious to know. I thought that it might be the effect of the ionosphere as we traversed it. I asked her if it was the ionosphere we had just passed through. She answered me readily, and with ease.

"'Yes, Adam, it was. Because you have asked and already surmised it, we can tell you. The molecules of our craft were tigthened a little so that the ionized layer around earth would not cause a glare inside. We have no need to do this for our safety, but we do it as a hint to you that we are going through what you think is necessary. The knowledge of it is already in your mind, or we would not show you. We cannot give you knowledge, but we can confirm what you already know. Our ship can adjust itself to conditions around it to quite some degree, especially to electrical and magnetic conditions. But you already had a good concept of this fact in your own understanding.

"'Every living entity on earth must rise to learning and knowledge through its own initiative. It is pre-ordained. What other purpose, Adam, could there be to existence? It is self-apparent, is it not? Even today your earth is a primitive jungle, in spite of all its progress. Most of its natives feel it is the final zenith of attainment. It is still a jungle of wild primitive-ness. Yet we cannot interfere, because it is ordained by the Heart of Creation that all life attain to perfection by evolutionary processes. You see, Adam, all the progress that your earth has made has been made by its everpresent resources, and by its own people. The glory to come is inherent within its bosom even now. Its people have not fully unfolded, and the materials of earth lie waiting to be known by its inhabitants.'

"Whether she was an angel or woman I could not know at the time, Orfeo, but she was real, and I asked her name. She said merely to call her 'Vega,' for it would be easier for me to comprehend than the knowledge of her true name. I asked her to continue speaking. She did so, in a casual manner.

"'Your world, Adam, is still motivated by personal successes, so short is the vision of the masses. Yet what are personal successes? All the old ones lie quietly in graves. The present ones are nothing but conflicts and strain, and soon they, too, will pass forever from the consciousness of those who pursued such ends. Is it not all in vain? Is it not infantile vision? What good is all that mass of humanity? Since the dawn of earth's creation it has not yet served itself. Its greatest violence against itself lies yet in the future. Of what use has it been to any other world? It does not even believe in the existence of other worlds, except in primitive derision. Oh, a few have the vision and the awareness, true. But a few on earth have always had the high and true vision. These ever-present few who, by the dynamic of the love of pure learning, keep the thread of essence alive, justify the hope that earth will come one day into the light of perfection.

"'What does earth have today, Adam, except the little fundamental learning that has been given to its history by these few? Yes, you may, say, human life is valuable, but without thinking and learning, human life becomes less valuable than that of a daisy. All humans would perish if left to survive as animals do, by nature and instinct. Without spirit and knowledge, a human being becomes ferocious even beyond the natural limits of animals. A human can devolve to as infinite a savagery as he can evolve to an infinite sphere of splendorous beauty.

"'That is the one and only purpose, all that is willed to your planet, earth: to one day stand at the decisive point, when it will devolve back to destruction, or evolve unto heaven. It will not be a time of gentle decision, Adam, for that decision must be made in the fire of Armageddon.

"'Our own world had to make that same decision ages ago. We entered our new estate from the ashes of our struggle. We have been aspiring ever since to a heaven-like glory. Evil in our world does not exist; only the love of pure learning. Anything short of the zest for learning, any ignorance due to apathy, and any consequences of these shortcomings are in our world what you would call evil in yours.

"'Do you not agree, Adam, that evil is willful ignorance?'

"With that she ended her introduction of me to herself and to her world. I nodded, looking into her eyes with understanding.

"'Yes, I do, Vega. You know I have always felt so, if only vaguely, or you would not have told me what you did. I know that I shall learn much more on your home ground. But for the moment, may I ask you why there are no implements in this ship? Why is it so bare? Am I dreaming, or is this all real?'

"'It is not bare, Adam,' she assured me, 'except for the absence of what you call implements and controls. This is one of our crafts which is controlled by a monitor ship, as a guided missile would be in your world. Our monitor is not far off. They see all our movements, hear all our words, and know precisely what to do and when to do it. You have but to wish to be back on earth, and they would respond so well you would feel as though you had originated the move.'

"Her face became a smile of rapture, and her eyes became gently fixed in distant reflection. Then she added, You see, Adam, our beloved superiors do not make mistakes of which you or I would be aware. They consider your safety and mine above their own welfare.'

SON OF THE SUN: The Secret Of The Saucers

"'Vega,' I spoke in surprise. 'What do you mean by your beloved superiors? To me you are the very zenith of human ascension. I can't even comprehend one more lovely, more elegant, or more perfect. I am so overwhelmed that I am giving little thought to this ship or to the trip. It is hard to take an interest in where we are going. For the first time in my life I am sure I am in love, if you will pardon my confession. Yet you speak of your superiors. Are there such?'

"'We will let that question answer itself later, Adam,' she said. You have other things to see and curiosities to satisfy, which is enough for the present.

"'Do you feel the gentle push of the ship upon your body? That is because we are still gaining speed, or accelerating. Would you believe we are traveling at two million miles per hour at this moment?' she asked.

"I was startled, but did not reply. I let my look tell her of my amazement, as she continued.

"'Yes, Adam, we are now going even faster. Soon we will be doing ten million miles per hour. But our sensation of the acceleration is unnoticeable. As you know, every atom of the ship and of our bodies is being vectored and impelled at the same moment as the ship, so we are not affected by the laws of momentum or inertia.' Vega spoke with such effortlessness it seemed as simple as reciting nursery rhymes to a sleepy child, and not like a relating of physical facts as yet remote from the sciences of earth. Then she asked me to tell it to her in my own words, as a teacher would ask a child to do.

"'Vega,' I complied, 'this force field which impels our craft is magnetic and gravitational. It is focused upon us by the monitor, or mother ship, which is not far away. This field includes every atom and fraction of atom of whatever lies in the focus of the field, moving each one of these together as a body. I venture to say that we could not even feel the slight push against our bodies by the seats if it were not being done merely for my senses, and for a demonstration. They could easily nullify that effect.'

"No sooner had I said this than the effect ceased. We felt free of pressure altogether, like sitting in an easy chair at home. Vega and I exchanged smiles in confirmation of their response to my words. Then she continued her conversation.

"'Adam, at this very moment we have attained the velocity of eight million miles per hour. If you will give your seat a twist it will turn until you release the force. Turn it around to the opposite direction, where a view is awaiting you.'

"I complied with her suggestion. At the same time, she turned her seat toward the back also. The entire rear hull of the craft became transparent, as clear as glass. But all was darkness. She put her hand to my eyes so I could not see, and asked me to open my mouth. She put a capsule in my mouth and asked me to swallow it. I did so without a qualm.

"It must have worked fast, for my body relaxed at once and I could feel my whole physical being come to a sensation of complete exuberance. She saw my face move into a smile, and she removed her hand from my eyes.

"'You can better endure the sight with that capsule,' she said. 'Also, your conscious and subconscious will receive and record it in more detail, and with deeper appreciation.'

"Even so, Orfeo, I could not suppress a sigh at the sight. Before my eyes was the earth in all its daylight glory, and I could discern the Eastern Hemisphere. It was surrounded by the stars beyond like jewels around the head of a majestic being. Its atmosphere made an auroral halo of rainbow colors around it. Our ship was going away from it at such velocity the earth seemed to fall back, diminishing in size, and the colors gradually were merging into the yellow band.

"The stars remained as if fixed, and they seemed to be absorbing our earth into their own environs. The earth light dazzled a bit, flared, and then flashed. We had reached a point where some of the earth's reflective mass had resolved the sunlight to a focus, like a reflecting telescope. Then, it became just a huge star, brighter than all the others, larger, and falling back rapidly.

"Suddenly, from the right side, another large orb came in view. Our field was so broad now we were seeing the moon, also. Like the earth, it, too, seemed to recede rapidly.

"I reached out and took Vega's hand and held it in my own. I could hardly speak, so overwhelming was my emotion. But I managed a few words.

"'Vega, I can see why they sent you to bring me to them. Never could I have been equal to it, either alone or with someone I could not love, as I do you. This experience demands a sharing, a spiritual merging, and the utmost of moral courage. Oh, Vega, how can I thank you? How can I thank you?'

"Her hand squeezed mine a little in sympathy and understanding, but her eyes were still gazing at the receding earth and moon with an expression such as a great artist would give to a goddess he was painting.

"The hull was now becoming translucent, now more opaque, glimmering as before. Vega released my hand and motioned for me to turn around to the front again—if there was such a thing as a front or back to this bubble-like craft. After we faced forward, Vega spoke.

"'We are now traveling ten million miles per hour, Adam, yet you feel not the slightest sense of motion. From now on we start to decelerate. In five hours more we shall arrive at our destination.'

"I had a thousand questions to ask her, and began at once.

"'Vega, tell me: Are the women of earth like this—I mean, like you?'

"Her face assumed a pleased expression. I could tell she liked the question.

" 'Well, Adam, I cannot answer that for you. You missed finding out firsthand in your lifetime, but tell me—did any of them attract you as I do?'

"'Yes,' I replied. 'They did, but there were so many of them, I thought I could wait before becoming attached. The one who could attract me as you do was never a living person, but always just in my mind, and just around the corner.'

"'Then,' she said, 'have you not met her in me?'

"'Indeed, Vega. I could be with you forever.'

"'But, Adam, nearly every young man has said things like that to girls, and has felt as you do toward me. Most of them have had their hearts shaken a bit by a few before the right one came along and really gave them a complete quake,' she said coyly.

"I noticed that for the first time she did not look at me during this line of conversation. But she enjoyed it. Was I just one of those 'young men' and she my first amour? She changed the subject somewhat.

"'Adam, don't you have any man's questions?' She still did not look at me. I had received my first blow. Gentle, perhaps, but a blow.

"'Yes; Vega,' I countered, thinking I would tax her feminine mind. 'Can your ships move with the speed of light?'

"'We will discuss that later. Meantime, you must take a nap for half an hour, so the nectar I gave you will have time to be absorbed fully, and it will give you equilibrium.'

"I fell back in my chair obediently, thinking I had given her the Waterloo question—a man's question. I still felt prankish, and even as I closed my eyes I thought I would give her the coup-degrace in the form of another 'man's' question.

"'How is it, Vega, that we have not seen the sun yet? Not even its outline through the hull of the ship? Is that too fearsome a sight to look upon?'

"She burst out giggling. Then she managed to say, between the most beautiful spasms of laughter I had ever heard, 'That is a real man's question, Adam! Even that will be answered for you ... by a woman,' she replied, still shaking in laughter.

"I had opened my eyes, seeing all her utter beauty in her amusement. I laughed in unison with her. Still, there was an enigma in her words, and I felt a new destiny awaiting me. Suddenly, I felt comfortably and pleasantly drowsy. I closed my eyes, but before I dozed I heard her say: 'Don't forget to ask me about that speed of light problem when you wake up, Adam.' Then I fell asleep."

* * * *

Adam paused a while in his story. We slowly became aware again that we were on earth, in Twentynine Palms, and in this little house. We felt wonderful, still under the balm of the nectar we had drunk a few hours ago. I made fresh coffee and warmed up some buns, and found an all-night radio station playing good music. Soon we would drift off once more, and live again Adam's experiences. He did not appear visibly moved by the memory of them. Indeed, he was forgetting them as fast as he related them, remembering only the part yet untold. I did not call this phenomenon to his attention, fearing I would disturb the flow of his story.

Chapter 3
THE SPEED OF LIGHT

We ate the warmed buns and drank hot coffee. I did not fill the cups, for we did not particularly need a stimulant. Our condition was holding up wonderfully. We indulged in some small talk for a few minutes, and then I asked Adam if he would continue his story. At this point I could see the reason for his having asked me at the outset to narrate his story in the second person when I wrote it, for it was becoming clear that his reactions and experiences could not be adequately told in the first person.

As he continued to unfold his story, I felt I was an eye witness to the events, hence I am following Adam's original suggestion for the rest of the story, and will relate it in the second person.

* * * *

Adam awoke from his half hour nap on the ship feeling alert, yet calm. He looked into the eyes of lovely Vega and reminded her of his previous question.

"Well, Vega, I ask you, can your ships travel at the speed of light?"

"No," she replied readily. "Nothing we know of can attain the speed of light in physical form. There is talk in our society that our superiors are looking into that possibility. There is not the slightest success as yet in their experiments. The only factors in which we have ascertained and measured the speed of light are magnetic waves, gravitational waves and light itself.

"However," she went on, "we are experimenting with the idea of propelling particles to velocities beyond the speed of light. The process is to focus a radar-like beam out into space, and then shoot particles into the waves of this beam and in the same direction as that of the beam. These particles may then attain speeds higher than the speed of the beam in which they lie. It can best be imagined by thinking of a surfboard riding the waves, or a canoe going with the stream. If either of these also used propelling force, they would both go faster —the one faster than the waves, the other faster than the stream—even twice as fast. But the ether has properties of its own, and thus far we see it yielding to none of our theories.

"The barrier of the speed of light is caused by the tension of the ether. It cannot be broken through as easily as the sound barrier in air.

"You see, Adam, the sound barrier in air is easily broken through, and speeds beyond that proceed smoothly. However, the sound barrier in water is more difficult to break through, and travel in that water faster than sound travels in it would be considerably difficult. In the case of the ether, this difficulty, which is the barrier of the speed of light, is apparently unsolvable. Nevertheless, our superiors keep at the investigation as if it were to be successful tomorrow morning. The imagination can see twice the speed of light, nay, thrice, and even a thousand times. But we have not yet attained speed equal to that of light in our material progress." She became silent.

Adam could easily cope with the facts she had just outlined, for he had previously formulated these concepts on earth. Vega had become in his eyes so charming, so deep, so soul-capturing, that he felt he was being drawn into her very bloodstream. He felt that their souls were so intermeshed that one was now but a continuation of the other. Vega stood out like a warm center amid the splendor and beauty of the ship's interior. What he did not know was that she was the first phase of his accelerated education, sponsored by a higher civilization. What he had missed of the mating bliss of soul and mind in his thirty-eight years, these supreme someones from an ascended world were now pressing into his whole being like a transfusion of life itself.

He did not yet understand such things as why she laughed so hilariously when he had asked why they could not see the sun, nor did he know that she was only the first of three women who were to put him through the intensified exercise of catching up on the void in his life to date in the love and romance department. He did not know that Vega was wholesome, yes, but placid compared to the two women he must encounter before graduating to the capacity for love in its deeper meaning, a love that could not be confined within the limits of the Milky Way.

Another thing Adam was not yet aware of, but which he awakened to later in his experiences, was that one does not learn the inner secrets of the universe without love accompanying the lesson—indeed, it may even precede it.

Basically good men learn through love. Basically evil men must learn through the hard laws of Nature. Adam had not yet learned that a mysterious force we call destiny had long ago, from the birth of time itself, sown a thread of preordainment, invisible to the physical eye but visible and sensible to the intuition of basically good beings. He did not at the moment know that the love of man for woman could attain the divine heights of man's love for God, that the one was merely one half loving the other half. He was not yet fully aware that every wave which roars onto the beach slips back only into its own sea. Every splash in a pool falls back into the pool . . . crashingly or lovingly.

At this moment, Adam was not conscious of the fact that all things come from themselves, and merge back into themselves in pulsating motions, like the beating of the heart, the flowing of the blood, the generation and regeneration of all the stars. To Vega these were elementary things, long ago resolved. To Adam they were things and thoughts yet to be learned.

Thus, two beings road on in a space ship at ten million miles per hour, worlds apart in evolution's scale, but close together in Creation's intent. One of them, Vega, who was from a world far advanced beyond the other's, continued her discourse on the speed of light, hoping to bring its truth to Adam's conscious comprehension as their ship sped on, splitting the emptiness or star-studded space like a light ray.

"You see, if you shot a block of wood through another block of wood of the same density, and at the speed of sound in that wood, one would not go through the other but an explosion would result at the point where they met. The same applies to everything known, be it air, water, iron, oil, stone, or the ether. Nothing can travel in a medium of its same composition faster than the speed of sound in that medium, for they merely burst at the same moment and become one. With the all-pervading ether, the speed of light is the equivalent of the sonic barrier in other substances. Is this fact not simple to you?"

"Yes," Adam replied, and then ventured to state the next question in his mind. "Then the theory of relativity is correct in postulating that nothing in corpuscular form can attain to the speed of light and retain its own form?"

"Definitely," replied Vega. "But remember, Adam, the theory of relativity, as all other scientific theories of earth, deals with observed effects, not causes. Therefore, the theory proceeds, knowing not what it is measuring nor why it produces certain effects. Thus the theory of relativity, at its extreme salients, fails as totally as any other theory can fail, its success and verity finally swept away because of that universal negative, ignorance. The ignorance inherent at the perimeter of this theory is as profound as the ignorance of a primitive being in the scale of ultimate knowledge."

Chapter 4
VEGA ALERTS ADAM

Adam smiled. Vega smiled also, but Adam had been "nectared" beyond wayward emotions which might overpower him, so he proceeded in thought and conversation to probe into those issues that all thinkers have wrestled with but never fully solved.

He saw in reflection the seething activity of earth and earthlings. Brothers were ranting and fuming over such small objectives, all of them in error. He wanted so much to call his brother earthmen to come and listen, but how could he? He could, he believed, set them all on a true and positive course at once, but who would listen and believe? Also, he suddenly remembered he had only seven months to live. Seven months, when seven years would not be sufficient to make even a start!

However, he thought, never mind earthmen. There were more questions to be asked; questions to which he already had the nuclei of answers within his own mind. He continued his queries.

"Vega, do you mind if I ask you why you refer to what you so loyally term 'superiors?' I don't like the sound of the word. To me it denotes a preferred side and a rejected side of life. We on earth have struggled for centuries to bring democracy into fulfillment. We have not succeeded, as yet. But you, and your society—how can evolved ones such as you use those words? If there is a superior side there must be an inferior side. Is that not so? It strikes a discordant note to my senses."

For the first time, Vega looked at Adam the way he had first longed to see her look at him. Her eyes assumed a soft pensiveness, and her voice mellowed into a romantic subtleness. Cosmic womanhood whispered its echoes in her every aspect. Her beauty reached the zenith of what to an earth- man would be the limit of his capacity to absorb in a state of sanity.

She answered him simply, "Adam, I'm so glad you asked that. You have released me to tell you why, and I will never again refer to them as superiors. But may I humbly, and rightly so, refer to them as our 'peers'?" she asked.

"That sounds better to me, Vega. I cannot conceive of your having superiors, in my definition of the word. I can't believe that a civilization like yours would tolerate an attitude of subservience." Adam's faculties were conditioned by the nectar tablet to speak on a plane nearly equal to her normal level. This in turn enabled Vega to speak freely.

"You see, we come from a planet which orbits around the star you know on earth as Alpha Centauri. As your astronomers have told your people, it is not quite four and a half light years distant from your sun. We are centuries advanced compared to earth, just as earth is centuries advanced compared to some other worlds. Thus, we are to your higher ones what they are to your aborigines. There are worlds as much advanced beyond our world as ours is beyond yours; and we know them no better than your world knows ours.

"We have overcome disease in general, and we live in comparative brotherhood. But even in our world there are some who have lagged behind. We are a minority, and we live apart from the peers, with no desire to intermingle. You see, we would not entertain for a moment the possibility of causing any backward slip of the peers in status, whether physical or moral.

"We have full freedom, including marriage to a peer if mutually agreeable, but the peers, knowing it would not be wise, refrain from this practice. A peer could not elevate the backward one by that gesture; in fact, the reverse would occur. He would at once descend and join the society of the backward ones. Only the slow process of evolution could correct the back-slip for himself and his progeny.

"It is easier to fall, Adam, than it is to rise. It is easier to spend than to earn. Civilizations rise one person at a time, but they can fall all at once. If a whole world rises, yet overlooks one lower being, that being could begin the toppling of the whole, no matter what the number involved or the length of time required.

"One tiny seed could replace a jungle with an orchard. Yet one tiny virus can blight in a week that whole orchard and turn it back to jungle. In life, the good seed is the love of pure learning, and the virus is willful ignorance. All things pass away to those who are involved in the evolution, but learning remains, and learning and love are halves of each other.

"At this moment, and only for a few moments, you love me and I love you. This is merely momentary, an outpost of love, and shall pass behind us as we move on. But we still love, and love is our final destination, no matter where we set our course. In a few hours, we shall have forgotten each other as entities.

"Adam, because of this awakened love you now feel, you will be seeking it forever. I was sent to you merely to light the spark, so do not feel empty, because I promise that for you it will be like swimming out of a pond into a great lake. And after that, Adam, after that, into a shoreless sea. You have not missed out on such love, not for one minute of it, for don't you see? No matter how late in life it comes it is like eternity, spreading both ways, into the past and into the future."

With those words Vega became silent, as she sat gazing into the emptiness ahead of her, trying to envisage the aurora of woman's love for man in its most highly evolved state, which even to her lay yet in the unreachable horizons ahead. Adam was spellbound by her motionless beauty. Then he managed to speak, just above a whisper.

"Oh, no, Vega. I do not choose to leave you or forget you. No matter what they have prepared for me, I shall need your nearness. Please add your desire to mine and make it the free will choice of both of us. Would they refuse us that sincere request?"

"No Adam," Vega replied, without changing her poise. "They would not refuse us our true will. But you are not master of your choice until you know all there is to choose from. You have not met her yet."

"Who is this 'her' that you speak of?" Adam asked, with a trace of rejection.

"You will spend a few days with her. You will just call her 'Launie.'

"To you she will seem superb. Yet she is one of the most retarded ones in our world. She thrives on occasional adventures, but I do not infer what the word 'adventure' would mean on your earth. She is not base. She simply resembles a humming bird in her motions. She hovers, tastes, and darts away to the next frivolity. You will find bliss with her, and she an adventure in you. Neither of you will be unduly affected. Both of you will learn much that will broaden your scopes, even after your stay together is but a dim memory.

"We, the retarded ones, will be sharing your rapture—yours and Launie's—for all of us have been informed of your stay with us. We learn more than you do from all passing events. By probing things we learn and rise. Our next generation will be that much closer to peerdom."

Although Adam took in every word Vega had spoken, it was difficult for him to realize that such an experience was to be his, not in dream but in reality. He did not know, however, that the pain which goes along with such experiences is just as acute in this reality as in the dream. During his young lifetime he had kept himself free of romantic entaglements on earth. Now he could not escape them, because he did not wish to escape them.

He had yet to meet Launie, and he felt as though the very cosmos held her in waiting for him. This gave birth to a new feeling, the feeling of guilt. For the first time he had said to a woman he wanted no other, and now his whole being was reaching out to touch the thrill of a new love.

Adam grew impatient. The ship seemed to be motionless, suspended in space. Vega sensed his impatience at once, and knew that her mention of Launie was in part the cause of it. In that moment she lost her sentimental attachment to Adam.

Adam looked toward Vega, and with a note of apology pleaded, "Vega, to be honest with you, I feel myself already in love with her, although I do not even know what she looks like. Never before have I felt this way. Who is Launie? Where is she? I feel that I have so much to say and to ask, but to say and ask only of Launie. Suddenly I feel no repressions, no inhibitions, and you now seem to me

SON OF THE SUN: The Secret Of The Saucers

like a distant goddess. But Launie—she beckons and nothing matters except finding her. Tell me, is she a spirit or is she flesh-and-blood? Can my hands touch her, or does she just fade away from my reach like a mirage? Yes, I know my thinking and feelings are conditioned by the nectar you gave me, but nevertheless it is my best self speaking.

"I love you Vega, and I love all your people. Yet I know it is Launie through whom all my feelings, my new lessons, and my new awarenesses shall be expressed. So I open my heart, and pray I may be worthy."

Then Adam became more practical. He suddenly realized he was going somewhere, somewhere into Vega's promised "world." It would be best to ask questions that would prepare him for entry into it. So his conversation became more academic.

"Are the peers greater in number than the lesser ones in your society?" he asked.

"Yes, many times greater. On our planet, which is no larger than your earth, the peers number twenty billion. We, the unattained ones, number not quite five hundred million. So there are forty peers to every one of us, the retarded ones. Yet a dozen peers would be sufficient to control all the activities of the five hundred million retarded ones. We not only obey them; we honor and love them. You will learn why very shortly."

Adam knew instinctively that he was not being taken to another planet, but to a gigantic space ship. He was recalling what Vega had said, that they would be but hours away from their destination. She had also said she was from Alpha Centauri, our nearest star neighbor, whose light requires nearly four and a half years to reach our solar system. From her words and manner Adam surmised that he was to be master of the situation at all times, because it was his world, his solar system and his sun, regardless of his stature in the scale of evolution.

All these facts his subconscious mind had evidently picked up, recorded, and now released to his intuition in a flash. Thus he not only felt but knew he was being transported to a visiting space ship in which were housed half a million "moronic elegants," ignorant by their own standards, but to the eyes of earthmen, gods and goddesses, cosmic "morons" held to a course toward ascension by their peers.

Adam was in reverie, and in its depths the entire universe lay bare its secrets before him. He murmured, "Oh, my God, why have you given me so much? My cup runneth over. I have so much of abundance. Like an egg, it is enclosed in a thin shell, breakable, but not vulnerable. Oh, God, wherever Thou art, whatever Thou art, since my cup runneth over in abundance, may You see that it spills over on those who so need even a drop of this . . . this essence of fullness."

With these thoughts, earth Adam had transformed into cosmic Adam, and he felt a sovereignty within himself that was new and strange to him. He knew in that moment that every one of the half million people awaiting his visit would be subservient to him. His slightest wish would carry more weight than their combined

147

will.

At the same time, this awakening also flooded him with the awareness that it would be more fun to be servant than master.

Servants may have vague backaches, but masters have acute headaches. He decided to take the middle of the road. It was the course already set for him, though he felt it was his own decision. These thoughts which seasoned Adam into maturity took no longer than seconds in his enhanced condition. He roused himself and asked Vega a question.

"Is it permissible to look into space again? This time not behind us, toward the earth, but before us, toward where we are going?"

"Yes," answered Vega, calmly and indifferently, "but not to the left of us. The sun is in that direction, and you would be blinded. Nor will you see straight ahead, for that is our destination. Look there—to your right—and you will see what you want to see, and should see."

As if it had heard Vega's words, a section of the ship's hull on the right became transparent. Once more there were bright stars suspended in a vault of space; large ones, small ones, lone ones, double ones, and clusters of stars in various colors. Something strange broke the monotonous evenness of that outer space panorama. A white fuzzy cloud, very faint, was suspended in space near the ship as they traveled. It remained constant and motionless.

"What is that white haze, Vega?" Adam asked.

"That," she responded, "is gas. It is nearly all hydrogen. Our velocity is so great that were we to smash into it, it would gradually wear down our ship's hull. We must have a clear path before us, so our monitor ship constantly beams a magnetic vortex ahead of us. This repels all atoms and molecules, casting them to one side, so it is like traveling through a tunnel as we go forward. The white haze you see is sunlight reflected from those gas particles. It seems motionless because our speed is so great.

"Small meteors in our path are deflected in the same manner. The larger meteors are detected by our monitor's automatic finders, even though the meteors are far distant. At the same time, our mass-ray guns are trained on them and they are disintegrated, that is, atomized. All this takes place faster than you could think."

She had hardly finished when there was an instantaneous flash of white lightning, its rays piercing the wall of their ship. The crystal hull reflected the flash into daylight, as if lightning had struck nearby. Adam jumped.

"What was that?" he burst out.

"You just saw a meteor atomized. Our monitor ship is not far away, remember? They detected the small object and vaporized it. It was in our path. This is space travel, Adam. You cannot travel in space without all these facilities. That meteor would not have harmed our strong ship, but it would have left a weak spot, and enough of them would damage our hull in time."

SON OF THE SUN: The Secret Of The Saucers

As she said these words the "window" in the hull became opaque once more and Adam felt secure again, like a frightened child hiding in a closet. More than that, he felt courage because Vega sat next to him. Whatever happened he would not be afraid, because she was not afraid.

Once more he realized why they had sent a woman to escort him on such a trip. Once more he knew that he could not absorb all that was yet to come, whatever it might be, without the buoyancy of spirit that a woman like Vega could inspire. He felt he could no more than perish, and what better way to die than in the vibrant presence of this beautiful creature beside him? Also, he sensed that what he was yet to experience would be beyond his most lavish dreams. Could their meaning be fully conveyed to him alone, alone with his own spirit, alone with his own soul?

The experiences would of course contain elements of things familiar to him, but without a loved one to share them, could they mean little more than a hearty meal eaten solo?

He was not alone in his thoughts. Vega was thinking the very same things. There was rapport between them, as though at heart they were one. Vega spoke a few carefully chosen words.

"Adam, it is this way: Knowledge in its highest sense would be but a skeleton without the warmth of love. The skeleton appeals to very few, but the clothing around it appeals to all beings. Love was not only the motivating force at the beginning of the worlds, but it is also the ultimate goal which we seek. We revere the concept and vision of God, but God seems far away. We, in our world, get no more response through our meditations or supplications to God than do your people. Yet we get much more response from His vital and dynamic universe than your people of earth. Therefore, you can see that in the eyes of the Fatherhead we all stand equal, but His creation, the universe, its heart and motions, respond much more to our advanced knowledge than to the primitive awareness of your earth. Therefore, Adam, as you already suspect, the straightest way to the Fatherhead is by the path of knowledge—knowledge of the truth, which is no more than knowledge of actualities. Not dreams; not fantasies; not traditions, which are nothing but stalemates; not swashbuckling abandonment to new adventures, which often goes in the name of progress, but adds nothing to it; but the love of pure learning. That is the only pathway toward true ascension.

"I feel that you already sense by intuition that Launie will not be the adventure you may secretly desire. But she will be a problem to you, and in coping with the challenges she presents you will have climbed another rung on the ladder of understanding."

Suddenly, Adam felt the fear of space again. Space, he sensed, was all about him; so vacuous that it seemed to be drawing at the vitals of his being. Only this gallant little craft was between its two occupants and the instantaneous explosive dispersion of their bodies to the hungry vacuum. This little ship; this elegant, strong, protective little ship. So silent, yet so treacherous was the fathomless space around him just outside the little ship. Vega sensed his fear instantaneously, and quickly reassured him.

"Remember, Adam, even a meteor could not harm us. Do not be uneasy. Not once in centuries has any of our ships met with damage or failure, other than those that bore into the core of some star. But you will learn more of that during your visit with us. Let us think of and speak of more interesting things for the time being."

Her explanation, given in simple words, made him feel completely at ease once more. She was a perfect guide, it was a perfect trip. Ah, yes! He must ask one more question.

"Vega, why is it you speak to me in such excellent English? Do you not have a language of your own? I would like to hear a few words of it, just for the sake of hearing it."

Vega rapidly spoke a few words and looked at Adam. He shrugged his shoulders to show they meant nothing to him.

"You see?" she pointed out. "Hearing our language means nothing to you. You have no time to learn it, and you have many other universally understood things to see with us. That is the best of all languages, understanding and knowledge. However, you did catch some phonetic delight when I spoke it, and earth shall one day have a similar language.

"I repeat it more slowly: 'un, doz e pez lo.' It means, 'No, you have lost weight,' and was spoken once before to another man of Earth, so I do not harm the code of non-interference with your evolution.

"In the grand and cosmic sense, Adam, there is only one language. Two complete strangers who are high in evolve-ment could carry on a conversation in silence, with a few mere signs and gestures. That is the universal language. Intuition first, and thought second, is the one language of the cosmos.

"In the navigation of infinite space, there are few words, and little deliberate thought. Knowledge comes first, intuition takes care of the problems as they are met, and orderly thought does the rest. The deliberate mind is useless in coping with space and astral rhythms. The dynamic of space is felt, as a bird feels its domains; it is sensed, as a good maestro senses the entire symphony. It is the domain of the stars and all the spheres around them, and the law and order which prevails for these also prevails for us all. Space requires the intuitive mind, the soul mind, for releasing and guiding its momentous yet subtle power tides.

"Our people come and go facilely in space ships. They study, make charts that add to our galaxial maps, tirelessly observe things, the little and the big. Yet, they seldom speak aloud, and never are they bored but feel always that they have spoken much whether by a word or in silence. Every second is exquisitely dynamic, but always in harmony with the moment and the place."

Her explanation was spell binding to Adam. "You are lovely," he said, in admiration.

"Thank you," she said. "But may I show you what I mean by quiet and harmony, and how within it you can awaken to much new awareness?"

Without speaking, Adam nodded in assent.

"Good," she said softly, preparing for moments of silence. "Now you must visualize that we are decelerating, erasing thousands of miles from our speed by the minute. We shall remain quiet for some time.

"The music you will hear emanates from the molecular vibration of our ship's hull, and is under the direction of our monitor ship nearby. To our right a round window will again be cleared in the hull, and it will move slowly leftward until it stops directly before us." She sighed softly. "Now, sit back and relax."

Chapter 5
VENUS, OUR SISTER

Thus a small craft hurtled through space, protectively conveying a man from earth and a woman from Alpha Centauri's system, to a destination not far as measured in astronautical distance.

As they sat comfortably inside, purposefully quiet, the music that Vega had promised Adam pealed through the ship's interior. A round section of the ship's shell became a transparent window, similar to a porthole.

As Adam related it to me that night at our small table, he was again listening to the music in memory. Once more he saw stars suspended in the vault of space. But under the spell of such music as he was hearing they were different to him.

There was a special message, silent yet clearly discernible, being communicated to him from that reachless cosmos. He knew with a conviction translated to his senses as wondrous, soft essences of truth that those spheres, those glaring spheres, were in their cores the embodiment of ultimate or absolute heat. More startling was his sudden awareness that every light ray is a small source or container of ultimate heat, for no body can be hotter than its components. It followed that absolute zero does not exist anywhere in the universe. If it does exist, he thought, it must be cloistered in the very archives of the Creator as the most rare jewel that is. That jewel would be a piece of solid ether.

In the quiet reverie within the ship, Adam's subconscious mind was yielding up to his conscious mind the highlights of his present earth lifetime, his nobler aspirations as well as his baser inclinations, passing like a pageant before him. He felt from deep within that he was being unfolded in preparation for his entry into Vega's society. He felt he was being readied by the minute, for he was so effortlessly grasping an understanding of all things—all, that is, except mathematics, in which he remained impoverished. Yet he felt that his mathematical poverty was amply compensated for by the wealth of understanding coming to him as a result of these immeasurable thoughts and visions. The music seemed to accent his intuitions.

Vega had spoken in wisdom. Things Adam had once merely assumed now became confirmed knowledge to him; false premises were quickly rejected by his enlarged scope. Yes, in the upheavals which were ushering in this new aware- ness, mathematics would dissolve even from the consciousness of a genius.

Indeed, he knew now that men of earth have not measured anything as yet. It was clear to him now that all the physical concepts of his brother earthmen were erroneous. Atoms were not spinning packets of energy; they were bubbles in the ether. The music itself was emanating from vibrating ether. The universe was one grandiose spectacle of spheres within spheres.

Something strange was taking place. The "window" had reached a position di- rectly in front of Vega and him, but it was also growing steadily larger, like a bal- loon being inflated. Its clear crystal structure began to turn cloudy. Soon it be- came soupy thick and the cloud surged and swirled, obliterating all the stars com- pletely. The music stopped momentarily, then began again, this time surely com- ing from that now enlarged window, as through a swirling, cloudy television screen.

The mood of the music changed to deeply vibrant, inspiring strains with lively tempo. Strain merged into strain. The clear window took on a fresh green hue, and Vega put her hand to her eyes as she ended the period of Adam's silent in- struction with,

"Adam, that is my people's anthem; the anthem of our own planet. When we land on our home ship you may refer to our social strata as the 'regulars' and the 'peers.' Remember this, the 'regulars' number nearly half a million, and the 'peers' number not more than one thousand. That is all you need bear in mind."

The green of the window now faded to soft yellow, then gradually became or- ange, then amber. Soon it evolved to the white of brilliant clouds.

"Vega," Adam said, in wonderment. "It grows whiter and whiter, cloudier and cloudier. What is the meaning of it?"

"That," she replied with a smile of contentment, "is the outer atmosphere of Venus. We are approaching home base. It belongs more to you than it does to us, even though you feel as a stranger. You see, it is the closest sister planet earth has in its own solar system. We are visitors, Adam, but you are a son. We shall honor your every mature wish. We visit, but we do not conquer and impose. We ob- serve, but we do not intrude and interfere. We inherit our estate, because we remain meek. We enter gates where so many meet with destruction. Adam, hold your head high always, but always in the fresh air of humility, of understanding. Let your soul cry, but let not your mind be dampened by its tears."

With those words she removed her hand from her eyes. By this time the planet Venus filled their entire field of vision. It no longer seemed as though they were going toward it horizontally, but rather as if they were falling down into the clouds. Thus Adam learned that the perspective of going down is only virtual. When an object fills the entire field of vision the sense of going down is experienced in- stead of the reality of going toward it. Gravity helps to produce the illusion of a downward fall.

SON OF THE SUN: The Secret Of The Saucers

Yet the surface of Venus must have been a great distance away, because Vega put her hand to Adam's eyes, telling him not to look until she removed her hand from his vision. During the next crucial moments she spoke mere nonsense to him, to help the time pass by.

Suddenly there was a steady roar, and the ship vibrated sharply. Adam knew the ship had entered the dense cloudbeds of Venus. For the first time he could sense a slowing down by the grind of the ship against the atmosphere. He was glad he was being spared watching this phase of the landing, and his regard of Vega swelled once more into love. She was so expert in her manifold roles, so spontaneous in her expression of appreciation for the opportunity that had been hers to serve a man of earth. Thus it had not really been love either of them had felt, but the exuberance of a new experience.

Romance, love. What were these things, then? She had promised Adam he would be introduced to them in their fullness. Even as his eyes were still occluded by Vega's hand and the ship roared to slower velocity, he could think only of his next great adventure. One name sought to fill his entire consciousness, the name of Launie. The wearer of the name would be touchable flesh-and-blood, he felt sure. But then, suppose it was to be merely an apparition in the mist? Would he be brought to the fountain to drink, and the drink be turned to mere vapor on his lips? No, no; space visitors would not play such earth-like pranks. With that realization he became patience itself, knowing his greatest fulfillment was immutably waiting for him. "Launie," he thought unconsciously hoping there would be no more to experience beyond her. Forever with her would be enough.

Though Launie was to give substance to the purpose of his existence he felt he had longed for her from time immemorial, this she whom he knew not, one thing was certain: Vega had become just another human being in his mind, and he knew he could live with or without her. It was Launie, he felt, who was his other half from the day he was born and would be until the day he should die, though she was a daughter of Alpha Centauri, and he was a son of the sun. Vega's role had been that of escort.

The ship came to a complete halt, paused a silent moment, then continued slowly forward. Vega removed her hands from his eyes, and before him appeared a new world. An ethereal horizon closed down sharply not far ahead.

"This is our home, Adam. We have entered on one side of it, and the horizon you see ahead is ten miles away. Yes, it is one large ship containing a self-composed world ten miles in diameter and housing five hundred thousand people. It is shaped like two saucers facing each other; or like the solar system. It resembles a galaxy, Adam, so how about giving it a name at once?"

"Good!" Adam exclaimed. "As long as I am involved with it I shall call it 'Andromeda', my nearest, or our nearest, sister universe, Hail, Andromeda; hail, wonderful Andromeda!"

SON OF THE SUN: The Secret Of The Saucers

Though deep in his story, Adam paused in his telling of it. We glanced at the clock and saw that it was 3:00 in the morning. The deep quiet of the desert was far from our consciousness, and there was no longer time for us. We felt only the life and imperceptible motion of which all things are. I felt that the very walls of the house had absorbed Adam's story, and remained attentive in their silence. He seemed to be apart from everything around him, including me, speaking his words as if they were meant for unseen people, and perhaps the walls, floor, ceiling, and the ether. The moment's pause was broken by the sound of a car passing by, going toward the marine base, a lone sound making a slight dent in the boundless quiet. As if aroused by the sound, Adam resumed his story.

Chapter 6
LANDING ABOARD ANDROMEDA

Placing her hand over Adam's eyes had no special significance. It was merely a whim on Vega's part. She did, however, feel that she wanted him to see the interior of her huge space ship suddenly, not gradually. Thus she had hidden from him the details of the entry from outer space into the safety of Andromeda. He had entered into a strange civilization with only Vega as his identifying requisite. He was not asked for his credentials by anyone.

Their small craft was now gliding at less than twenty miles per hour, gracefully weaving and dipping toward the center of this little artificial world. Adam saw the area below him as they soared in midair over the beautiful city; a city inside a huge space ship. Vega threw kisses with her hand to the waving throng just below. By the thousands they kissed back, with graceful hands and child-like smiles. Adam was in the fifth estate. It was like looking upon his earth fellows transformed into angels, viewed from his "magic carpet."

Their craft was overtaken by a long ship which went forth as if oblivious to the waving people below.

"That is the ship which monitored us here from earth," Vega announced. "It is going to its hangar."

Their own little craft descended to barely ten feet above the grassy streets, and slowed to a glide. The people cheered by song as they waved, bowed gracefully, or danced about. It was one grand symphony of welcome for Adam, the earthman, and for the historic adventure that was Vega's.

Here indeed was an interstellar floating island containing a beautiful city of half a million population. Full ten miles in diameter, it encapsulated a small, self-sufficient world. The ship was now nearing the center of the city which seemed to be entirely engulfed by a slow, lazy fire as the buildings marvelously changed color, billowing and merging beautifully from hue to hue. The walls themselves were active. They appeared to be made of plastic materials and every square inch of the walls could glow with light as required. Adam knew this from the demonstration he was witnessing.

SON OF THE SUN: The Secret Of The Saucers

He felt himself flickering rapidly inside, a sense of unworthiness seizing him and then suddenly leaving him to spring into euphoria, alternating back and forth. His reasoning mind told him he did not deserve this sublime experience, but the nectar he had drunk affirmed just as strongly that he did, and this rapid vacillation finally ended when the better decision of feeling worthy permeated his consciousness, and he made an agreement within himself to learn all there was to learn from it.

Finally they reached their destination, the center of Andromeda, the horizon now being five miles in each direction, and the sky ceiling five miles straight above. The perfect symmetry of the interior of the ship formed a wonderful half-sphere, crowned by uniform cloud overcast all around, yet all was clear daylight within Andromeda.

Adam and Vega were preparing for the landing in this center, which was composed of buildings of great size, larger than the ones they had passed over on their approach. These were evidently their governing facilities. A large pool of water nestled like a jewel amidst the verdure of grass, where a few swimmers were enjoying themselves. The grass, trees, and other foliage were of many colors, so that vegetation served as flowers. In the air a few craft were cruising around—ships within a ship.

Outside, at the ceiling of the clouds, there were constant lightning, fireballs, St. Elmo's Fire, and other phenomena produced by electrical discharge. Adam had read of such displays in the book, "The Secret of the Saucers," but the author had made no attempt to fully explain them. He gave the matter no further thought now, because he felt that in due time all would be clarified to him.

They landed slowly amid a cheering but orderly crowd. There was nothing physically different from earth's people about them. All appeared to be typical of Vega, healthy and radiant.

There were blond-haired, dark-haired and red-haired people. It was like seeing the inhabitants of earth possessed of physical health and mental understanding that were transcendent. So gentle did they seem that Adam felt as one among happy human lambs. He felt himself becoming one of them, from deep inside.

But something in him made him also feel like a lion among the lambs, and at intervals he felt like an ape among angels. He was indeed a dual personality, vacillating from the high estate to worthless dust.

Suddenly, from the very center of his life, he yearned for one among these who would be more on his level, yet be from among them. Ah, yes, he felt this person was somewhere in Andromeda. He had not seen her as yet, but his soul's need vouched that he would surely find her. This one would make him feel at ease, at home, secure in the port of his true love's heart.

Adam reflected that his sponsors had of course anticipated that he would feel this way and he need have no fear, someone more on his own level would be

SON OF THE SUN: The Secret Of The Saucers

provided as his hostess and guide during his stay here. Yes, he concluded, he was already being prepared to expect her, so in eager anticipation he felt ready for all that awaited him.

The little craft came to a halt in an open grassy area, and Adam and Vega stepped out of the opening which had quietly appeared. A man took him warmly by the hand, while another took Vega's hand. The one who greeted her seemed to impart more than just a welcome. Adam saw that it was love claiming its own, and he knew she was now out of his life, leaving him free for the one his heart awaited. The man embraced Vega, and their lips met gently in affection. Then, with a look of approval, he came and put his cheek to Adam's. At the same time, Vega kissed Adam on the forehead. He noticed that at the side of her beloved, Vega's eyes became more beautiful than ever.

As she said goodbye to Adam, she warmly thanked him for the opportunity that had been hers in picking him up from earth and escorting him to their space ship, Andromeda. The experience, she assured him, had elevated not only him, but had also lifted her another rung on the ladder of learning.

"I am going now to see our entire trip reviewed by recording. A group of our peers waits to review it with me. Among them will be Lyra, Orion, Neptune. Saturn also will be present."

As she spoke the name "Saturn," the crowed pealed a melodic song. The mention of his name enraptured these people. Vega walked away with her escort, and as she did so, some girls touched her clothing gently in admiration as she walked by them. Girls will be girls, thought Adam, the universe over. He followed, with his guide holding his hand as they walked, much like happy children.

"You need not name me, Adam," said his guide. "You will meet too many of us to recall each by name. You are not gifted at recalling names, so do not even try.

"Saturn is our chief here on the ship Andromeda. His name and the ship's name, as you know, are so given merely for your benefit. His name suggests the planet of your own solar system. It represents the beautiful symbol of the atom, hydrogen. It is also the symbol of the universal systems after their attainment to perfect symmetry. Our chief is that to us, so the name you give him fits well.

"On Andromeda, there are one thousand of our peers. The rest of us, nearly five hundred thousand, are what you might call retarded ones, still having much to learn to reach the peers' status. Just call us the regulars, as you already have been advised. Our peers seek much deeper insight and knowledge than we regulars, but all of us are as yet learning, and we love the motivation of learning. The regulars have much more to learn than the peers, so we seem to evolve at a faster pace to you. However, we are aware that what to us is yet mystery is to our peers elementary knowledge.

"For instance, a child appears to have a more aggressive initiative to learn than an adult. This is no reflection on the inherent intellect of either. Individual pur-

SON OF THE SUN: The Secret Of The Saucers

pose is what matters. Without wisdom, without logic, without intuition, there is no attainment of the fruits of Purpose. Each one who rises lifts the rest of civilization—indeed, all of creation—a little higher. Thus our reception of you and of our own Vega."

As his guide thus spoke, Adam did not notice that the crowd of people had been left behind. Still hand in hand, they walked across a grass-carpeted square and straight toward a large building, its plastic structure glowing with a translucent green color. A large golden dome shone above it. Since no one had followed Adam and his guide, and no one seemed to be gathered to greet him at this building, he suspected a surprise of some kind.

Apparently there was no door to this building. At least, he could see none. The opening before the two men was wide, and they proceeded through it into the interior. There was no need here for doors, Adam realized now. The temperature inside was the same as that of the outside, and such things as stealing or destructive mischief did not exist here. All weather conditions were uniform within the ship Andromeda, inside and outside its buildings.

All at once, from various entrances to the room in which the two men stood, children came rapidly, singing to joyful music that pealed forth from out of the air. Some brought with them large squares like table tops, from which they drew down folded legs and then stood upright in the floor. Soon the entire area was filled with small tables set neatly in rows. The walls and ceilings were ivory color, but Adam felt that these could change color to suit the occupants. The floor was blue-gray, at least at the moment.

The bee-like activity of the children, still singing as they moved about, produced chairs in place at the tables. When this was accomplished, they did not walk around or stand idly about not knowing what to do next, but continued singing and swaying to the music. It was singing unrehearsed, swaying that was spontaneous, and all was harmonious and melodious.

Flowers were brought in by some of the little ones, and adults began to appear, coming in streams through the doorways. Adam saw one long table being set at the front of the large room, with chairs placed at the outer side only, like the speakers' table at a banquet. His guide took him to the center chair of this long table, where the chairs on either side of him were being taken by others in orderly fashion. He was introduced to the gathering, there were brief nods, and all sat down. At each adult's place was a small bouquet, different from its neighbors in color and fragrance.

Now the children were seen busily bringing food in with their small but deft hands, through the entrance ways. Trays, plates, saucers, cups, silverware, and napkins were quickly put in place at the tables without confusion. How marvelous, in such little time, to see a great banquet set up by children-children who had learned to learn. As Adam said, "it was all beyond words."

159

SON OF THE SUN: The Secret Of The Saucers

His guide had not sat down. He had gone elsewhere, but now he returned with a young lady and led her to a platform near Adam. There was instant quiet and attention when she spoke.

"Well done, and very lovely too, young ones," she said, addressing the children. "We greet Adam from earth. He will partake of what to him is breakfast, and we shall join him in what to us is lunch.

"At this time, Adam does not distinguish one from the other, for he has lost the sense of time for awhile. But the eggs, the butter, and so-called coffee you have placed before him begin to orient him even now." True enough, Adam could feel himself beginning to distinguish morning from evening again. The lady went on speaking.

"Please rise, one of you, and say what to Adam would be Grace." The young woman's speaking voice sounded like a song. She was not quite as beautiful as Vega; yet something about her captivated Adam with a relentless pressure that must end sometime, or explode.

Would they never have him meet Launie, who would be more on his plane, and allay his emotions for more important learning? Why must all these people have such a unique attraction? His thoughts were quieted as a boy arose from a table to volunteer Grace. It was obviously a spontaneous gesture, and everyone bowed in reverence as he spoke these few words:

"For the gift of life we are happy, and for all things that sustain us we give thanks to the Bosom of Creation. We promise to remain aware of the ever blessed love of learning, thereby to be led to the Light of Knowing, and to love our fellow creatures. Bosom of Creation, we thank Thee."

The young lady on the platform then directed, "Let us sing now for Adam."

Introduction music played a short time. Then, like a heavenly choir, they sang Stephen Foster's "Beautiful Dreamer." Such an arrangement as Adam heard that day has not yet been captured on earth. He looked at the young lady, who was still standing on the platform, and she returned his glance through moistened eyes.

Adam did not know whether to thank Stephen Foster or these people. Whatever pertained to Adam in the most minute detail— past, present, or future—was a completely open book to this woman whose glance met his in complete understanding. What passed between them in this brief moment even Launie would be incapable of erasing. Yes, even Launie.

Adam, the novice, thought he was the first ever to feel such sweeping emotions. He was oblivious to the fact that millions of people on his own earth had been either lifted up or devastated by them. He forgot this was part of the briefing on these basic emotions he was being given by his hosts in preparation for embracing grander vistas of learning. Neither did he yet know Launie.

Now the young woman stepped down from the platform, joined the man who had been his guide, and together they walked to a small table that had been set for them. All began eating and engaging in affable conversation. Adam's eyes, however, were still on the two, and as if reading his thoughts, the man sitting next to him explained.

"They are not wedded mates. They are, however, in love, and when they fully decide to become partners they shall wed. They will not vow loyalty lightly such as your people on earth do. One will merely say to the other, 'In the presence of all goodness, seen and unseen, I am yours.' That is our wedding ceremony, be it performed in the presence of witnesses or not. Their announced word of it is sufficient, and it is then recorded. Wedding festivities, if any, are a spontaneous expression from among their close friends.

"Both of them are teachers of our children. Yes, we have schools right here on Andromeda. The pupils are given the semester schedules, which are reviewed by the peers, and from there on the teachers have full sway. Results are what matter, and we find this plan works very well. The latitude of our teachers is equaled by the freedom of the pupils. If a teacher shows signs of slipping back into retrogression, she or he is then retired from public teaching for life. Children who are faster in learning than others are given more to assimilate, within their limits and needs, of course."

They continued dining. After a few moments' pause, Adam asked his neighbor, "What is the secret of such health and physical beauty in your people?"

"That is only in your perspective, Adam. We regard our peers somewhat in the same way as you regard us. You should behold our chief, 'Saturn.' Such stature, such understanding.' He is friend, physician, and patriarch all in one. All mortals must feel a sovereign orientation to some degree. We must be able to look down from where we have climbed, and up to where we are going. Saturn assures us that he also looks up to a stretch of stairway which extends beyond his own vision," he said, noticing that Adam's expression had changed to one of perplexity.

Something just said had caused him to reach back toward memory. A word echoed throbbingly in his mind, the mention of which had catapulted him from this hall. Physician! Physician! Yes, Saturn was even physician . . . He was breathing heavily, trying hard to think. The word came laboriously from his lips . . . "physician, physician." A word so dear, yet so futile to him now. He felt a little shaky, with a panic creeping into every reach of his vital self. Every nerve in his body felt some pain, some numbness, fear. He was in the throes of one dying, yet he was living. He needed more than "physician," more than his former self. He needed another person, his other half, who was heir to the same despair, but who gave that despair a hue of glamour, a note of infinity.

Then a blessed numbness enveloped his body. In it he was more alive and responsive to sights and sounds about him, but unable to move. Haziness was all about him. Was he dying? he asked himself. If he could only see that one person who would give him courage, whose face would render him glad no matter what was to be! He looked wanly toward the table where the young teacher sat with her fiancé.

But she was not there. She was walking toward Adam, deep concern showing in her lovely face. She was approaching him rapidly, walking with a speed that denoted urgency, all the while looking steadily into his eyes, and Adam knew she had assumed the role of nurse. Adam, physician, was now Adam, patient.

With graceful haste, she put a pellet in his glass and filled it with water. As it fizzed and bubbled she put it to his lips. Her eyes remained on him while she both appraised his condition and responded to his need for affection. Both felt drawn toward each other, meeting in spirit at that indiscernible place where tides meet momentarily. Adam, the earth physician, accepted in warm comfort the fact that he was in the hands of a better physician, a unique nurse, average in her world, but resplendent by earth standards. In his moment of distress, this exquisite being had rescued him. There was no doubt in his mind; he knew now the painful sublimity there would be in loving a woman.

In a moment the nectar began to take effect. Adam regained control of himself, while his nurse explained what had happened.

"The first nectar, which Vega gave you, had almost worn off. Then your breakfast of regular eggs, bread, butter, and milk activated your digestive processes and your metabolic cycle, and these subdued the slight effect of what was left of the nectar. Your entire system was flickering dynamically between your normal state and your enhanced state. You were not dying physically, but dying from our estate back into your own. You began to sense your true identity again, that of Adam, the physician; the physician of earth.

"As you have guessed, I was entrusted with your welfare, and accordingly felt close to you and your feelings, sensing immediately what you were going through. In helping you I rise also. Now drink the rest of your nectar, and feel again as one of us."

With that she took her leave, returning to her table. As she sat down, her companion smiled at her in appreciation of what she had just done. She was a source of ecstasy to Adam as he gazed her way in deep admiration. He felt strong again, healthy, and equal to all that might occur around and to him.

A young lad came to Adam, breaking his reverie, and put a newspaper on his lap. A little girl accompanied him, and she laid a magazine on top of the newspaper, saying they were both for him. They were his favorite newspaper and magazine on earth. He was amazed, for they were the latest issues.

"They were not delivered to us," said the boy, vibrantly. "We have hobbies here, just as your people have. Some of us telemeter photos and news of events on your earth every day. We have reproduced these two copies for you, Adam. We trust you will feel at home because of them. Just tell us if you want anything else reproduced for you."

SON OF THE SUN: The Secret Of The Saucers

Adam put his arm around the boy and asked, "And this is just a children's hobby here?"

"Yes, it is. We make our own apparatus, such as presses, radio, and radar-telephotographs, also ink and paper such as earth uses. But these are simple things, so do not ponder on them," the child said, chuckling with inner glee.

The little girl came close to him and asked if she could whisper in his ear. Adam consented with pleasure. Thereupon she drew herself up and whispered to him.

"Adam, it is time for you to get some sleep. No one will leave this room until you get up to do so first. You are an honored guest."

He was overwhelmed. They had left such little things as manners up to their growing and learning children on Andromeda. He gazed into the sweet face of the child, who was closing her eyes and turning her head upward to receive a kiss on the forehead. As he held her small head in his hands she clasped a

bracelet around his left wrist, and lovingly kept her hands on it for a moment. This was another surprise to Adam, but the little girl had an explanation for her act.

"This," she said, "is for your identification. Should you become lost in the cosmos, all travelers of space would know where you hail from, and in whose care you are. When you are returned to earth, it will be converted back to vapor, but until then nothing can take it from your person."

Adam was touched by her concern for his welfare, and he noticed that it was the same type bracelet all these people wore, each having a separate identity by numerals, symbols, and size of beads. It was metallic in a sense, yet it was warm and silken to the touch. It would identify one anywhere, should he become stranded among civilizations of equal or superior evolvement.

The little girl nodded to Adam, then toward the teacher and her escort at the table where they sat. It was evident the teacher had coached these children, at least to some degree, for their reception of Adam.

Becoming aware of wearing apparel, he noticed for the first time how simply everyone was dressed, although the clothing was appropriate and modest. Colors, motifs, and styles were according to the taste, the nature, and the inclination of the wearer.

Every piece was fresh and new looking; every garment enhanced the wearer. Each person seemed so satisfied with his or her apparel that it added further vibrancy to each personality and to the air about the individual. These people impressed Adam as being perpetually poised for alertness to any new event and eager for any opportunity to serve their fellowmen.

Adam began to feel a pleasant drowsiness. In a voice that only those sitting near him could hear, he said, "I feel I should go to sleep. It is more pleasant here than I can express. But sleep calls me, and I beg leave of you."

All those at his table stood up at his words. The young lady and her escort rose also, and came directly to him. Music sounded again, and everyone in the hall sang softly. The young woman and her escort indicated to Adam that they would see him to his cottage, and the three of them left the hall together.

Adam noticed his drowsiness did not increase, but that he took on new zest while walking. Outside, he asked his two escorts what all the lightning and electrical flaring far above them meant. It never ceased. He could even hear the rumble of thunder accompanying the lightning effects. The man answered his question.

"Our ship, Andromeda," he said, "is afloat in the atmosphere of Venus. The solar energy causes the electrical turbulence you see above us in the cloudy atmosphere. Our ship is deep enough in the atmosphere to prevent seeing the sun, or its outline. On the night side of Venus there is no lightning. No need for more detail to your ready assimilation, is there, Adam?" he asked.

"Wait a moment," said Adam. "How can such a large ship as Andromeda remain firm and strong? It is all of ten miles in diameter."

His guide replied without hesitation. "Our ship is built on the principle of the structural arc. It will neither collapse nor burst. The large floor beneath us is thick at the center, and not so thick at the periphery where it joins the shell overhead. This gives our floor the strength of rib and suspension. Besides, we have developed materials so strong you could not comprehend their strength even if you knew the composition. However, the entire body of Andromeda is similar to our smaller ships, namely, plastic-crystal molecules held together by absolute polymerization. Know that you are safer on Andromeda than on the vulnerable surface of your own earth, Adam. Need I say more?"

"No; oh, no," Adam faltered. "But may I ask you this: Do you not have any questions of your own to ask me, for a change?"

"Yes," smiled the guide. "Tell us, how did you enjoy your trip from earth to Venus with our Vega?"

The young lady at the guide's side walked away from her place as if impelled by an unseen force, coming closer to Adam and looking deeply into his eyes to get the full effect of his answer. Once more he was under the spell of a feminine beauty, who seemed to have forgotten her own betrothed at her side. Adam instinctively used this opportunity to hold her attention. He was learning to use one woman to attract another woman, even on Andromeda. She is jealous, he thought. I shall make sure that she stays jealous. He pursued his momentary advantage, speaking with concealed rapture.

"How can I express it to you?" he asked, glancing from the guide to the beauty whose eyes were gazing into his own. "I asked her about such things as the masterfulness of our little ship, its speed of ten million miles per hour, about my earth and its moon, and about Venus. Her gentle nature and complete beauty gave me the answers. I was so overwhelmed that the incredible nature of all I was experiencing receded beyond my consciousness. In her presence, everything else turned into the usual and ordinary. I was lost in her sublimity."

The guide was deeply attentive, as Adam added, "It was all of this, of course, but what it really was to me is beyond words. How can I tell you? To me it was just incredible," he concluded.

"Do you mean," asked the young lady, "that you could tell of your recent experiences and include Vega as just a part of them, having no special place for her in your memoirs?"

Adam did not speak. He merely smiled and nodded in confirmation to her question. Yes, his intense nod said, but at the same time his eyes said to her that this would not be the case with her. His hands fidgeted, for they wanted to hold this young woman closer. Her eyes found his depths and bound him into slavery.

Then he spoke, in a voice weakened by his emotion. "Yes," he sighed, "it is one thing to me; categorical record, and nothing more. I will bear up under all that your people can give me in experiences, and I will merely relegate it all to history in written word. Even you; even you, my Waterloo; even you shall be a mere written name in my records. So, I am to learn first the meaning of woman in the consciousness of man. That, I know, is what I am now going through. But I shall forget it. Believe me, I shall forget all of you, reducing you all to mere names and events."

His male guide remained in his place a few feet away, fixed in concern by his strange behavior. He looked like a statue, so much aloofness was he assuming, as he entrusted to his beloved the responsibility of administering unto Adam's fragile emotions. He did not interfere, nor did he speak a word.

"Shall we go on to your lodging, Adam?" the young lady suggested.

"Yes," he replied, "I am not tired or sleepy now, but I feel it is time to be there, so I am ready."

"Well," said the young woman, "walk right in. The cottage before you is yours." They had stepped onto the lawn of his assigned cottage. She turned her eyes from Adam to her escort, then to Adam again, back and forth from one to the other, hardly realizing she had just spoken in such a detached manner. The man who had been Adam's first guide on Andromeda bade him a casual goodbye, inferring he was leaving the situation henceforth in the capable hands of the young woman. His services seemed to have come to an end.

The little teacher turned to her friend as he turned and walked away. Suddenly she burst out, running toward him, "Leo! Oh, Leo! I know now the folly of follies. Your absence will leave a void of many moments in my life. I would come with you now if you say so. I would, Leo, if you truly say it."

But Leo merely smiled into her eyes. His emotions were not the emotions of woman, and in his masculine steadiness he seemed to know that she would soon be over her little outburst, for he nodded his head, not in accusation, but in gentle approval and understanding.

So, Adam reflected, this man was to be known to him as Leo. He walked over to where the two stood. Leo looked directly at him, his eyes penetrating deeply into his as he approached. Then Leo spoke.

"I am not your guide, Adam. No one is your guide here. We are all host to you. When I leave she beside me becomes your hostess. Not only you shall gain knowledge, but she will also. Her next sphere of learning can only be reached through a few moments of romance. On earth you denied yourself that phase of experience, but you will soon be matured in this phase. Do not be uneasy at any time. You cannot hurt us, and we would not wish to hurt you. Tomorrow you will meet in truth your Launie, who will give you the finishing touches of what all mortals must have for fullness of living and learning."

As he paused, Leo was interrupted by Adam.

"But I do not know her name," he said, looking toward the little teacher.

Wistfully, she answered him herself. "My name, as you know by now, would mean nothing to you. Whatever name you give me I shall accept, with pleasure."

Immediately through Adam's mind swirled the vision of a misty pond at evening time, with a lone lily gracing its surface.

"May I call you Lily?" he asked. And Lily smiled assent. Then Leo spoke. "She will make you comfortable, Adam. When you awaken, it will be our evening time, and you will be just as one of us. Keep your aspirations on the better things, and you will do no wrong. Know that the best things to come are only a little beyond the present, and that awareness is your best guide. It lifts you upward, and it insulates you against unwholesome temptation.

"Do not wallow in the present, and crawl not after the past. See all things in relation to the 'now,' and see them as sliding before you at the speed of light; and before you shall forever stretch the infinity of things. To the enlightened ones, Adam, the past, present, and future are all just 'now.' Motion gives that 'now' life and infinity. Please know that I leave you both with that admonition."

"Leo," Adam commented, "I see why I have been asked to call you by that name. It was assumed beforehand that I would see in you the Lion, yet holding a lamb in his arms. A lion becomes handsome, gentle, and understanding. The lion becomes sublimated into Man, as promised. You don't mind, do you, that I voice my perceptions?"

Leo merely shook his head with a smile for reply and, waving his hand, turned and walked away.

Adam stepped closer to Lily, who was looking at neither Leo nor himself but at the lawn, with mischief dancing in her eyes as though she had just made some kind of conquest. She was now alone with an earthman, to be his nurse and hostess for a short while. This was indeed a new experience to her. Thus Adam thought, and thus she confirmed by her next words to him.

"Adam, you have justified Leo's faith in earth's people. You have made him glad that you and I will be alone for a time. This is one time in your life and mine that

SON OF THE SUN: The Secret Of The Saucers

Alpha Centaurians, my people, have removed all recording facilities from our two lives. Higher beings from other worlds no doubt record us just the same. It will be my pleasure to bring you into my world for a while, and it is for you to bring me into yours. I believe we shall find them to be essentially one. Do you not feel as I do?"

"I have always felt so, Lily, even if only subconsciously. But I never dreamed so much would be revealed to me. I thought ages must pass before earth's evolution would bring any of us to such heights of realization."

Lily walked rapidly, and almost ran toward the cottage entrance. How swiftly, Adam thought, these people change from one attitude to the next, and how smoothly, almost as if their actions were timed to music.

He ran to catch up with her at the doorway, and followed her inside. A teacher she was, but she was many other things. She was a youthful girl chasing the butterfly in a meadow. She was a girlish beauty, knowing nothing but rapture in all things. She was the vision that appears in the morning mist on a little hill. She was not a temptation but an exquisite sensation, never consumed, always fresh. She was like an eternal fountain abundantly offering its cool effervescence to all within its radius without stint.

Was this exuberance of Lily's due to knowing that Leo would never be more than five miles away from her, or was it due to the interval of absolute freedom she would spend with Adam? He was suddenly introduced to one of the questions man forever asks, and woman never answers. He was suddenly in love, in love, as the phrase means in its higher sense.

He was sensing the bittersweet, the web which is interlaced with threads of jealousy; the flames that leaped within him dampered by the pain of unrequited adoration. In the light of love he saw her body as the gateway to her shining soul. He longed to look at her in leisure so his being could merge with hers.

Instinctively, he called upon all his training as a physician, and all his knowledge as a science student. She was, he reminded himself, merely a mass of molecules brought together in organisms and consciousness. This analysis only aggravated his emotions, however. He loved her that much more. After all, was he not also a mere agglomeration of atoms and molecules? How could these be assembled by Nature so as to feel, to see, to hate, to resent, and ultimately, to ... to love? His heart was tearing at his ribs. His limited earthly learning served only to accentuate his burning emotions, which became a million scorpions stinging every nerve in his body.

So this is what love can do to one, Adam thought, as he stood in the doorway with a semblance of outward calm, while the object of his worship continued her brisk pace to the kitchen. If she would just stand motionless while he absorbed the essence of her with hungry eyes! Why would she not keep still?

"Was she, after all, like earth women? Even earth women were beyond his inexperienced knowing, he remembered. Would Launie finally bring him the love and peace that "passeth understanding?" Launie, Launie, he thought. Why are you so long in appearing to me?

But Lily, delectable, lovable Lily, was delicious to his inner vaults of feeling. He remembered suddenly that he was here alone in the doorway, lost in a kind of limbo. He nearly ran into the kitchen so he could feast his eyes on Lily, who was cosmic livingness itself. She was preparing two glasses of refreshing beverage—water and pellets—those never-ending pellets! She offered him one of the glasses, with its liquid bubbling amber. She took the other and they drank thirstily, Adam rising under its effect, and Lily descending. As they put their glasses down, they looked into each other's eyes with a deeper understanding than before. Lily saw in Adam the small essence of Leo, and Adam saw in Lily only the promise of Launie. One thing was certain now, and that was that Adam was no longer tired or sleepy, but wide awake and expectant. No, not anticipating Launie, for he must first understand and fathom Lily. He had learned the ways of these people, and he must master each phase of his learning before progressing to the next. Thus ran his thoughts.

Having drunk the nectar, and now meeting on an equal plane, Adam felt his masculine strength assert itself. Through his vocal chords it spoke, almost as a thing apart.

"I do not wish to meet any other woman of your world. I want to be with you. I will learn whatever I must learn, and I do want to learn, but I want no more of your women in my life. Please spare me from any more such pain and pleasure. Really, I cannot stand more. You have been my nurse. You are beautiful beyond words. I long to be near you and with you. That is all I feel at this time. Must I go through more than this? I am only an earthly mortal, and you give me all that I can possibly receive. Won't your people let me be at peace within myself, and let me remain only with you?—Lily, aren't you listening to me? Where are you going?"

As if she did not hear Adam, Lily proceeded to make the cottage comfortable, seeing that everything was in good order-She busied herself in the kitchen, putting things in the oven of the small thermionic range, taking them out again. She arranged dishes, cups and saucers in a scurry of motion that left Adam breathless. Her eyes, blue as the lakes of northern America, set off by the Helen-of-Troy features, finally looked into his own, as she paused in her duties.

"Be open, Adam, but be still. What is your own will come to you. You asked for a meeting with another world, and now you are in the fulfillment of that wish. I have not called you. You have called us. But we answer as though we have called you. Ask for whatever you may, Adam, and if it be existent, it shall respond to you. Thus, I am and you are. You call and I hear you. Call upon an angel, and an angel will respond. Call upon something lesser, and it, too, will respond. You have called me, and I am here. Now, if that is clear in your mind, you are on our level and no more special preference will be given to you. Unless you become one of us in spirit you can learn nothing, and nothing shall be added unto you." Thus spoke the elementary teacher to Adam, who loved her.

He drew close to her, and looking into her eyes, said, "I am sorry, ma'am. I have yet to meet Launie. But I do not want to meet her alone. I want you to be present. Whatever she has to add to me will be welcome, but I do not choose to lose what you have already given me. I want your person and your spirit to be at my side at all times. I need you. Even Launie could not overcome that need. Please, may I ask that much in humble sincerity?"

Lily thereupon assumed a formal attitude, and charged him, "Adam, you are letting yourself be carried away by emotion. You are not the only thing on my mind, nor are your little wants all I have to attend to. This is my cottage, and will be your home during your stay on Andromeda. An extra room has been added as your bedroom. You would hardly know it was not part of the original design, yet it was done by our young boys within hours. In less than twelve hours, our people have given you such an experience of wholesome and idealistic love, and now a sense of home, that you feel you have always had such things. You may be sure we will have company soon, and you have yet to know Launie. This will still be your home after you meet her.

"You see, besides all that is yet to come, you have been subjected to quite intensive living. Now I must be getting ready, for we are going to have some distinguished visitors."

With this, Lily disappeared like a nymph into her bedroom. Adam was in no mood to be thwarted in the discussion he had started. He followed her, planting his feet solidly across the doorway of her room as though ready for a long siege. Words filled with emotion poured from his lips like a cloudburst.

"I'm sorry, I do feel that I want to meet Launie, after all. I am not sleepy or drowsy any longer and I feel capable of any new experience that awaits me. But I still wish you would stay with me for the duration of my sojourn among your people. Let's go meet her, and please stay close to me."

Lily smiled to herself with a joy somewhat exaggerated for the occasion, as though she knew more and saw more than Adam, but she promised not to leave him as long as he fervently wished it. As she started toward him, something stopped her suddenly and, transfixed, her ears attuned to a sound he could not hear, her eyes tried to see what she heard. Then Adam heard it too. It was music, faint but growing stronger. Lily swept past him and ran into the living room to turn a small dial, and at once a section of the wall became a television unit. Adam followed her.

In three-dimensional view they saw three men and one woman walking side by side. They were moving with a grace like that of a waltz. Lily's fingers crept to the sides of her temples, her eyes wide with awe.

SON OF THE SUN: The Secret Of The Saucers

"I can hardly believe it," she breathed. "Adam, that is Saturn, Neptune, Orion and Lyra! They are on their way here to see you. Never have all of them been here together in my lifetime. Your presence brings them to this cottage. Oh, Adam, see how important you are to them, and to all the rest of us? Every hair of your head is counted. A sparrow does not fall but is noticed and recorded. Remember that eternal lesson, Adam? This is what is meant by it. Look whom you bring here—our own Saturn, our chief, and three of the peers with him." Lily was in ecstasy. In a sweeping move, she left Adam alone before the set.

"Out of the way, Adam! I must prepare for them. I must give my dance of welcome for them." Then, pausing, she asked him hurriedly, "Oh, yes! it must be for them, but in honor of you, also. What song do you wish me to dance to when they arrive?" Her expression was changing rapidly. Like a chameleon, she was transforming from a young milkmaid into a devastating Salome, her hands already groping into the ether for the touch of rhythmic perfection. Her eyes were focusing even more distantly within their own mists. Turning the small dial, she spoke as if to the wall.

Adam heard the name "Antares." The other words were strange to him, yet sonically delightful. She had spoken to one called "Antares" in her native tongue, and the music ceased. Then a low rumble began to swell from the set before him, filling the entire room.

Lily rushed to her bedroom. Adam was truly perplexed for a moment. Then he saw what he thought was a vision, but it was no vision. It was Lily emerging from her room in time with the crescendo of the familiar earth tune, "Siboney." He had been unaware that he had requested the song when she asked him to state his choice.

Adam beheld a new Lily. She had changed rapidly, not only in aspect, but in clothes. Her skin had not a flaw. Gleaming synthetic material composed her scant apparel; scant, but artistic and proper.

The rendition of Siboney swirled into its melody, and Lily became a figure inspiring the very notes. Adam stood entranced. She had timed it perfectly, for at that moment Saturn walked in, followed closely by Neptune, Orion, and lovely Lyra.

Trained monarchs never entered anywhere on earth in equal elegance. Every motion was majestic, purposeful, progressive. Their clothing, was simple, fitting perfectly, and looking like silk sprinkled with diamond dust.

"Welcome, Adam, welcome," Saturn greeted him, with vigorous ease in his voice.

"Welcome, Adam," the three others joined in. Lily went on dancing, with joy through all her being. Siboney had reached the ultimate in music as her dance gave faithful interpretation to each note. As the number ended, she came gracefully to Saturn, and bowing slightly, kissed his right hand. She repeated this gesture to Neptune, Orion, and Lyra. Lyra took her hand in her own, and kissed her hair.

Thus Adam was ushered fully into another world. Had he known these elegant ones for all that they were, he too would have greeted them in a dance of joy, baring his innermost feelings physically for their benevolent inspection. Lily was simply carrying out one of their customs, namely, that the lesser ones in evolution present themselves to the greater ones in the fullness of their entire beings, such as the dance through which she was now expressing herself. It could be compared to the shaking of hands among men of earth, but the grandeur of the greeting was symbolic of the vast gulf between their civilization and Adam's.

He was privileged to taste both phases of their civilization. Lily stood erect now, once more her former self, and begged leave of Lyra to change clothing. More than merely assenting, Lyra accompanied Lily to her room. Adam was left with the three men. Men, these were! Orion spoke to him.

"Adam," he said, "we will not stay long, because you need sleep. Trust us not to say or to teach you what is utterly new to you. If it should sound new to your mind, then someone else on earth has already come upon the same knowledge. When you awaken from your sleep you will be ready to learn all that your whole being as a man of near perfection might learn. You are in good care. Be joyful, and feel secure. Tonight shall pass quietly for you. Tomorrow you shall be submerged in grandeur. Everything will be new to you only by confirmation. We give thanks to the Creator for this opportunity to share with you what we have."

As Orion finished, Lyra and Lily came out of the bedroom and went into the kitchen to prepare refreshments, talking together as women do everywhere.

Saturn went directly to Adam, who sat comfortably in a chair. He looked intently under Adam's right ear and put his finger there, rubbing the spot gently.

"All gone, isn't it?" he asked.

It was gone, indeed. The little lump, the herald of doom, was not there. Adam could hardly believe it.

"Yes, it is gone," Saturn said. "The beverage Launie gave you a little while ago destroyed all the nuclei of the cancer cells. Metastasis has ceased temporarily. The sarcoma has been returned to its root origin. It will evolve again, but a month has been added to your earth days, Adam."

Adam had forgotten his doom. He had forgotten he was in the presence of the peers, one of whom was a master physician. He had heard the name "Launie." It had lifted him in spirit to another realm. Was he dreaming. "Launie? I have not yet met Launie. How could she have given me the nectar to drink? I beg of you, Saturn, where is she?"

But Saturn remained silent, evaluating Adam's health in general. Neptune now took the opportunity to speak. He came close to Adam, and as Saturn -stood thoughtfully looking on, he said,

SON OF THE SUN: The Secret Of The Saucers

"Adam, our hostess and yours, whom you have called Lily, is in truth your Launie. She is one of our little fun-makers here; it is just a harmless pastime. She has much to learn, so she is a teacher of some of our children and thereby learns through teaching. You have been with Launie since you first set foot on Andromeda."

Adam felt rushing relief from his guilty conscience, his feeling of duplicity in having been drawn from one lovely girl to another. Lyra and Launie had suddenly become silent in the kitchen. Now, for some inexpressible reason, Adam felt wedded, wedded to a girl he scarcely knew. He looked toward the doorway of the kitchen. Launie was standing there, draped in a white dress, in which she looked like an exotic flower in full bloom. She had won her first little conquest, and she had not only won through a harmless scheme, but so far as the peers were concerned, had won eloquently and regally.

Lyra came out of the kitchen, spoke her native tongue into the wall near the dial, mentioning the name Antares as Launie had done. Presently there was music, subdued for the occasion, so conversation would not be disturbed. Launie had returned to the kitchen.

Adam recognized the music as a familiar one of earth called "La Vien Rose." It fitted the flowing presence of Lyra perfectly, but it was the lesser Launie who held his whole being spellbound in total love, for Launie was on a level he could fathom. After all, Lyra was one of the peers, unreachable to his appreciation and to his less evolved senses. Lyra was almost of a mirage, but Launie was warmly real.

Before long Launie and Lyra were bringing in two trays holding glasses of beverage. Lyra took over most of the duties of serving, noting that Launie was lost in a dream. She was in deep reflection, trying to comprehend the meaning of these present moments. She fumbled a bit but Lyra turned the occasion into perfection. What flustered Launie was the realization that four of her peers, including their chief, Saturn, were guests in her little cottage.

Their genuine interest engendered an atmosphere of intimacy and warmth that taxed her equilibrium. In all the five hundred thousand population on the ship Andromeda, at this moment it was she, Launie, who was entertaining the top ones. She was delighted to the point of being overwhelmed by it all. To think that one such as she was given this experience!

Potentially, she was a daughter equal to any and all the daughters aboard Andromeda, and the moment confirmed this feeling within her. Also, she was to sponsor a man of earth in his extraterrestrial experiences. What more could her lovely heart ask? And Adam was the cause of it all. Insignificant, plain, earth mortal Adam, was able to bring to the house of Launie such peers as Saturn, Neptune, Orion, and Lyra. Thus, if only superficially and for a passing time, she loved Adam, shutting her true love, Leo, deliberately out of her mind.

Adam surrendered himself to the ecstasy of this new-found love, unmindful of Saturn, who had not yet completed his examination and was exploring around his ears for any sign of upsurge in the lymphatic ailment. To Adam, the sight and presence of Launie submerged concern regarding his physical condition, and made him oblivious to others around him.

Saturn and Adam now joined the others and they all sat quietly for a moment, sipping the delicious nectar. Launie sat on the floor next to Adam's chair. He felt unworthy of her nearness, but it was so irresistible he accepted it in silence.

Launie lifted her glass to her lips, and suddenly broke into tears. Lyra gave vent to her own emotions, following with tears of equal volume. The men were at a loss to understand this outburst.

Orion looked intensely at Lyra. Saturn and Neptune held their poise, but glanced at each other as if to say silently, "Thus be all learning and true ascension of soul; painful, delightful but progressive; and thus even the lowest rises up, and becomes a glorified one."

Adam, feeling a little of the mood of the others, concurred with Saturn and Neptune in thought. Wisdom was asserting itself in this moment. Why should tears move him any more than they moved Saturn and Neptune? He, a mere earthman, was more poised than some of these Alpha Centaurians. He was equal with Saturn, the chief, and with Neptune, a high peer.

Launie had spent her emotion. With eyes still damp, she turned smilingly toward Adam's own eyes, asking of them their inmost history, their very reason for existence. In that instant Adam the master became Adam the slave. He knew that for her he would forget all else, for her he would nullify a segment of the universe itself. For her he would become selfish desire personified. There was not now, and there never had been, in his present senses, any kind of existence anywhere but what Launie had not now at last given to it meaning and fullness.

The living universe was she. If she could understand atomic function as he now understood it, she was truly his mate and not the mate of Leo. But with this thought Launie seemed to recede from him. She was once more distant, once more strange, once more a ravishing beauty seeking nothing but surface romance.

This time Adam was not hurled into a lonesome limbo. Even though Launie was aloof, Saturn, Neptune, Orion, and Lyra were close in spirit with him. They talked small talk and bigger talk, and no talk. The peers were taking in every detail of what Adam said or heard, and his every reaction was recorded in their minds like photography. He knew this though they had not stated it, but he did not object. Indeed, he was grateful, for in his own way he was also recording them in his mind.

The music from the wall slowly faded, and Saturn announced they would be leaving. When Adam awakened on the morrow Launie would escort him on short sojourns. He had only one question to ask of the group. It surged within him so strongly he felt it proper to ask.

"How is it that I heard Launie and Lyra speak your native tongue into the receiving and sending set? Vega told me I would not hear it during my stay on Androm-eda."

"Because," Lyra spoke up, "you remembered five words which I had spoken sometime ago to a man of earth, and you quoted them to Vega correctly. Thereby you freed us of needing to take extreme care in order to spare you any undue confusion or feeling of inferiority. You have gained nothing and lost nothing. Every second of your trip here was recorded by our Antares, whom you will meet on the morrow." Lyra's loveliness reminded him of Vega. Ah, yes, he had another question.

"I never saw such loveliness before as when Vega laughed heartily, laughed like a warbling youngster when I asked her why it was that we had not seen the sun, nor even its bright outline. Why did she laugh so?"

"Because," Neptune replied, "you asked it with an air that told Vega you had finally reached a point where she was defeated. You had the pleasant aspect of an intelligent victor. In reality, we have simply not come to the sun on your tour as yet. Do not feel slighted on that account. Your chance to see it will come. For the time being, get on with the present things, Adam, and trust in us."

* * * *

"With Neptune's words the remaining half hour was spent in social talk, and getting better acquainted. When Saturn arose to leave, the rest of his party followed suit graciously', and soon Launie and I were once more alone," Adam said. "Believe me, Orfeo, I felt in love up to the zenith. It was romantic love, to be sure, but wholesome. She reveled in her own beauty, and was pleased with her success in molding my emotions thus far. At times I felt she was more like a distant relative to me than someone I wanted as my own."

We looked up to see the early desert dawn beginning to light the open spaces. Adam seemed energetic in spite of his narration throughout the night. I was not feeling tired, either.

"Well," he suggested, "let's continue this tonight. Meantime, we should both get some sleep during the day. It is Saturday, and you do not go to work. Are there any questions in your mind before I leave?"

"Yes," I replied. "You said the lump under your ear was gone after you had taken the drink, when Saturn examined it. Yet I see it there. It is small, but present, nevertheless."

"I know it is there, all right, but if you feel it you will find that it is no longer hard, but is very soft. The malignancy was decidedly destroyed in the area. The slight swelling left has merely flared up somewhat, that is all. Remember, they would not cure me, though they could have easily. That would be interfering with earth's own evolution, and they never would risk it."

"But, Adam," I rejoined, "they added one month to your lifetime. That is as much interference as if they had taken over your entire life. How can that fact ever be reconciled with the 'no interference' policy they so magnanimously practice?"

"Orfeo, are you trying to be a Sherlock Holmes? If so, then don't conclude until all the facts are assembled," Adam neatly remonstrated.

"You see," he continued, "they knew I would eventually submit to surgery at the focal point of the sarcoma, namely, at the neck. This would have given me another month of life, at best. So they merely extended the time of its progress where I would have had surgery anyhow, and diffused the total sarcoma unilaterally. Not one minute has been added to me. How they did it is still a mystery to me, but where is the interference? This phase of it means more to you than to me, but you are already giving the problem study, so again, I'm telling you, it is not interference. Whatever we of earth do is not interference of one world upon another, but merely evolution. Now, are you satisfied, and do I have leave to go for the day?"

He smiled benevolently. A beautiful man he was, doomed in this lifetime, yes. but he had found life, or life had found him. What matter which it was? His minute was another man's year. He got up from his chair, prepared to leave. As he walked out of the door it was like the dawn of nature meeting the dawn of man.

"Oh, Adam," I called out as he got into his car. "Where shall we meet tonight?"

"Same place, Orfeo; Tiny's Cafe, at about the same time as last night."

He started his car and was soon driving away. Suddenly I realized that I did not know where he was going if I should need him. The lonesomeness of the eternal desert gripped me, for most people had not yet awakened and all was still, all but the rising sun and Adam's car now climbing the hill toward town.

I looked to see if a lizard would dart from one bush to another, or a jackrabbit rear its head and run off, but there was nothing alive at the moment except the rising sun and me. For ages it had never failed to rise, nor to set. Everything else had some flaw, but not the rising and the setting of the sun. How beautifully earth spun on its axis! I thought, as I went back into the cottage.

Yes, mankind slowly and painfully unfolded unto the glories nestled in its bosom, for man alone was the destined heir to all that lay just beyond his primitive vision. For man alone earth turned steadily and danced on in its own orbit, hugging that sun.

The wealth of the earth came from the sun, and that of the sun came from the Milky Way, and that of the Milky Way, from . . . from where? Even these space visitors came only from a stone's throw from our sun. They had not yet fathomed the Milky Way. Why, then, should I try to ponder it? A cup of coffee, yes, warm up a cup of coffee. That would be a more practical thing to do. And then sleep.

* * * *

I awoke about 2:00 o'clock in the afternoon, refreshed, invigorated and peaceful. A new well-being made the desert sands more meaningful to me than they had ever been before. The life around seemed like the surface activity of a sea with hidden depths. I felt more in communion with the huge life of its silence than with the small life of its surface. I had not known the mystic spell of the desert before, nor of the sea, nor of the river, nor of the mountain, nor of the meadow, nor of the sky. Below all surfaces are quiet but steady messages, having one ultimate thing in common, the sense of eternity.

I went into town about an hour later. There I found the bustle of tourist activity, people coming and going. I saw nothing of Adam, and did not look for him. Rather, I used the late afternoon mingling with friends and tourists. It is easy to start a conversation in Twentynine Palms. A stray marine is glad to speak to anything that moves. A widow in retirement has yet to meet the purpose of living in human form.

A hotel or motel keeper greets your hello with the rate of rooms, overnight or weekly. A real estate operator thinks you are a millionaire in pauper's clothing, ready to buy up acres with a "river view," which river turns out to be a dry wash. It is dry 364 days of the year, except when the cloudburst comes. Then the river washes clean through miles of desert, surges through the Colorado, and lands in the middle of Nevada. Thus thrived this little community and therein lay its appealing beauty. I loved it, and thousands of others seemed to love it too, for they have braved its every challenge.

Today Adam was among these people somewhere. I was hoping inwardly that he was not out buying up a thousand gopher holes with the ten thousand dollars he had promised me.

By late afternoon the effect of the nectar had almost completely worn off. I began to feel listless yet restless, and to doubt that Adam was real. Time slipped by and the sun went down. I did recall having washed two cups this morning, but it could still have been just a dream of some kind.

I looked at my wrist watch. It was 7:00 o'clock, and Tiny's cafe was just a few blocks away. I drove slowly and parked not far from its door. I could already see a man who resembled Adam sitting at the same table where I had met him the night before. When I walked in the door the same smile, the same man waited for me.

This time I could understand how he knew, and why he was here. He lost no time in preparing a glass of nectar for me. Tonight there were only two glasses, his and my own. There was a loneliness within both of us without the presence of the third glass, but the nectar soon elevated us into the next octave of consciousness. This time Adam ordered two vegetable dinners, which was just what we both seemed to want.

As we were getting ready to enjoy our food I noticed the waitress looking at me, then she asked if there was anything else I wanted. Oh yes, I thought impulsively, and I asked for another glass. Not minding her surprise, I poured water from the pitcher, and occasionally looked into the glass. It remained there with just the water. Nothing happened. Adam smiled to himself, shaking his head a little as he ate.

"Orfeo," he said, "it was you who taught me that you cannot initiate a contact with them. They do the contacting. Why do you even try?"

"Anything, Adam, anything at all," I replied, "to see her dance once more. I see her anyhow, even in the clear water."

We did not linger too long over our meal, and soon drove our cars onto the driveway of Earl's little cottage for the second time. I could hardly wait to hear more of Adam's narrative. Tonight we would have tea instead of coffee, and I went to the stove to put some water on to heat. As I held up Earl's package of tea bags, Adam grinned his approval.

We sat down, and neither of us said a word for a few minutes. Then Adam asked me not to turn on the radio this night, for he would need to feel as if he was living it all again and I must absorb every word. With that request he began at once, and we were promptly catapulted aboard the space ship Andromeda.

Chapter 7
ADAM MEETS ANTARES

After Saturn and his companions had left them alone, Adam felt a pleasant lethargy, then a desire for sleep.

"Adam," Launie said, "go to bed whenever you wish, but go before fifteen minutes are up or you will be asleep wherever you are." She laughed winsomely, as Vega had laughed during their trip together. She came up to him, put her forefinger on his chin coquettishly, and added, "That is so, Adam. Tomorrow I am your guide, tonight your nursemaid. Now goodnight, you handsome, untamed earthman."

After Adam was in bed he heard Launie singing, and as he drifted off into sleep her voice became a background of smooth velvet. He remembered nothing more until he awoke in the "morning" and heard her singing again. He could smell breakfast being prepared by this dainty miss. Never on earth, Adam thought, had such a lovely woman been so attentive to a man and yet belonged so completely to another man.

He felt fully awake in a short time and called out, "Good morning, Launie. Have you had any sleep?"

"Oh, yes indeed," she called back. "But not quite as much as you."

Adam washed, dressed, and presented himself in the kitchen. There she was, the human meaning of morning glory, too innocently lovely to look upon by a crude person like himself, he thought. How could she be one of the "retarded" ones among her people? He was indeed learning to love. The next problem was how to forget. At that instant Launie looked at him with a Mona Lisa expression, as though reading his thoughts and conveying the message that teaching him to forget would also be her task.

He seated Launie at the table and then he sat down. Before them were eggs, bacon, potatoes, toast, and a pitcher of milk. It could not have been more like home anywhere on earth.

They ate with few words spoken. Just before finishing, Adam asked, "Launie, I noticed yesterday that the children and adults in the banquet hall were feasting on delicious steaks. Do your people still eat animals? Most of us on earth do, yes, but your Alpha Centaurians, do they?"

She answered without looking at him.

"Yes, Adam. We eat steaks and all else we desire, with pleasure and with gusto, but we waste nothing. To waste any essential is the same as destroying, the same as killing outright. Such things as waste are so remote from my people that only the most retarded of us ever speaks of them. As for the steaks—have you seen any animals thus far on board Andromeda?" she asked.

"No. No, I haven't. That is strange, especially since you feed me eggs, milk, meat and other animal products. There is an unreality about it all. It makes me feel I am drifting in a lagoon halfway between a Paradise and limbo."

Launie replied warmly and reassuringly. "We at home or on our base ships produce everything synthetically, as you would say. Does not what you have eaten taste even better than the natural foods of your earth? Furthermore, Adam, remember that all things are natural. Eventually the people of earth will duplicate much of nature's own creations. It is merely a result of learning, remember?"

Adam nodded his head almost imperceptibly. No longer did this seem unreal, but all was alive, superb.

"We do have animals on our home planet," Launie continued, "but very few. Our people number twenty billion, so there is little room for animals. But ages ago, Adam, we also had a moon. Our ancestors finally landed upon it, and in time we gave it an atmosphere and cultivated it. It remains our satellite to this very day. We have made it into a small planet and transferred most of the animal creatures there. There are also a few million of our retarded ones, like myself and the others here on Andromeda, who make their home on that man-dressed planet. Even the animals evolve to final gentleness.

"One thing to remember, Adam, is that for every pound of weight we brought to our moon we removed a pound of moon matter, to keep its weight original, and to keep the orbits in balance. Indeed, we found we could not shoot too many objects away from our home planet into space if we were to avoid affecting the mass of our own planet. This would have the effect of disturbing the orbits also, if carried to a sufficient extreme."

In a few minutes they had finished breakfast. But Adam's thoughts were still on what she had said.

"Launie, do the scientists and engineers of earth consider that fact? That is, to replace a ton of moon matter with a ton of earth matter when removed, and vice versa?" he asked.

"If they don't," she replied, "they will eventually. But let's drop that subject for the time being—and never mind the dishes. The children know I am busy with you, and they will be eager to come in and set everything in order, clean and neat."

SON OF THE SUN: The Secret Of The Saucers

They were soon outside, where Launie took Adam by the hand. On the grassy street was a small platform, about four feet in diameter. It had circular plastic railing around it about three feet high, and a small gate which had been purposely left ajar by someone who had anticipated their use of it. The platform was in effect a small craft, and the two stepped aboard. Launie took her position by a small control box, moved some dials, and they rose up and away. There was not a sound coming from this amazing gondola-like craft.

The sky above Andromeda itself was dark, but the whole interior of Andromeda was as light as day. There were no longer lightning flashes above. Adam asked Launie the reason for this.

"Because, she replied, "we are now on the night side of Venus. That is why you see no lightning and other effects. The center of our ceiling is five miles high. Andromeda is a large half-sphere ship. She can stand anything but the interior of burning stars. Although we are still in the cloudy atmosphere of Venus, as I said, we are opposite the sun, and it is the sun's intense rays which cause the constant electrical displays on the side facing it. We are going to meet our chief astronavigator. For your sake, we shall call him Antares, after the great star."

No sooner had she spoken his name than hundreds of humans soared into the air. Children and adults, like a flock of birds, rose in even ranks, then broke the uniformity into myriads of individual positions, elevations and directions. There were objects under their feet which looked like round skates. The people looped and zoomed up and down, they twirled like toe dancers and some tumbled about with dizzying speed. They were skating in thin air, and then their skating area was filled with waltzlike music, accompanied by angelic singing.

Launie had anticipated his utter surprise and, smiling happily, was ready to explain to Adam, who was too mute to ask.

"You see, Adam, they wear crystal-plastic shoes, which simply ride the magnetic waves. The entire floor of Andromeda functions in the same way, as do our little craft here and our larger space ships, and as do the solar systems, the galaxies and the cosmic spheres-within-spheres. It is really very simple, once you know how," she finished, with her hearty but enchanting laugh.

Very simple. Indeed! thought Adam. Their simplicities were his perplexities. At last he found his voice.

"Launie, don't laugh that way or I will be tempted to kiss you. I will call you 'lovely one' instead of Launie. I . . . I . . . oh, I don't know what I'll do," he managed to say, laughing with her.

"Go ahead, handsome one," she said, laughing still more beautifully. "Leo would like to hear you say it, too."

With those words, she regained her composure. Adam was beginning to see the real Launie. What to him was akin to a spiritual unfoldment was adventure for the sake of a little bit of learning to her. He felt he was among angels and so, he reasoned, she must feel as if cavorting with a primitivelike creature, yet he could not have been made to feel more at home, nor more delighted. Soon there were many craft rising up and going to and fro, of various sizes and shapes, weaving among the hundreds of "skaters."

"This is more normal," Launie informed him. "They all stayed grounded until you and I appeared in the air. It was a fine gesture on their parts toward you."

"Launie, do you not feel somewhat flattered with all this attention you are getting along with me?" Adam wanted to know.

"No, not flattered, Adam. We rarely are flattered. We know joy and communion of spirit in such displays as these. When any one of us receives a privilege or widespread attention, the rest of us are glad, and confirm that one's singular joy of the moment with some form of rejoicing. Some day your own earth will know this fullness of living."

Their little car slowed down and soon landed on the flat roof of a large building. Other crafts of various colors were parked there also. Launie opened the little gate and they stepped out. Adam looked at the roof, which was like translucent ivory.

"Hmmm," he murmured. "No leak through this solid beauty."

"Leak what, Adam?" asked Launie, smiling. "This roof is fully one inch thick, but never worry. It is stronger than a foot of your strongest steel. This building is our central astro-navigational headquarters. From here we control and keep in contact with all our smaller ships in the sector of Andromeda, including Andromeda herself. There are a few smaller buildings at compass points here, and they are extensions of this. Each houses a particular branch of research. Antares is the chief of the department."

Launie took his hand in hers and led him down a stairway. After a short walk through door-lined corridors they came to the main office, and walked directly in. Adam got the impression he was in a sort of broadcasting station, and that this office was the very center. There sat Antares at an average, earth-type desk, his demeanor one of calm expectancy. Launie walked to the desk, spoke his name with a slight bow of her head, and gave him a look of gratitude for this opportunity to be with him. Antares returned her sincere greeting. Then, turning his eyes toward Adam, he merely said, "You are welcome, friend; most welcome, indeed."

"Thank you, Antares," Adam responded, with ease. "I pray that 1 will prove worthy of being here. Please forgive any shortcomings you find in me. All that I see and learn is appreciated, and I revere it. At this moment it seems I have lost the dividing line between what I once called matter and spirit. I wonder if there ever was a dividing line?" Adam turned his head from Antares to Launie. For once, she looked intimately, deeply and exquisitely into his eyes, finding her way into his soul. Adam was learning of the future, while she was learning of the particular awakenings of evolution in this man who was far behind her in cosmic time.

SON OF THE SUN: The Secret Of The Saucers

"Adam, do you think you would have appreciated all this if you had not met Vega and Launie?" Antares asked, motioning for them to be seated, one on each side of his desk. Adam sat to his left and Launie to his right. Adam made haste to reply to Antares' question.

"No, I wouldn't. I would have seen everything as merely material knowledge, which would soon curdle my spirit, and my whole being with it. I must admit I love Launie, but she is so elusive! I find myself forever chasing an unreachable promise of ecstatic love. As for all things, material and spiritual, I now feel they are one and the same. I feel the merging of the two must occur before the final attainment of great happiness is possible. For the first time, so-called spiritual things have come to mean even more to me than so-called material things. Am I to know the dazzling finality of this supreme understanding?"

"No, Adam, not in this lifetime," replied Antares. "Even our civilization has not yet found it. It awaits us all on the last rung of the upward ladder. Nevertheless, you will learn enough to give you peace of mind, and the rapture of awakening to some extent. Your material life ended when you closed your office for reasons beyond your control; but because there was the slight spark of the angel in you, you ascended, as it were, another rung up the ladder of spirituality. Even the one rung is rapture, is it not?"

For a moment Adam was stunned. Then he found words to say, "Antares, are you the chief navigator? I expected to find a brilliant but methodical and cold wizard. Instead I find you, as I have found most of your people, including the peers, unpretentious and warm-hearted, rather than highly learned ones intensely absorbed in their work."

"You will never find us tense and strained in your perspective, Adam, and you see we do get results through our attitudes. Good health offers us good and orderly energy. God is not violent with the understanding ones. The more we find the more is bestowed. It is ignorance and disease that struggle. Comprehension exerts its excess energy in rapture and thrill; not reckless thrill but objective thrill, which evolves into the rapture of the cosmic splendor eventually. Now, let us get on with some things you should see."

At that moment the walls of the room changed slowly to another color. Little wonder they did not need decorative touches. The walls, floors and ceilings were equipped with all enhancements required for any occasion, although for furniture this room had only Antares' desk, a plastic cabinet with dials and switches, and the three swivel chairs in which they sat. The clothing of these people did not vary greatly from earth's apparel, other than being more simple and of finer texture. Antares rose and rolled the cabinet near to his chair, then sat down again. He pushed a button, stood up again and went toward Launie. She arose as if in response, accepted his arm around her shoulders and his kiss on her cheek with such docility Adam felt a pang of painful jealousy. Antares had sensed Adam's reaction, and reassured him.

"When I pushed that button," he said, "Andromeda could tune in on us by sound and vision. You may be sure that Leo too is tuned in on Launie, not to spy but to look upon her. We do not know such emotions as jealousy, having forgotten them ages ago. Besides, every person in this building has been alerted that visitors are here. Come, let us look around."

Nevertheless, Adam had tasted jealousy which refused to ebb away completely from his mind. On all of Andromeda, he was the only being who knew such an emotion, mild as it was becoming. Thus to him the whole universe became flavored with some of the bitter in all its sweet. He had lost the bloom of his youth's blossoming, and like a ripened fruit would know that bloom no more.

They walked along the corridors, looking into the rooms on either side. The simplicity of everything, of the building itself and the many rooms, of all visible facilities, belied the complex purposes and activities to which everything herein was devoted.

The experts seen working appeared to be engaged in light and meaningless play rather than in works that not only would tax the most brilliant people of earth, but would be far beyond their comprehension in most instances. All was being done by the retarded ones, supervised by a few peers such as Antares, which made the tour of inspection that much more awe-inspiring to Adam.

On the way back to the office of Antares, he was informed of the true nature of the building.

"This is the very center of our ship Andromeda," said Antares.

"We have four other control buildings at compass points. Any one can fully function in the event that all the others should fail for some reason. We have had no trouble in any one of them for some centuries." Launie exclaimed at his words, as if she had not known this fact before.

Finally they were once again in the office of Antares. He asked Launie and Adam to sit in their swivel chairs, as he drew the cabinet with the buttons and dials close to himself.

"Now, Adam," he began, "you will see something few men of earth—in fact no man in many centuries before—has seen. The import of it is self-evident, and there is no final evaluation. Even we wonder as to the nature of what we have, captured by our instruments, so your surmise in this case will be as good as ours. A child's would probably be even better," he said, with calm but eager voice as he manipulated the buttons on the cabinet. This caused the room to darken except for one section of the wall across from them, which maintained an ethereal glow. It gave a beautiful, three-dimensional effect.

As they watched, the glow took on the darkness of space, visible only because stars merged in motionless suspension at the same instant. This was an actual photograph of space. Antares' fine voice began to narrate the film for Adam's benefit.

SON OF THE SUN: The Secret Of The Saucers

"You are looking at one of our televisions, my friend. All our walls and partitions have this same capacity for electronic function. Now, watch carefully as we bring in a close-up of the center section of this scene. One of the stars will enlarge. Our crystal telescopes give details that show only as indistinct light on the best telescopes of earth. See, Adam! Do you notice that star in the center getting larger? Our film has been speeded up so we can bring in this close shot hundreds of times larger than we originally were able to photograph it. This, of course, is merely a fastmotion type of moving picture, and does not mean we have attained velocities exceeding the speed of light."

As Antares spoke, all the stars seemed to move off to the sides, while the center star became larger and larger. Then the focus on the center star revealed the beauty of the planet Saturn, with its concentric rings in bold relief. There, before his eyes, Adam saw one of the most beautiful sights of the universe. Shown in the suspended relief of three-dimensional photography, it would be difficult for one to imagine a more awe-inspiring scene.

"There, Adam," Antares explained, "is your solar planet, Saturn. As you look upon it, know that you are looking upon the exact replica of the atom, hydrogen. Yes, your nine planets are replicas or symbols of some dynamic function of nature that underlies invisibly what we perceive visibly. It is as though the great Creative Intelligence gave to our eyes a macroscopic replica of what goes on in the microscopic realms. Thus, you see now not only Saturn, the planet, but the atom, hydrogen.

"Now, let us go directly to the surface of Jupiter, the largest of your nine planets. Does it tell you anything? Indeed it does."

The scene shifted, bringing Jupiter into focus. Even from a distance it bespoke hugeness. Its zonal divisions, clearly defined, gave it a "split personality", an aura of mysterious strength. There was a small red area on its otherwise mono-form sphere; monoform, that is, except for the zonal belts. Adam wondered if his guess at the nature of the red spot would be confirmed or reversed. Even as he was wondering Antares softly began explaining this strange bright area.

"Now, Adam, let us go directly onto the surface of Jupiter, and right into that red spot. You will hear the sound emanating from this seething sea of red, that you may fully appreciate what you see. Remember, that spot is so huge several earths, strung side by side, would well fit into it.

"Notice it is becoming larger and larger, more red as we approach it," continued Antares. "The misty vapor you see is that of molten metal. We are now entering its cloud, then it thins out so you see it no more. The red spot has become a huge sea of bright orange color, and you cannot see its shores. It appears to be smooth, but wait until we are closer to it. It is still several thousand miles below us, so the clouds you saw were reflected, not real. Now we are in the true metal vapor clouds, which you see only as a hazy mist."

SON OF THE SUN: The Secret Of The Saucers

When Antares finished speaking these last words there was silence in the office, the scene before them dominating every thought of the three people watching. In the darkness the lifelike televised projection of the planet's red sea loomed like some fiery ghost. Adam was still feeling the effect of the nectar, and the presence of Launie and Antares gave the moment something akin to his idea of heaven.

The spell was soon broken by a deep, guttural and ominous roar. It was the voice of Jupiter's red ocean of molten metals. The surface was no longer smooth, but had become a heaving and billowing mass, bright orange with angry heat. Now the eyes of the watchers were brought to within scant yards of the seething turbulence of metallic geysers and whirlpools.

There were waves of mountainous proportions, swells like oatmeal boiling in a vast cauldron. The beauty of the scene lay in the merging of brilliant hues, when orange heat cooled to red, then soon heated to orange again. These two were the only colors on the screen, merging into and out of the seething madness that was this red ocean, Jupiter's red "spot". No ship of earth could have withstood this madness, this inferno, for an instant. Adam had suspected its nature, but the actual sight of it was a little too much for him and he waited tensely for Antares to say more. However, his suspense was broken by the sudden appearance of tiny moving objects, three of them, flying over this forbidden, deadly sea like insects over a living volcano.

The objects were brought into full-sized perspective, where they could be clearly seen as three spherical craft with men visible aboard them. They hovered over the vastness of liquid spouts and turbulence, liquid so dense aluminum would float in it, Adam thought inadvertently. Antares, breaking the silence, narrated the facts.

"Those are three of our ships. They are spherical for the purpose of strength, not only in the vacuum of space but for the pressures of submergence in any ocean, or in any medium." Even as Antares spoke, the three craft plunged straight into the blistering metal ocean. It seemed suicidal, and Adam felt a wave of deep compassion sweep over him for those poor souls in the three little ships. But the voice of Antares reassured him.

"That boiling sea is more than ten thousand miles deep, Adam. Those ships you saw plunging beneath its surface actually went to its full depth. Can you imagine diving into a cauldron of molten metals more than ten thousand miles deep? To us this is what you would call routine. The floor of that blistering ocean," he continued, "goes to the very center, or the core of Jupiter. In fact, the whole ocean is born because of the seed-cell area, which is only a few hundred yards in spherical diameter in the very center of old Jupiter. Your earth has the same hot cell in its center, born of the great pressure that gravity exerts, and all atoms in that center are smashed to shapeless energy, fuming and seething to regain symmetrical form as atoms. Your sun is so much greater in mass that it smashes a far larger area in its center into formless energy, and it asserts itself throughout the entire sun body, rendering the whole sphere radiant and lighted. Your earth expels this energy by way of volcanoes, hot geysers, hot springs and earthquakes. Jupiter expels its inner core heat by way of its red spot, which you now know as that burning orange sea. The sun shines forth in majestic, life-giving light, radiance and heat. This is the secret of all the bodies of the universe," Antares concluded.

Adam, excited by the words which verified his own theories, was quick to interject questions and suppositions.

"In short, Antares, the seething sea of Jupiter gives birth to some matter, while the sun gives birth to much matter. Yet," Adam rushed on, like a student hitting at all the answers, "it takes a great mass of matter to exert pressure on a central core, which in turn gives birth to matter non-existent before. We are now more deeply into the question, then, of 'which came first, the chicken or the egg?' It requires the core of massive stars to create matter; yet it requires much matter to bring about the great and massive bodies enveloping such a core. Which, then, came first?"

From out of the dark came the soft voice of Launie.

"Adam," she asked, "may I answer that one for you, in the best and only way I can? Feel sure that Antares can offer you no better answer to this question than I can, and even my answer will be no more accurate than a child of your own earth could give you. Which came first?" Launie almost sang, like some invisible siren.

"When you find the answer to that question you will find the answer to the source of all things. In the meantime, you must be content with observing the results, or the effects, or with just observing things as they are. Then you will notice an orderliness in everything, and after that you will see a purpose. That purpose extends into the infinity of origin, and proceeds on to the infinity of the final end. It is the origin, and it came first. No matter how you approach the study of nature, you come upon that intangible, elusive yet vibrant thing called Purpose and Order. It always lies exactly in the middle of the effects we observe and the causes we seek. That intangible middle, Adam, came first. Yet, even that seems to be but the third harmonic of all things. Not only does it respond as an end product of action, but it also appears as the cause of all action observable. It has an infinite intelligence of its own, and remains aloof from any and all decisions, be they from the intuition, or from the calculated.

"For instance, think of the terms 'Positive and Negative,' 'Action and Reaction,' 'Cause and Effect.' What have you in the final analysis? Just the same two essentials. But in between these terms there is always the word, 'and.' So, there is the essence. Positive is positive because negative makes it so, and vice versa. Effects exist because of causes. Reaction is because of action. Even if you reverse the words they are just as accurate. It is safe to say that any cause we observe is actually an effect of something else. But you see, Adam, the word 'and,' which is always present, in any term, is the eternal essence, the third harmonic, the end product of the mutual exchange, the infinite hairline point where exchange is made between action and reaction. It is always at the center, at the word 'and,' that life emerges. It exists first, last and always. It is what our peers are seeking at this very moment. It is what all intelligent life is seeking. What is that middle? What goes on in that word, 'and,' which separates all countermotion? Only there will we find the ultimate answer. Only there can we find the Eternal Being of life. Do you understand what I am saying, Adam?" Launie concluded.

"Yes," Adam answered. "In other words, the real action, the real place where life lives is at the point of exchange, where action becomes reaction, where positive buffets the negative, and so on. That point is consciousness, life, and purpose."

"You have put it well in few words," Launie said. "Jupiter stands in space as proof of that dynamic. It is a planet ready to burst forth as a sun, yet it is a sun gone out of light. If it gained much weight it would become radiant as the sun. If it lost much weight it would become dormant, like any of the smaller planets. Thus is the universe. Mass and weight determine the radiance of any star. As with the sun, it is not action that gives it radiant energy, but pressure upon its core that makes the action and the radiant energy."

For a moment, Adam felt as though he understood all the basic dynamics of the universe. The quiet following Launie's words helped his assimilation of their deep meaning.

"Now, Adam," Antares said, breaking his long silence, "we bring you the return to the surface of the three ships in that hot ocean of metal."

From the seething turbulence the crafts emerged, not even dripping from their hulls.

"There they are," said Antares. "They have been near the floor of that ocean, where the heat measures thousands of degrees, and have taken up many kinds of metal in various stages of molecular states. That ocean in its depths produces materials which can duplicate anything we can make artificially. Nature is always ahead of its own creatures, Adam."

"Incidentally," Antares continued, "that ship in the center was piloted by Leo, whom you have met here. Now we shall take the roar you hear from Jupiter's red ocean and convert it to music by our crystal modulators. Listen."

The horrendous roar became beautiful music. Adam was listening to Jupiter's sea and all its radio emissions, modulated into a harmonious symphony. Antares spoke again, this time in a reverential tone.

"Now, Adam, we want to show you our prize astrophoto. This you have never seen. In fact, no man of earth has ever seen it."

His words brought a sudden gasp from Launie. Caught by surprise, she asked, "Oh, Antares, not the Corona?"

SON OF THE SUN: The Secret Of The Saucers

"Indeed, Launie," Antares assured her. "Is that not our prize photo from the cosmos?"

"But I am not prepared spiritually or morally. I may feel I am not worthy to look upon it. Adam is innocent in his ignorance, and you are worthy. But I . . . Oh, Corona, it is with humble eyes I will look upon you. With God's grace I will be pure in thought, and deeply pondering as I look upon you. Oh, Heavenly Corona!"

Adam was taken by surprise by Launie's sincere supplication. He felt as though he was to look at something which would move him from the depths of his soul. He could not see Launie in the darkness of the room, though she was close beside him, but he felt close to her, closer than he had ever felt before. It was a warm intimacy, mingling pure affection and inexpressible love. The atmosphere about them took on something of a divine essence so he could hardly wait to see the Corona. Antares sat motionless until he felt Launie had prepared herself, emotionally, then turned on the photo, a photo captured by the best molecular telescopic camera in the possession of the Alpha Centaurians.

To a novice like Adam the sight was indeed breathtaking. There was a central star, emitting light much as earth's sun radiates. A majestic planet appeared some distance away from this radiant star, where two moons, one on each side, came into view. Around these were six great satellites, each one the exact replica of Saturn, each a symbol of the pure element, hydrogen.

The Corona appeared to be a small constellation in itself. Its perfection bespoke a purpose and a function lofty beyond human comprehension. Studded here and there in its environs were golden stars which were set aside from other stars, serving to enhance the cluster.

Antares spoke in a tone that betrayed his humble attitude in the presence of this photo, his voice subdued in rapt humility.

"We have never been able to hold that majestic cluster in view, Adam. When we lose it we do not find it in the same area again, but once in many years we relocate it in an entirely different section of the Cosmos. It is the only celestial object that behaves so, and we have a theory about it. Perhaps it is only one of a number of such objects, and they go out like a light turned off at the will of some Intelligence, which causes another to light up as one goes out. However, that is mere conjecture, pure guesswork.

"We find that the Corona differs in many ways from any other spacial entity. One of these differences is that the bodies resembling Saturn are huge crystal lenses, being capable of sending, receiving, emitting and absorbing any dynamic function of the universe. Each object is as large as the planet Saturn.

"By this time you may be ready to ask, could this be part of the very Throne of Creation? We ask the same. Your answer would be as good as ours. Sincerely we ask you, is it? Is it the very Throne system? Could this be God's Chariot Galaxy? If not, Adam, is it not then the estate of God's archangels and His legions?"

SON OF THE SUN: The Secret Of The Saucers

Adam responded with a silence that was as much an affirmative answer as if he had spoken aloud. His eyes had become adjusted to the darkness of the room, the light from the three-dimensional television scene of the Corona giving whatever illumination relieved the darkness. Something was happening to Adam in this moment of silence.

He felt for the first time like a full equal to Antares and Launie, and to any mortal being in the whole universe. To his chagrin, he even felt flashes of superiority in understanding which, in a sense, were well-founded, for Antares and Launie had known of these things, and were merely reviewing them for the benefit of Adam.

He, like a child learning something new, felt his understanding soar so high, that it must surely leave the Centaurians far behind him in knowledge and awareness. Now he could look upon Launie, not as one inferior to her but, alas, perhaps even superior; and with a pang of regret he turned toward her.

In the eerie glow, close beside him, she presented a vision of sublime loveliness. Her calm, detached absorption in the Corona made her unaware of Adam's feelings. Her eyes were wide open, her lips parted softly. It was exquisite, thought Adam, to watch Launie surrender herself from the very soul.

Strangely, he was her master, for she was reachable, understandable. Why, he could supersede Leo in understanding now, and Launie was his by every law of nature, by every human right. Even her smile seemed to be waiting merely for him to decide to make her his.

The Corona shone brightly on the screen, the resolving point of all thoughts, of all desires, the fountain in which all things were cleansed. Launie was being cleansed spiritually, and suddenly Adam was not sure of himself. She could not look so bewitchingly lovely and not be attainable. She must, by any means he could use, be included in his little world, to be forever held in it, protected against any harm, to be loved as she should be loved.

He turned his eyes once more to the Corona, then back to Launie. Why, she had already changed in perspective! In his rapid changing of focus, she now stood out for what she truly was.

In the pure light and glory of the Corona, which again overcame him, Adam could see Launie as an equal and as a woman. She was at once a beautiful creature, free of negative qualities, and a fellow being in the vibrant universe who lent her beauty and her feelings to soften the otherwise grinding friction of mere existence. Her feminine attributes gave warmth and happiness to his masculine appreciation. She took on and nurtured what he merely observed, discarded. His history was given to her to be preserved for posterity. At this moment he was far ahead of her mentally, but it was only for this moment and only because she had agreed to bring him into the present experience.

Adam felt that he would lead her into new and better things, but Launie believed there were no better things than those she had already encountered, and which she absorbed with her entire being. Having become the epitome of womanhood to him, Adam saw in Launie not only a flower which would adorn the barren life of a man, but a delicate flower to be nurtured and cherished unto its fullest bloom. He saw her hidden beauty, saw that sometimes woman was unaware of the role she had to play, just as a man was unaware when he was being led on by that which he believed he was leading.

With so many thoughts and emotions racing through him, it was now difficult for Adam to know whether it was the Corona which revealed Launie in her true self or if it was Launie's presence which gave the Corona its divine semblance. Only one thing was he sure of: He could put the Corona into a file for future reference which would always be part of his inmost self, but he could not push Launie into the same memory file. She was not to be put into any cold storage for future reference. She was warmth and beauty; she was livingness and oneness now, not yesterday, not for tomorrow.

Suddenly Adam felt that a sin was laid bare before him. After all, he had a yesterday with Launie which he had nearly forgotten. He had forgotten the Launie of a few minutes ago, and the Launie he dreamed of tomorrow would be only the Launie of yesterday on the next day. But Launie did not fade and reappear with the march of time. She was always the same. She looked upon the Corona with that removed and distant look, far away from any man, yet in reality she would shortly be with some man again.

That man, no doubt, would be Leo.

Adam felt lost in an abyss where there was no time. Actually, only seconds had passed during these ponderings. Antares put his hand on one of the buttons of the cabinet and the Corona slowly faded from view. At the same moment the room became fully lighted again, and a man walked in without announcing himself.

It was Orion, one of the peers who served in duties around and with Saturn. Antares excused himself to attend to one of the units of the department. Adam, hardly over his meditation inspired by the Corona, found Orion fitting easily into the peaceful atmosphere. Launie rose from her chair and bowed slightly in greeting, which courtesy Orion returned to her. Adam rose from his own chair and added his greeting in the same manner.

"Adam, how would you like to spend the rest of this day in our elements and physics department?" Orion asked. "Tomorrow you will learn some of our ideals and aspirations, which are a strong part of our religious convictions. We long ago learned that matter and spirit are intercompounded, and we have not yet been able to find a single instance where one is apart from the other. But then, we still have so much to learn. Today you will be prepared in regard to our knowledge of the physical world so tomorrow's interview with Saturn will not be unintelligible to you."

"Indeed!" responded Adam happily. "It will be an experience I will look forward to with eagerness."

The group left the viewing room to stroll along the corridors. The next room they entered was rather large, with glass partitions marking it off into smaller areas throughout. Through the glass Adam could see section after section, in all of which people were busy at their work and study. From everywhere they looked up and smiled, all of them knowing this was Adam, the man from earth. Shortly, a young man came from one of the rooms and warmly welcomed the three of them, asking them to be seated at one of the round tables.

"This man is head teacher and student in the physics section, Adam, so you may call him Mercury. He is all science, and close to your sun in his observations and study. Also notice how handsome and alert this realist is," Orion said, in a spirit of light humor.

"Now, Orion," Mercury quickly retorted, "you know that I preach in our schools periodically. Sometimes I think I am more cut out to be a theologian than a physicist, or a 'realist,' as you call me, just as Adam, here. He knows well what I mean," he said, turning to Adam.

"Yes," Adam replied in a low voice. "Yes, I do understand. How you people surely know me, my actions and my thoughts! How on earth do you manage it?"

"Not on earth, Adam; on Andromeda," Launie quipped.

"Yes, Adam, on Andromeda," Mercury joined in. "We know, for instance, that you have read the treatise called 'The Nature of Infinite Entities'."

"Yes, I did read it. I found it so absorbing I still cannot take it from my mind when pondering any physical phenomenon," said Adam. "But, do you find that important in itself?"

"Adam," Orion offered, "one of the reasons you are here with us is because you did read that treatise and absorbed its meaning so fully. It grasps the truth of nature so well, so fundamentally accurately, that in abstract hypothesis it reaches out even beyond our practical accomplishments. If the science of the earth were to know it and comprehend it, the earth would be on its way to incredible scientific unfoldment. So busy would it become evolving materially that thoughts of conflict would simply cease to exist. Earth scientists would find all matter so awesomely beautiful it would respond to their probings like something conscious.

Your being aware of these things makes it obvious they are already known on earth, Adam, and thus you absolve us from interfering in any way with the predestined plan of evolution on earth. Now, nay I ask you if you feel you truly want the audience with Saturn tomorrow?"

"Yes, Orion. It may be the highlight of my entire visit on Andromeda. I feel greatly privileged by the invitation."

"Then I take my leave, and Saturn will prepare for tomorrow," Orion said, and he left Adam, Launie and Mercury to continue the discourse.

Chapter 8
NATURE OF INFINITE ENTITIES

"Adam," Mercury asked, "do you know how the author felt when he came upon the concept of the treatise, Nature of Infinite Entities?' "

"No, I do not know how he felt, but I also read the story of his experiences with visitors from space and, putting the two together, I can imagine how he must have felt."

"No, Adam; you cannot imagine. You have had a similar experience, called the sudden moment of enlightenment, the cosmic consciousness and many other names, but we shall call it the Cosmic Splendor, for it is just that. It comes only once in a lifetime. Many people seek it from the fountains of others and thereby lose any hope of attaining it. You cannot seek it, for in seeking it you lose it, but if you seek the truth and the light which makes a better person of you, you will one day know this moment of splendor. No one on earth can retain its fullness for long. The evolutionary stage of earthlings is too primitive as yet for your mortals to sustain its grandeur.

"Yet, remember this. There was one being on earth who was born with it, grew up in its glow, lived every moment in the fullness of it and lost it not even in the torture of the cross. Yes, read the story of Christ, and you will note this fact to stand out clearly throughout his thirty-three years."

"Wait a moment, Mercury," Adam interrupted. "I like this tremendously, but I thought I was in the physics department, and in the presence of a true physicist."

"Adam, Mercury is a true physicist, as you will see," Launie said, quick to defend Mercury even though Adam's words were far from challenging. She continued, "Our physics are somewhat ahead of yours; in fact, they are ahead by many hundreds of years. True physics merges into metaphysics, and true metaphysics must come upon physics. Neither is of the highest order unless it comes face to face with the other."

"All right, Adam," Mercury resumed. "You have seen our ships and observed their functions in outer space and within Andromeda, which is herself as superb as any of the craft we know. Indeed, you see a little world in Andromeda, selfsufficient, and evolving, though we are nearly four and a half light years distant from our home planet. These accomplishments come from reverence as much as from applied physics. We cherish everything about us, and our peers live with the delight of the Cosmic Splendor pervading their consciousness.

"Now, the physics," Mercury went on. "Try to recall the Nature of Infinite Entities' while I bring some of your own type of ginger ale to you. It was in such a bubbling liquid that this concept was first conceived in the author's mind."

Mercury left to get the ginger ale and Adam's eyes sought Launie's. What he beheld sent a warm thrill through his veins. Launie was looking at him as she had not looked before.

"Oh, Adam," she said, with a sigh. "Adam, I believe he is going to cut the thin veil that is between you and the Cosmic Splendor. Oh, Adam . . . you will see things that cannot be seen normally. You will hear music you do not hear now."

"Launie, how can I thank you for all this? Already I feel something of a new splendor. I do hope you have some way here of making me forget. Even a few months back on earth will be unbearable away from you. I will not be able to look upon another star without my heart breaking."

"You will not forget me, Adam, nor I you, and I promise, you will be more than just normally happy in the days to come," Launie reassured him, as Mercury returned carrying a tall glass filled with ginger ale, which he set on the table in front of Adam. It was sparkling and bubbling. Already, in anticipation, Adam thought he could feel the atmosphere becoming rarer and himself becoming lighter.

"No, Adam, this is pure ginger ale. There is nothing else to it. Take two sips and bring the glass up close to your eyes so you see nothing but the depths of the liquid," Mercury instructed.

Adam followed his advice. He drank, then looked into the glass, watching the bubbles rise steadily and gracefully to the top, small bubbles, little silver spheres fully enclosed by the sparkling liquid. How beautifully they remained spherical, in spite of their rapid upward ascent! If they would only stop for a moment and remain suspended so he could see them and ponder them. They were beautiful and they were intriguing, but it was much more exciting to look into Launie's eyes, to see her enticing smile.

Certainly, thought Adam, looking at these bubbles would not lavish the Cosmic Splendor upon his soul. Mercury spoke, slowly and encouragingly.

"Soon you will not see mere, gas-filled bubbles. Can you imagine how a man feels when a long search and hard work suddenly result in a new discovery? Can you imagine how one feels when his entire being, in one flashing moment, comes upon the truth that God is? It is not like the thrill of a child in receiving his long-wanted toy or gift, nor is it the same as the flush of love at first sight which is equally requited.

"Now see a man who is consumed with the desire to know the secrets of nature.

SON OF THE SUN: The Secret Of The Saucers

One by one, the known laws parade before his eyes, only to meet with the dead-end theory that atoms are little systems of spinning packets of energy, and such other erroneous notions as are held by contemporary science in general, including the theory that the sun will one day dim out and become dead, and that the universe is slowly dissipating into a frozen nothingness where all things return to limbo. No, this man felt there was more in the dynamic of nature than such unproductive ideas. Now, Adam, you may set the glass on the table.''

Adam complied. He noticed that Mercury and Launie had taken on heightened expressions of happiness. Their faces were calm, yet fully alive with some inner glow. Whatever their feelings might be, his own were at their very highest point, so, he thought, how much more joy could he hold?

"One day," Mercury went on, softly and slowly, "in the late summer of 1946, this man felt a change in everything. The ground seemed to become one with the air, with the sun, and, as the night approached, one with the stars.

"His sensitive nature was under perpetual stress, just in the effort of living. This night, his nerves tightened so he could not sleep. It was a typical summer's night in New Jersey. About 2:00 o'clock in the morning he was under the strain of a nervous headache, and rose from his bed to go to the kitchen. His wife and children were asleep, so he did not turn on the radio, although music would have helped him. Feeling hungry, he made a sandwich, filled a tall glass with ginger ale, and sat down at the table.

"He took a drink from the glass and munched on the sandwich. Why, he thought suddenly and inadvertently, does nature guard her innermost secrets so well? Why does she reveal them only slowly to man, and only after centuries of complex and exhausting research? At this moment, he was a materialist of the first water. Facts, logic and matter were all that made any sense.

"He had some saving grace, however. He probed wherever observation led him, he felt that the universe as a whole was rather intelligent, orderly and purposeful, and he was ready to admit any error he made, ready to admit another was right the instant he was proved right. These were the qualities which were to reward his confused and haphazard gropings, the qualities which alerted him to something strange in the atmosphere of this early morning.

"Roosters were crowing nearby, and the wind was blowing, yet in all this sound he sensed an unheard whisper. It was not in the air, but within him. He lifted the glass to eye level and stared into the liquid, seeking some relief from the tension in his head. The bubbles rose rapidly from the bottom. 'Why can't I know the true nature of the universe?' he asked, half of himself, half of the glass. 'After all, there is the Ether. I see the liquid as the Ether. Look at those bubbles going on and on, indifferent to my plea for knowledge. Just bubbles in the Ether, yet so hard to really comprehend.'

"He set the glass down on the table and began eating the sandwich. He felt a little better. The wind had died down to a whisper outside. The ache in his head was lessening as he relaxed. The kitchen in which he sat seemed to be receding, becoming surroundings more rare, more unfamiliar than wood and plaster. Once more he lifted up the glass to look into the 'ether' and the bubbles in it. Once more he pleaded, this time to a universe which was becoming more alive around him. 'Why, why can't I know? After all, every atom is only a bubble in the ether'. He had finished his sandwich and was now holding the glass with both hands.

"At that instant it struck him. His entire being fused explosively with a flash of glorious light, as white as the sun but casting no heat. Glory of glories! He had hit on the answer the first time. Yes, bubbles in the ether. Atoms were in reality bubbles in the ether!

"His head ceased to ache. His entire body now felt completely healthy, completely relaxed. There was strange but lovely music he could hear, and looking straight up into the air, he could see dazzling little faces smiling. They were as tiny as the bubbles in the glass, but much more dazzling. The hosts of the universe were acclaiming the fact that he had finally been ushered into a better concept of all Nature. He felt it so completely there was no doubt in his mind that the simple idea was being confirmed by actual Intelligence of some sort."

As Mercury finished, Adam lifted his own glass to his eyes once more, this time with something noble in his manner. Launie was carried away with the feeling that she was about to witness a man enter into the Cosmic Splendor. She thrilled from head to foot. Mercury, careful not to obstruct such a possibility or to force it, went on as if noticing nothing.

"At first, the music he thought he heard was in his own mind, but then we produced some real music for him, barely distinguishable from that which he imagined, so he did not know we were observing. Yes, there were faces looking on, smil ing and beaming, and there were voices from a million choirs truly singing. We on Andromeda celebrated openly. Nearly five years later our home planet received the news, and by that time we were making open contact with this man. It was Orfeo Angelucci.

Chapter 9
ADAM'S MOMENT OF ILLUMINATION

"His realization was such a simple truth. The complex part was to come. Could a mere bubble concept explain the grandeurs of nature? Not quite. Orfeo was momentarily in a world of his own, yet in communion with everything in the universe. He could see its pulsation, its rhythmic movement.

"He was new to such experiences, and he felt God was blessing his discovery. In the broadest sense it was blessed, but there are hosts in the universe to whom God gives the sublime pleasure of being His intermediaries, and it was these whom Orfeo saw in the ether, floating around with the bubbles.

"We have perfect motion pictures of those minutes. What a transformation came over him! His eyes were transfixed in high rapture and, like a musical record, the cosmos revolved around and around, giving up one secret after another. The simple became complex, then returned to the purely simple state of complete oneness."

Adam did not hear these last words of Mercury's. Both his hands were holding his glass. He was mesmerized by it. His right hand broke away and waved about as though leading an invisible orchestra, slowly and gracefully. It was not music he was directing, however. He was depicting to himself automatically what his mind was seeing abstractly, as though to capture each unveiling with confirmation of the hand. To him, at this moment, Launie and Mercury did not exist.

Mercury kept silent. The faces which now looked in deep interest from every room within the many glass partitions knew what was going to transpire within Adam. These people lived in Cosmic Splendor. They could sense its dawning in any other being. Launie was the only Alpha Centaurian there who was beside herself with ecstasy. Her face did a dance in expressions that were utterly beautiful, and her ever-fresh spirit gushed like a fountain within her and sprayed its mists about her. Everyone around was in love with Launie. She knew it and felt it, but her love was now for Adam. She was his godmother in this moment of his being born again. A new Adam would emerge from the baptism of the Cosmic Splendor. This new Adam would never know the meaning of the words death or

SON OF THE SUN: The Secret Of The Saucers

oblivion. Indeed, Adam had never known their meaning in a negative way, but he had before thought they existed, and that thought alone was death. The new-born Adam would know the truth of Nature and know that he had always been a segment of it, and always would be. He had a glimpse into the inexhaustible womb of Nature, and had seen that it is ever creating, never dissipating.

Launie and Mercury left their chairs and went to a window. Neither said a word. Their main concern was to leave Adam undisturbed, incubating his new self in the bright light of truth.

After a time Launie turned to look, and saw Adam sitting in faraway meditation. Perhaps it was her mother instinct, perhaps it was her mating instinct, but she could not stand this gap between them any longer and hurried to Adam's side. As though it had been planned in advance, so well was the attunement of their minds timed, that a new Adam looked into her eyes as she stood close to him.

"It's all right, Launie. I see the real you now. I see the real Mercury, the real things as they throb in life in all their motionless being. I see with new understanding the greatness behind all those lovely faces looking at me.

"Oh, Launie! Would you believe I saw Eternity? Please sit down, both of you," Adam requested, as Mercury also came back to the table. "Do not tell me any more about physics. Rather, let me tell you. Stop me if I make a mistake, but I must tell it; I cannot hold it. Even though you know these things, I must repeat them. Please bear with me."

Mercury could see that Adam was speaking more to himself and to the universe than to either Launie or him. The people who had been still in rapt attention behind the partitions went back to their work, knowing that Adam had broken through the thin veil.

"I came face to face with Eternity and Perfection," Adam said, speaking into infinite space and to no one in particular.

"Perfection took two forms. One was the Ether and the other was the Absence of Ether. The Ether is the only substance that truly exists. If it existed by itself and were not separated evenly and equally, one particle from another, there would be no light, no life, and no motion. Only absolute zero would prevail in the entire universe. No power known to man could convert any part of the ultimate particle of that Ether to anything lesser. It cannot be ground or cut down.

"There was a separation of these particles, though, and the separation was exactly equal in volume to the volume taken up by the solid ether itself. This separation, this moving aside of the particles, caused a space where there was no Ether, no anything, and the Ether tried to fill this space again. As it did so, new areas of the Absence of Ether emerged. Some of these became permanent as little spheres or cavities or bubbles, which were formed by the placement of Ether particles in a curved position, or in the form of the arc. Once formed into spherical shapes, these little vacuums could not be filled again because Ether particles had placed

197

themselves in a spherical and arched position around an area.

"Throughout all space the Ether heaved up and became separated, in exactly one-half. Its action could be likened to a huge block of metal which appears solid. Suddenly something separates all the atoms from one another, leaving a space between them equal to that occupied by the atoms themselves. This block of metal would no longer be solid, but would be fluid, gaseous and in motion. The atoms move around and try to fill up the dividing vacuums, but for some reason cannot. Thus, half the volume would be absence of Atoms, and half would be Atoms, but motion of the atoms would be the rule.

"Yet, the atoms themselves are mere bubbles in this Ether. Some of these bubbles are too large because they were formed at the speed of light when the Ether tried, by its own pressure stress, to fill in the vacant space, and the arcs of the bubbles are wobbly and unstable. Eventually each one collapses, and again at the speed of light is formed into a smaller and more perfect bubble, very stable. Part of the bubble is now squeezed and pushed around in the Ether. It moves the Ether aside as it wiggles about. This elongated, formless cavity is eventually directed toward the perfect bubble, because that perfect bubble causes the Ether to be disturbed. This disturbance is the cause of waves, both gravitational and magnetic.

"Countless trillions of these arrangements all over the infinite reaches of the Ether make all the things that exist. There are only the absolute and solid Ether and the absolute and perfect spaces of the Absence of Ether. The Absences of Ether appear as formed spheres and halos, such as the planet Saturn symbolizes, and the elongated darting forms make what we call light rays. The motion between these two states makes all motion and is even what we call Life.

"In the same instant I realized this truth, I saw Eternity. Eternity is not time, which never was and never shall be, but is Motion. Eternity is that which occurs in the smallest particle of the Ether or the smallest part of any vacuum in the Ether, and occurs at the speed of light. Thus it is always Now at all places, under any circumstance. Absolute energy and motion can be attuned to, anywhere in the universe, and we know this attunement as magnetic dynamic, or gravitational dynamic. There is no other force existent anywhere, any time. The Ether acts, and the vacuum reacts; or the vacuum acts, and the Ether reacts, always at the speed of light. Life is the result, and is the third harmonic product of these motions.

"Because of such perfect balance between Ether and No Ether, and the one condition upheaving with universal force against the other, I see what earth sight identifies as atomic energy, the force of Life, the contact with God, the Intelligence of the universe, and the cause of causes, the effect of cause.

"Ah, indeed, I see it all. If the Ether occupied all space, it would be frozen into motionlessness and absolute zero. By the same token, if nothingness occupied all space, it would also be a frozen state of absolute zero. But the two states exist together, therefore there is no absolute zero condition anywhere in the universe, and no man or being can ever make it exist. Yet, and I say 'yet' with my whole soul, the states of absolute heat and light do exist. They exist in every light ray, in every photon, in everything that has motion. The overflow of absolute light results in what we call Life. Life, therefore, is the left-over energy of the entire Cosmos. It is grounded back, like electrical currents, to the source from whence it came, to come forth again like flaring energy captured in symmetrical forms and functions we call man, woman, and angels. It is neither added in the universe, nor is it ever diminished. What we use in one place is not exhausted but is directed back to origin, or converted into another symmetrical form. In atoms it is expenditure. In human beings it is death. Yet the conversion makes for new births, be they of new particles, or of new living entities. Therein is the Eternity of both matter and life. There is no death. There is no such thing as oblivion.

"Even as the zenith of Illumination ebbs back from me into the cosmos, I am as bewildered as before, for I still cannot know the why and wherefore of it all, why man and woman, why the seed must exist before the end product and yet the product produces the seed. I am now further from the answer to which came first, the chicken or the egg, applied to all things, but I have seen where the egg is born. I have seen the dynamical force, the essence behind all eggs, behind all entities. This force, though it be the inherent force of the universe, though it be the exact measure of the stress of the ether in its attempt to fill the empty spaces which divide it, also manifests as the gentle force of life, of love, and of intelligence.

"In a flash, I have also seen that the gentle flux of that force which is life and intelligence can arrange it and bring it to a focus for tremendous expression, whereby the atomic bombs explode. Yet there is no destruction, for it takes intelligence to bring together the atomic bombs, and no force is greater than its creator.

"I see now the potential of love, be it partial love which attracts man and woman, or be it total love which ultimate ascension to knowledge bestows upon a being.

"I see that all matter originates from motion of the Ether, its first manifestation being in the form of a hydrogen atom, and that the additional stress of the Ether gradually forms more complex expressions as other atoms, all being basic molecules of hydrogen-within-hydrogen. Thus, for example, iron is not more than a number of interwoven atoms, and some excess vacuum given off as what earthmen call energy, which forms other atomic particles, and so on with all the elements. I can see that substances made by such atomic interwoven matter can produce materials able to withstand even the universal forces which have welded them together, dissolving only at the dynamic point of equal stresses.

"Even spirits shall not be at-one until these truths are met face to face and understood in pure knowledge. We must learn. We must learn every inch of the way. We cannot jump to spiritual perfection and remain indifferent or resentful of material facts, nor can we learn material perfection except through spiritual awareness. Indeed, I beheld in the Ilumination that they are one and the same, and in my consciousness they shall remain so.

"From the atom to the solar system, to the galaxies, to the universe and to the beyond-the-beyond, Purpose remains unaltered. In that Purpose, in that Eternal Light, my whole being tells me the Throne of the Creator is. I can never understand it nor describe it, and no one in the whole universe may describe it, be they primitive beings or Archangels. Any descriptions of the Creator written, voiced, or otherwise enunciated, have been distortions of the Truth, as all earth records are. We must aspire and learn, step by step, to know the real truth, and the truth shall make us free only when it fully responds to every call we send forth to it.

"Now I feel I understand the universe as much as any mortal being, and more than many who are still to come upon the Illumination. I could build superb space ships and conquer disease, but I need the help of millions who would understand my plans and blueprints with keen perception. There would be much work and play for everyone. There would be no room for hate, jealousy, or ignorance. Indeed, one person having such negative characteristics would impede the work of millions. There must be no imperfection in perfection. Even within Andromeda we could be short of such an enterprise. On earth there is not one being who would qualify. Now, with this illumination having pervaded me like an exposure to radiation, where can I go to fulfill one first small step toward this end? The lips which would claim to be worthy are the least worthy, but the lips which will say, 'I wish to learn,' reveal the hunger of the heart, whose need is for the light. Churches fall and crumble by the thousands, but not one school has ever receded into dust.

"Preachers give up in disgust because of their own ignorance, but not once has a scientist fallen to say he has no faith in what he has learned. Empty temples flow and ebb, but schools only grow. God does not want imperfect or ignorant angels among His Hosts. He wants only those who have attained the fullness of understanding through evolution and learning.

"We find that all material is wealth, and all spirit is material understanding. Man thinks that gold is the noble metal, but he will learn that gold is worthless, and that silicon, the most abundant mineral, is also the most priceless, for it will give him not only crystal functions, but plastic strengths. There we see another aspect of Purpose—whereby God has lavished in abundance that which man will need most. Man must learn the true values from the false, yet to this day he knows only the false, for he has pursued only the false."

Adam was coming out of his illuminated moment. Mercury and Launie were transfixed at his words by the light which shone upon his face. As soon as he had regained a more normal composure, he looked at Mercury and Launie and said in conclusion:

"Whoever gave me the name Adam in your society did rightly, for Adam was the name of the symbolic first man of earth. I will be dedicated to bringing the light of illumination, much like a rebirth, to my fellow beings on earth, no matter how much longer I am to live upon that sphere. I will fear no evil, for truth is with me." Thus Adam finished speaking of what he learned in his "physics lesson."

"Yes, Adam, indeed, Truth and one make a majority," Mercury added, to affirm and to welcome Adam back to normal perception.

"I encompassed the innermost dynamic of the universe, Mercury, and I saw that there is no such thing as evil as it is generally regarded; at least not on earth, for evil is nothing more than the behavior of ignorance. Even the willfully malicious are nothing more than ignorant ones. Evil in itself does not exist, for it would mean action opposite to action, and such cannot be. What is called evil is nothing more than action resulting from the morbid minds of the ignorant. Thus, physics analyzes the most dynamic or the most subtle behavior of life." Adam was ready to speak again, but Mercury cut him off masterfully.

"Well, Adam, do you wish to visit our physics department and see what we have that might be new to you?" he asked. But Adam was wise. He was in the Light, and could reason and speak on the same level with Mercury. He could see through any subterfuge also.

"I do not believe so, Mercury. This glass has given me all I can absorb in physics. I feel that anything you can now show me would be anticlimax. With humility, I can say that I understand all you have accomplished on Andromeda, and can even foresee, as your peers can foresee, what you are yet to discover from time to time. I have had decades of academic learning here in a few minutes. Unless, of course, you feel there is something that would be very new to me, why should I take up your time?"

"No, Adam, there is nothing that would be new to you. Whatever there is here that would be new to you cannot be shown, for the divine code of no interference with your evolution must be kept. My part with you is ended, although the fruit of our meeting has just begun. I leave you again with Launie. Thank you so much for spending this irreplaceable moment of your life with me," Mercury said, in farewell.

"And I thank you, Mercury," Adam replied, "for the most wonderful lesson in pure science."

Launie rose from her chair, bowed slightly, and soon Adam and she were atop the roof again and entering their small basketlike craft. Once more she manipulated the small control box which started the craft off, becoming one of the hundreds that went to and fro in this little enclosed world of the ship Andromeda.

Launie was quiet, a smile of satisfaction on her face. Adam looked at her, completely lost in admiration and love.

"I have had a few lessons already, Launie, and I seem to have graduated from them with little effort. It seems to me that my longest lesson is the one you are giving me, and I still can't know what the nature of it is. When do I graduate from your department?"

"Never, Adam," Launie answered. "From some courses and lessons there is no graduating. You just go on and on, like everyone else does. The pupils and teachers may change, but the lesson, never. Everyone is a pupil and everyone is a teacher. Before you leave Andromeda you will see someone else reflected in me, and your lesson shall proceed from there."

Adam could not take his eyes from her. The universe, true enough, was filled with infinite expressions of itself, and she was at this moment one of its masterpieces.

"Where are we going now, Launie?" he asked.

"Directly home. You have had a full day, and you shall spend a few hours reading. Tomorrow we have an audience with Saturn. Here we are over the cottage," Launie said, as she directed the craft to the solid floor of Andromeda.

Inside the cottage, a boy and girl awaited Launie and Adam. They had brought a book and had laid it on the table as they turned to greet the two adults. Both appeared to be about ten years of age.

"We have brought it, Launie," said the boy, picking the book up again and handing it to Adam. "We completed it just a short while ago."

Adam looked at its title, "The Secret of the Saucers," and asked, "I have never heard of this. When was it published?"

"It has not been published as yet on earth, but it is soon to go to the press," said Launie, "and this is the finished product as the publisher has decided to print it. It will be released within three months on earth."

Adam got down on one knee, and the children came close to him.

"How old are you?" he asked.

"Oh, in your terms, Adam, we would be ten years of age. However, we are a little older than that," the girl replied.

"You are as pretty as Launie, little one. It makes me feel so happy to know that beauty and grace are abundant in this grand universe and that nobleness goes along with it, as the young lad here proves," said Adam, kissing both on the cheek.

"Rise up, Adam," came Launie's somewhat emotional voice. She came up to him and kissed him gently on the lips, saying,

"Happy birthday."

Adam was pleasantly surprised. "But it is not my birthday, Launie."

"You have had a new birth in awareness through your unfoldment today, Adam. You have emerged into the grand world of our science, having broken the veil from the Cosmic Splendor. You were not aware of that. You did not even hear all of Mercury's words as he spoke. Oh, indeed, Adam, happy birthday," Launie added. "You can never again fall low in consciousness and awareness."

"You are a fortunate man, Adam," the boy said lightly. "A kiss from Launie is

SON OF THE SUN: The Secret Of The Saucers

rare. It would behoove you to have an unfoldment daily."

Launie shooed the youngsters out. Laughing, she said to them, "Now, both of you go back to the classroom. I shall be there soon, and we shall discuss Adam's experiences of this day. Tell the others to be ready for the discussion."

Launie then went into the kitchen and returned with a glass of water, handing it to Adam. As he took it in hand, she dropped a small pellet in, bringing the water to a sparkling fizz.

"Drink it, Adam. It will give you calm vitality for a few hours. You can read the book while I am gone, and you will have finished it by the time I return. It is not very long and is easy to read."

Adam took a few sips, then sat down in an easy chair. She looked at him enchantingly and asked, "What number do you wish to hear, Adam?" She remained poised for a dance she felt coming upon her.

"Siboney!" he exclaimed, and in two seconds there came a most enchanting rendition from the wall. Launie whirled into her dance. Sheer delight of being alive gave her the impetus and the expression. Her vigor was modulated by the grace of her swaying and pausing, by her foot and arm movements. There was not a flaw in Launie's dance, though it was unrehearsed. As the music neared the end, she danced toward the door, and soon was gone.

Adam drank the rest of the nectar and began to read the book. He read on, page after page, until the end. Then he turned again to the chapter, "My Awakening on Another Planet," trying to comprehend some of the symbolism and various points which, even to his reborn awareness, seemed inconsistent with reality.

But he decided that he would need the help of one of his hosts, perhaps Saturn, to clarify some questions in his mind. It was comforting to know that another man of earth had been here before, even if not in physical reality. Certainly this author must have been given the exact description of things here to have written of them. He, Adam, was not only here in fact, but learning much more than this book revealed.

He closed his eyes to meditate, wishing there were music to be heard. As if by magic his desire was granted. Soft music pealed throughout the room. These, he thought, are systems of the highest order. His eyes still closed, he felt a faint breeze close to him and looked up. Launie stood smiling before him.

"Well, Adam, my day's work is done. You look as though you have read the book thoroughly. Tomorrow we visit Saturn. Tonight we dine out, as you would say on earth. This will be better than New York, Paris, or Hollywood. We shall have music and singing and dancing such as ...."

"Wait a moment, Launie!" Adam exclaimed jubilantly. "Say those words again, please, and include Seattle. I had forgotten there were such places. Seattle has beautiful women, too. Yes, it is a beautiful world, no matter what its state of evolution. Shall I dress?"

203

"You are dressed, Adam. Look at yourself."

Indeed he was. His clothes were of a different color, soft and silken looking. He went to the mirror in his room. Blue background, with starry dots and gentle rays. How on Andromeda did they do this? He went back to Launie in the living room.

Her clothing also had changed in the moment he had left her. She just stood there facing him in her loveliness, smiling like one who had just given her friend a cherished present. He could say nothing in reply but laughed aloud with glee.

"Do I have to tell you how it is done," she asked, "after the lesson in physics you have had today?"

"No, Launie. I guess I should know as much of your possibilities as any earthling could."

"Adam, feel at home tonight. Remember that even though my people are not native to the solar system which is yours, we are native to your grand galaxy, the Milky Way. So, celestially speaking, we are one and the same," Launie said to him.

"I won't feel strange," Adam assured her, offering his arm for her to take. "We're off, Launie. Where to?"

"Oh let us just say to the Cafe Venus," and arm in arm they went out, to walk along the grassy paths and streets.

Chapter 10
A NIGHT OUT ON VENUS

The Cafe Venus was ready for them. Tables had been bedecked with gay table-cloths. Plates and silverware were familiar to Adam. All was arranged much as a fine restaurant would be in any city of earth. An elegant stage and elaborate scenery adorned the front of the large dining room. The music was soft and soothing. No one made Adam feel conspicuous by undue attention, though all knew he was an honored guest from earth.

They were escorted to a table, and as soon as they were seated one wall became a three-dimensional television screen. Sailing ships on a realistic sea were shown, and Columbus' landing on the eastern shores of the Atlantic—an actual picture four hundred and fifty years old—was viewed, the voices of Columbus and his men plainly heard. Then the Mayflower giving its passengers to America, as well as many other outstanding events of earth's history were shown, all of them actual recordings.

After dinner there was an hour's stage show. Adam knew it would be many centuries before anything like this could be reproduced on earth. Had he not taken the nectar it would have been too much for him to see and hear. Included were a few of the best compositions of earth, arranged in the incredibly beautiful orchestrations of the Alpha Centaurians.

Among the several hundred diners this evening, not one of the peers was there, but all of the diners were elegant in appearance and behavior.

On the way home, Adam noticed nearly no traffic overhead. In the dome-like sky above Andromeda he saw the heavy clouds again, all moving in one direction, with occasional darts of lightning flitting here and there. Strangely, there was no thunder.

They approached the home cottage, which Adam noticed was the third one from the corner. He paused awhile and looked at the corner house. Then he looked at the second. His face lighted up as he looked at Launie, who was already smiling at him in advance confirmation.

"Launie!" he exclaimed, pointing to the corner house, and to the second one.

"Yes," said Launie. "It is. You have really read that book, haven't you? The comer cottage is Lyra's, and the next one to it is Orion's. The third is mine, and for a while yours also. You go to sleep now and rest, Adam. When you awaken we shall go to Saturn. Neptune will be present, as will Orion, Lyra, and myself. Our meeting will be in Lyra's dwelling."

Adam looked up to the center of the five miles' high ceiling of Andromeda. Funny, he thought, that since he had left earth he had not seen the sun, nor the slightest sign of it.

Chapter 11
ADAM LEARNS ETERNITY

Adam paused in his story. We noticed through the window that it was getting brighter outside.

"Well, Adam," I said. "Speaking of the sun, you are about to see it soon. Here comes the dawn again. We have consumed two entire nights."

"Yes, Orfeo, and tonight I give the climax of my story to you and, I hope, to the world," he said. "Shall we have breakfast in town together this morning? We won't discuss the story to come at all. We'll talk of other things."

I was glad to be with him as much as possible, and agreed to breakfast. It was Sunday morning. Little by little the town awoke to life, the people preparing to go to various churches. After breakfast we parted, and I rode around town for awhile, wondering if Adam would be among the churchgoers.

Perhaps earth's evolutionary stage is young as yet, I thought. Perhaps it is un-knowing in comparison to the higher estates, but it felt good and homey to be snuggled in its environs; to know that at least its past had brought it thus far, and the future would most certainly bring it further upward. After two nights with Adam and his story, the normal pace of the good earth seemed restful to me.

So I decided to attend a church, any church; it did not matter which one. I went as far as the door of one but did not enter. I tried another and found myself unable to enter that one, also. Then I thought I would drive over to the Catholic church, my own church. Once more, at the very door, something within me made it im-possible to go in. Not far from this church is the Oasis of Maru, where eighteen palm trees still survive out of the original twenty-nine, from which the town of Twentynine Palms derived its name.

For many centuries it was a drinking place for local and wandering Indians. This morning, as I looked toward it, I felt an urge to go see it just to find out how high the water at the natural well was.

The water was slightly below the top of the well. I walked through the vegeta-tion and came upon the stone marker of a lone grave which I had seen many times. It was the burial place of a little girl who died there in the 1800's while crossing the desert with her mother and father, pioneers of the West.

My thoughts went back many decades, trying to visualize this family crossing the country, braving its hazards and hardships. A little girl, tired and dying in the desert, far from her own civilization of the time, alone. Alone, that is, except for her communion with her Creator.

Where was God in that lonely moment? Was the Father-head indifferent to the plight of this little girl and her parents as they moved on westward, leaving her small body buried in a lone grave? And the parents, was there anything in life for them that would justify existence itself? Death awaited them also, as it awaits everything that lives. The happiest existence would be grotesque if one stopped to think about it. If God had forsaken that little girl, was His attention with other people? If so, His Infinite Omnipotence surely was limited.

No, she was not forsaken. After all, was it not this very indifference of Nature, which is of God, with which all the patriarchs and prophets had argued? No man is a true believer unless he can stand and argue with Nature, call for some manifestation, call for assistance. God cannot be hurt. A man who is aware of the all-presence of the ultimate Intelligent Power knows that no supplication, no plaintive argument, can faze It. A man of little faith will not argue with God, feeling he is only talking to himself.

As I thought these thoughts the very desert floor, the oasis, the little girl, everything, seemed to be welling up with an answer. An airplane droned overhead, a passenger plane. People were coming out of the nearby church and driving off in shining automobiles. Modern homes were everywhere in the distance.

And there were graves of those who had passed on since. I had my answer. Nature is not indifferent; it merely waits, having all Eternity to accomplish its Purpose. For untold centuries this desert lay here as if by some accident of Creation. Some years ago a little flower from its own civilization came by and lay her body down in seeming bleakness and loneliness. But in a few years a transformation occurred. As her eyes closed did she perhaps see that day not too far off, when other graves would surround her own? Could she see the desert around her adorned with better and better homes? Could she imagine such chariots as the automobiles, or her own humanity in flying machines zooming over her resting place?

No, no place is so remote that God has not laid out a plan for it. I felt satisfied; my church this morning was the well in the Oasis of Maru.

Was I not directed by some unseen Power? Why was it that I could not enter any of the three churches? To come to the Oasis was the last thing in my mind at the start. Ah, yes. Perhaps these things would come out tonight, when Adam concluded his story.

* * *

That night, knowing he was close to Lyra's cottage and Orion's abode and anticipating the audience with Saturn and the others in Lyra's home, Adam thought he would be long in getting to sleep because of his restlessness. He had not seen any sign of the sun in such a long time, yet was closer to it by millions of miles than he ever had been on earth, and the idea suddenly cast a sleepy mood over him. He went to bed and indeed he did sleep, waking up the next morning fresh and sprightly, ready for anything. He heard Launie moving around in the cottage, but after dressing he found no breakfast ready.

"This morning," she said, "we shall have breakfast with the peers in Lyra's home. Oh, Adam, it is hard for me to realize the pleasures of these times that you have helped me obtain. You may feel the equal of each and all of us today, for the things to be talked of are not better known by one than by the others. Today, in the presence of such speculations, you and I are equal with our peers. Can you get the full implication of that; can you feel the warmth of Creation which will make itself manifest to us?"

"I do, Launie. I surely do," Adam spoke, fervently. "Even now I have climbed the ivory tower, and have reached you."

"Fine," she replied, looking tenderly and understandingly into his eyes. "But everyone is already at Lyra's and waiting for us to arrive, so we must hurry. Saturn, Neptune, Lyra, and Orion—all waiting for us. Just imagine," she concluded, half dreamily.

Within a few moments they walked into Lyra's house, which was made to resemble one of the fine homes of earth, and Adam felt a glow of comfort and welcome surge through his entire being.

Six teenagers served them — three young lads and three maidens—one for each guest. They went about their business of serving without a flaw, not interfering in any way with the dining or the conversation of the guests. They served the table with delight and enterprise, as though it were a high privilege. At the end of breakfast the guests went into the comfortable living room, while the young ones set everything back in order and left unobtrusively.

All sat down in the living room except Neptune and Saturn. Saturn walked around slowly and majestically. Neptune stood in quiet reflection. As Saturn came toward Adam, he asked, "My son, what do you consider to be the finest piece of written matter pertaining to earth and its life?"

This caught Adam by surprise. He had never given such things any thought, but, being straightforward and honest, he answered in the best way he could.

"The Holy Bible, of course. It is the foundation of my very civilization."

Saturn reached his chair and sat down. Neptune sat in his own chair only after Saturn was fully settled in comfort.

"What would you say, Adam, about the Bible? Is it a detailed history and prognosis, or is it in the main an allegoric and symbolic scripture of human life on earth?" Saturn continued, after he was seated.

"I would say," replied Adam, still vigorous and alert, "that it is entirely an allegoric scripture, and a very good prognosis of the future of my civilization. If it were a detailed history and an example of the accomplishments of genius, it falls short and is superseded by many other written records, and even by novels. Why, there are Homer and Shakespeare and Scott and Bacon and Dante and so many inspired, accomplished works of literature. But not one is greater in all its fullness than just one page—any page—out of the Bible. For the Bible is allegoric and symbolic to a degree that reaches Infinity."

"Would you say, then, that it is the Word of God?" Saturn asked.

Suddenly Launie stood up, looked tenderly at Adam, and said, "Wait before you answer that, Adam." With that she was off to the kitchen. Quickly she returned with a glass of ginger ale, and handed it to him.

"There is nothing but ginger ale in that glass, Adam. Take two sips and look into it before you answer Saturn."

"You have a good lawyer, Adam," smiled Neptune. "Not that you need her, but she is one of countless millions on your side. So feel free, and feel sure that the universe itself listens to you at this moment."

Even as Neptune spoke, Adam could see the smiles on the faces of Saturn, Orion and Lyra, and the somber, loving depths in the eyes of Launie. Once again she was his nurse. He drank twice, and looked into the glass. The crystal clear liquid was the ether before his eyes, the bubbles were atoms, molecules, or entire galaxies. He was one with all, and all was one with him. He could ask any question, he could answer any question.

"Yes, Saturn," he spoke up. "It is the Word of God. Just as much so as the truth from the mouths of babes is the Word of God. Just as much so as what I am now saying or will ever say is the Word of God. Just as much so as any word, from any source, is the Word of God. Some words are mistaken and some are correct. It is not God which is mistaken, but His creatures who grope for their way back to Him who make mistakes, hold on to them for awhile, and then cast them aside for the more true things which lead to Him. There is as much room for error on the way back to God as there is for the correct. Like pioneers, we must forge our way back to Him and His Glory. For that the Creative Fatherhead awaits, nothing less, nothing more."

"Whether you are right, Adam, or whether you are wrong, I frankly admit I do not know, but I agree with your attitude completely," Saturn said. "Now that you have assumed a position equal to the moment, may I proceed to speak, promising at the same time not to break through any premise or salient that has not already been established somewhere on earth?"

"Indeed, Saturn, speak at will, and I will not disturb you unless I have a question or a challenge," Adam replied.

All faces turned to Adam, including Launie's. All seemed to ask in silence, "A challenge? Challenge Saturn?" But all faces melted back to thoughtful truth, a truth which silently said, "Why not?"

And Adam looked at the glass of bubbling ginger ale, symbolic of the ether, of all matter and life. After all, he was a son of bubbles in the ether, and Saturn himself was no more than that.

"And then, Adam," Saturn went on, "there was Genesis and there were Adam and Eve and their sons Cain and Abel, the first beings on earth. Yet Cain went forth eventually to meet the wrath of whole nations. From where did these nations arise so fast, and how did they know that Cain had the sin of slaying his brother on his conscience? Is that not just allegorical? Yet, could any playwright be so brief and so symbolic?

"Then there was Daniel in the lions' den. And Elijah went up in a flying and flaming chariot. And Ezekiel saw the wheels. And Noah and his Arc survived the deluge. And Samson alone stood up to nations. And David, the boy, wrote psalms and slew Goliath. And then he became sinful, king, and pure again. And Moses was born into the palace of a Pharaoh, to turn and lead a slave nation back; back not to freedom, but to wickedness and the wilderness.

"You see, Adam, Moses led a mass of people out of bondage of other people, but not out of evil. The people had to find their own way out of evil. And Joshua did not do better by breaking down the gates of Jericho, or its walls. Remember always that evil in itself is ignorance, and therefore ignorance is evil. Shed light on any darkness and it is no longer dark. Shed knowledge on ignorance and ignorance no longer exists. The love of pure learning is the only true virtue that exists, and apathy and care-not attitudes are the only sins that be. The rankest atheism is nothing more than the manifestation and expression of lazy minds and ignorant souls. Allegories and symbolic expressions are the underlying and steadfast truths of things that were and are yet to be. No building project could be started without the blueprint, just as no blueprint could be produced without the ideal. People gawk at a building but admire it not, for they do not consider the architect, the builder, or the conceiver. And so all things that are not comprehended in the fullest shall crumble, but first shall crumble those who have not comprehended what was lavished upon them, and then the lavished plenty shall topple upon them.

"This is not materialist idealism, for what is made as a result of man's thinking and ideal is of a high order. Some may frown on the very notion of seeing a material product assembled by man, but these same ones will bow their heads and thank God for bread and fruit, thank Him at every meal. Yet, is not food as material as anything could possibly be? Some thank God for health, but is not the seeking of health, with no effort to learn why it should be, as materialistic as anything could be? Indeed, in my concept, it is far worse. People who seek spiritual healing as something given them by God for nothing and not given others by the same God, are seeking material repairs for a material body. Not in all the history of our Alpha

SON OF THE SUN: The Secret Of The Saucers

Centaurian home has one plea for healing by merely praying for it or asking for it been answered by God directly. Neither have we observed it to occur in the history of any other planet.

"In the beginning there was the thought, and the thought became Word and the Word became worlds and life. That still remains as the dynamic, the beginning and the end of everything. From imperfection all things must evolve to perfection, and the order and the wherewithal abound within all things to evolve. Once set in motion, God has spoken to or replied to none of the lesser creation. As the lowly beginnings rose to high perfection, the risen ones were given much dominion. It is these who are intermediaries between man and the Supreme Intelligent Power, for whom the name God so well fits. Of course, 'God' is not God's name, for every language has a different name. No one knows the true name of God. A thought is the best means by which we can approach the truth of Him."

Saturn spoke calmly and smoothly. None would disturb him before the end of his talk.

"I do believe that neither God nor His Hosts favor a little old lady in fervent prayer over a tyrannical and fierce overlord of people. At times, it does seem as though pleas and prayers are answered, but always there has been a third element entering the situation. A time may have arrived for a given law or condition of nature to turn the events in the other direction, or in other cases some intervention, not interference, was in order by the higher hosts. We are mere mortals, even as you, and we have interceded many times when the situation warranted. Your visit here is such an example.

"Now, Adam, feel free to speak or ask any question you wish," Saturn concluded.

"I find myself in harmonious agreement with what you say, Saturn, or you would not have interfered with my evolution by telling me so. But for the sake of discussion, and for the record, I do say that the Bible gives many references to man speaking with God. Moses and others have let it be written so, and did not Christ, at the very end, ask the Father to remove this cup from him if it be His Will? Did he not ask why the Father had forsaken him?" Adam inquired.

"To be sure, Adam, these things are so written. But was the cup removed? No, it was not. Was there an answer to why the Father had forsaken His son? No, the events went on as if only the people of earth existed, and no Higher One at all. There was no answer or interference. As for Moses, remember it is written that he did not see God, but spoke with a 'Spirit.' In other words, he heard a Voice."

"But, Saturn," broke in Adam, "one of the crucial things of the Scriptures is the tablet whereon the Ten Commandments are written. Were these not forged into the stone by God?"

"It is a point well taken, Adam," said Saturn. "But notice the simplicity of the Ten Commandments. They are commandments, and there is not one element of learning contained in them. Even the most primitive human could have originated them. That a mass of people had to be commanded such simple facts by a Supreme Being only shows that the morals of the people must have been base. It would be ridiculous to have to remind a highly civilized person to adhere to such commands, for such a person would not think of behaving in a manner contrary to them anyway."

Launie rose, went into the kitchen and quickly returned with a plastic plate, setting it before Saturn.

Saturn looked at it momentarily, glanced at Launie, then asked Adam:

"As for the fusion of the commandments on the tablet; do you mean like this?"

As the plate lay on the floor Adam saw the Commandments burned into it, and heard plainly a slight purring sound. That was enough. Adam needed no more. But he had another question, which he asked sincerely and slowly.

"Saturn, was it your people who conversed with Moses?"

"That we cannot answer. No, in no way can we offer you any answer. But there are hosts far above us in stature. Inasmuch as all high orders are learning, learning toward God, everything is in a sense the Word of God.

"There is a purpose to everything; and the purpose is the plan. So it is the Word. Whoever can see the purpose and the plan, even in a small way, he speaks in the essence of the Word. Thus, remember that allegory and symbology live long after history dies. The symbology and allegoric nature of the Scriptures make them of eternal value.

"Many ages ago, our civilization was where yours is today. Our sciences were theoretical and problematical, our creeds and doctrines rested purely on allegory and symbolism. Then, one person brought forth a concept of the nature of nature which served as a point of departure from the bottom up, and answered all questions that could be raised. It not only served us materially but opened up the human vista to such truths that our spiritual essence gradually rose with it.

"Before that we had many differences. There were those who would not eat meat because it meant the slaughter of animals, and on that single premise they warped their own souls, killing not the body but the soul, which is far worse. They could not see that by not eating meat they were killing millions of animals by merely not creating a demand for them. They could not see that in the final analysis everyone kills by merely being born. Parents are killers, for their children must die. People kill many germs and step on many insects, and never know or give it a thought. Also, they must themselves die. Is it not all killing? Since all life must die, creation itself is the greatest killer."

Saturn continued. "You see, there is a plan and a purpose, and those two are the only eternal life that is, the only things which cannot be killed. Has it not been taught on earth that you must not fear who can kill the body, but fear those who can kill the soul?

"Thus, you can see that whosoever would mislead a child, or anyone, is a killer of the first water. Such a one also holds back evolution and retards the time of perfection."

As Saturn finished, Adam quickly commented, "Saturn, we all speak and think of perfection. But since all action is learning, and we must have positive and negative action, what do we really mean by perfection?"

"Perfection, Adam, already exists in all things. The only imperfection is the ignorance of beings who should but do not see that all things already are, and that any future attainment can be made only by use of the materials on hand, by minds and hands that see the potential.

"In our abject ignorance as primitives, we wallowed for centuries on pure instinct. That goes for your earth, for ours, and for all the countless others. One day someone was struck with an idea, and he and all his kind went that much further forward in progress because of it.

"As long as we needed horses, there were millions of them, but when there is no longer need for them, horses shall disappear.

"For centuries man wanted dogs that were fierce and barking for protection, but today man wants gentle dogs, pet dogs, and so the fierce breed is dying away from the face of the earth, like the horse. One day, when man has so evolved that he is self-sufficient, he will no longer need pets and then even the gentlest of dogs will disappear, as will other pets. Many animals which fit into the chronology of the periodic table of life are extinct, and others are gradually becoming extinct as time goes on.

"At the same time, as animals disappear you will find that the number of humans increases and their intellect increases also. Thus, no life has really disappeared. It has merely sublimated into a more intelligent form. As man moves into the desert, the rattlesnakes disappear, as do the coyotes, jack rabbits and so on. One day these will have no place to exist on earth. Man will have occupied it all.

"Mountains will be cut down so winds will bring more perfect and gentle weather conditions throughout the year. Automobiles and airplanes and rockets will disappear, and everything will become born of silicates or the abundant sands, put there purposely for your people, and moved about by magnetic propulsion such as you see in our ship Andromeda. These elements and forces are inexhaustible and they existed before your eyes all the time, but only learning will enable you to utilize them. Glory to the Providence which foresaw all this in the Plan, the Purpose, the Word!"

Saturn stopped to meditate a moment in his rapture. When Adam felt that he had come to the end of his meditation, he took the opportunity to speak.

"Saturn, you always say 'you' though I am the beginning and the end of life on earth. Actually, I am thirty-eight years of age, and have only seven or eight more months of life. What can it mean to me, whatever it is?"

"That is a good question, Adam. Look at it objectively. In all the world's history there have been important people and nondescript people. Whole civilizations have come and gone. Take them all together and at this very moment, in the eyes of God, who is more important, all they who are no more or you who are?'' Saturn countered.

"Why, true enough, I am, and so is any one or any thing else that exists at the moment," Adam replied.

"Why, then, do people put forth such efforts to promote their ideas or ideals, giving up their very lives? Even a so-called atheist is interested in the history or origin of earth and its life, and he is concerned about the future of the earth as is the most pious person. He will exert effort and give his life for his own ideal, yet he professes to believe in nothing. You see, there is no such thing as an atheist. Such a person is merely ignorant of facts and blind to truths. But the hypocracy of the pious one levels him to the same order as the atheist.

"So, we are all really one in essence, and since we are all concerned about the future, we must agree that the concern is a natural instinct. A natural instinct is always unerring. Deep inside our subconscious we all know we do not really die. As long as life exists anywhere, none of us dies, and we feel intuitively that this is so. Some of us see it clearly and plainly, and we call ourselves enlightened. It is nothing more than knowing our own instincts. The moment you die from your body, Adam, you cease to exist as you are, but you can- not go to oblivion, because oblivion has no consciousness. Wherever life exists, you will again feel yourself as one unit of it although the entire universe became devoid of all but one mortal. If that one were to disappear, then all life would have sublimated back to God, from whence it always was in the first place.

"Life is everlasting, both your life and mine. What we leave behind when we go out, that is what we shall inherit when we come in, at the very next instant. It becomes plain that, if only for selfish reasons, it pays to learn and to teach. If there should be twenty billion people on earth near perfection and one should be either ill or unlearned, all attention would be focused on that one. He would be the best known individual on earth. He could start that civilization back to retrogression, like a germ in a body.

"By the same token, Adam, if all the billions were primitive and one was endowed with learning and vision, he could eventually bring that whole populace into enlightenment by teaching and by breeding his kind among them. You have been told that our retarded ones are kept among themselves in our world. Andromeda is such a concentration area, and Launie is one of the hindmost. But she is not offended. She wants to be among her own kind, to learn, to generate better and better, and so it is with all the others. We cannot risk falling back. A perfection awaits us all sometime, somewhere."

"Now," Saturn offered, "do you wish to say something?"

"I do. It is a question," said Adam. "If learning is the very basis of human life, which came first on earth, for instance, the school or the church?"

"Both came at the same time, Adam, like the chicken and the egg. There was no division between them at the dawn of time and there really is none now, except the division that ignorance thinks exists.

"You will notice in your history that be they Scriptures or history books, both feature highly the accomplishments of man such as arts, literature, symbols, numbers and upheavals of whole nations.

"A modern university feels pride in graduating its students. The higher they go in life the more credit to the university or the grammar school. In turn, the graduates give to the university and the school what they find in their forward trailblazing.

"On the other hand, churches have become mere cults, holding in psychic and spiritual bondage those whom they should be helping and enlightening. It is the churches that must become as free as the sciences, or they will disappear. A church should teach its congregation and then graduate it, to try other churches. If they fear to do this, and on earth they all do, then they have no faith in themselves. A modern priest or minister should also be a scientist. If he cannot see God in any manifestation of matter, then he is not fit to minister to the souls of others."

"But, Saturn," Adam broke in again, "there are ministers and priests on earth who have pondered on these things called 'flying saucers,' and they are truly consulting their consciences as to whether or not they should speak of them from the pulpits. That they are helpless is no fault of theirs. Science has merely stepped ahead of them."

"Ah, Adam, just what I told you! Why should science have stepped ahead of them? How can they teach of God when they do not even understand God's lesser doings? The Scriptures of every major religion on earth are filled with such manifestations, and form the basis of religion. But the modern clergyman says these are miracles of the past and occur no more today. Yet they occur more today than in the past. As they know so little of science, so little do they know also of God and His Infinity. The churches swelled in membership soon after the atomic bomb, and they were swelled even more by the advent of the 'flying saucers,' as you call them. But it is a false swelling, and it will deflate faster than it swelled. All things swell before they burst. True growth and evolution is slow and solid. They shall all topple into the dust, leaving only the foundations which were built upon the rock, not the sand, and from these small stumps shall rise your new churches. They shall be Churches of Learning, replacing the cold and equally empty schools of learning. Everything must change, Adam. Everything must give way to discovered truths."

"Then," Adam rejoined, "is the religious structure bereft of truths, and has science so far exceeded it that there is no hope for the present theological institutions?"

"No, indeed, Adam. Quite the contrary. Not long ago the materialists rushed to

Darwin's works, hoping to upset all that religion stood for and they found not one iota of support for their dead reasonings. They received a death-blow with finality. A few ignorant ones still seek for some sign that man evolved slowly from the amoeba. Their ignorance grasps the amoeba because science discovered its existence. They do not know that the beginning of the amoeba is the hydrogen atom. Nowhere in all earth can they find one form of life migrating over into another. If they were true scientists obeying only observed facts, they would have long ago observed that all the evidence, not a part but all, is clear proof that no one can understand how the various forms of life occurred. Thus religious concepts are far ahead of materialistic concepts. Please, Adam, never confuse real science with the ignorant few who find more pleasure in a false and negative belief. The true intellects are highly religious, in the positive direction.

"Let the dead bury their dead. That is all these thwarted few are doing. Even that is an expression right from your New Testament, but you have never heard of it. Indeed you haven't. Too many are busy at it, the dead burying their dead, and so no one likes to give it much voice, either from the pulpit or from the masses. The best and most dynamic parts of Scripture are seldom, if ever, promulgated into the minds of people." Saturn stopped, waiting now to hear from Adam. "On earth we have our social divisions, these being the state, science, and religion. Are not the three of these working side by side equivalent to your monolithic structure, whereby you have merged all into one magnificent enterprise?" Adam asked.

"With people of high culture and intelligence it should work out well," replied Saturn. "But even they would soon see that there would then be no division between any of these elements and they would naturally merge into one anyhow. On earth it is different. One vies against the other, rather than cooperates. Greed, selfishness, and ignorance is the rule, and they cannot merge under those conditions. If they do not merge, eventually the stronger will absorb the weaker of them. There must come a new light unto them. A vision must come to them from the very bosom of Truth."

"Saturn," Adam spoke, "is there not some group of people, some institution, some church or some nebulous thought pattern now generating on earth seeds containing the fullness of these vistas?"

"No, Adam, not one. Now and then there seems to be an embryo of something good, but it flares up and dies down. Of course, it is a good sign. There are viruses in formation, and that means there will be a growth. It will be a wonderful dawn when the birth of such an institution takes place. Here on Andromeda we shall rejoice a full seven days in commemoration."

"Saturn, in regard to Eternity,—do you have a clear and vivid description of it? Is there no way in which some idea of it might be grasped? Does time really exist?"

"One of the prime laws of Nature is that no two substances can occupy the same space at the same time. How big or small do you think the shortest split moment of time is?" Saturn asked him.

"Well, I imagine it is so small and fast that no human mind can conceive of it, no instrument measure it," replied Adam.

"No, Adam. It is enormous. It is Infinite. That shortest split second fills all space at once, extending from one no-end to the other no-end. And since it fills all space at once, there is no room for any other moment of time to enter therein. Thus, it is always now, everywhere.

"If it were not that time is at rest everywhere, then I could ask you, 'Which is longer, the past or the future?' Is there such a fool who would venture to say he knows?

"The same applies to space. It is Infinite, for if it were finite, I ask, 'Which is farther, that way or the opposite way?'

"No, Adam, time is not parceled. It exists as a state of Now, everywhere. Motion is what gives us the impression of time. There are space and motion. It is easier to grasp a thought with your bare hands than to define Time. God is Time, as God is many other essences."

"To be spiritually on the right path, is it essential that man believe in visitors from neighboring space?" asked Adam.

"If the possibility remotely exists, how can man help but have such a conviction? The thought of it alone elevates him in minutes to a degree that would require years otherwise. Many who profess not to believe in space visitors have no compunction in saying that there are angels with wings. Imagine such a grotesque sight as a human form with wings! The believer himself would faint in fear at the sight of such a monster. Also, of what use would wings be out in space? Again allegory and symbolism come in. "Wings were invented for space beings by earth people, the blind leading the blind."

Adam was left without a question in his mind. He passed his hand over his face and across his forehead, trying to determine whether there was anything further he wished to ask Saturn. His hand went across his cheek and to his neck, below his ear. He could feel the lump, now small and soft, but it was there just the same. He was shocked back to the reality of Adam the earthman, Adam the dying. There was something akin to panic surging up within him. Once more Launie looked at him as she had the first time in the dining hall. She was all attentive concern, all tender care. She was beautiful, warm and soothing, as she hurried to the kitchen for some of the bracing elixir. Soon she had placed a glass in Adam's hand. Thirstily he drank of it, and almost at once felt the wonderful effect.

Yes, indeed. He had one more question to ask Saturn, chief of Andromeda, physician par excellent. As he looked toward him, Adam could see that Saturn had already anticipated, not a question but a request.

"Saturn, in all sincerity I ask you: You can cure me of this thing, I know. Is it at all possible that you would do this for me?"

"Yes, Adam. Possible, yes. But probable? That is another thing. I would need the consent of Neptune, Orion, Lyra, Launie; I would also need the consent of everyone of our people here on Andromeda, and then wait ten years to get word back that assent was given by every one on our home planet. For my curing you would amount to interference with the timetable of evolution of the earth. My act would be the act of my world, and God's detailed plan would have been interfered with. Two worlds would need to start all over again from the very beginning, yours and mine. Simply put, Adam, it means that God would begin all over again from the primitive beginning, like a man playing solitaire and cheating a move. He would just shuffle the deck to start the game anew. That is what the whole universe is to God, an endless shuffling of worlds, each to fit into perfection by its own allotted elements.

"If you were an Alpha Centaurian, twenty billion of us would not rest until you were cured, and on earth, no one shall rest until such blights as disease, war, and ignorance are things of the past. One world cannot interfere with another world which is behind it in evolution. It would be cheating God's plan, and such things are not done with impunity. Would you hazard such calamities if it would mean having you live a few more years, only a few more years anyhow, Adam?"

"No, Saturn. Assuredly, no. I am sorry I brought that up, and you may be sure I will not again," said Adam humbly.

"Well, now that you feel that way, I can add this. Besides disturbing the Plan, there is another thing to be considered. A dying man is very wise. A doomed man is resigned. When either is brought back to a measure of assured longer life, he is not like other human beings. He does not fit any more in life's motion. You would find nothing on earth interesting, for you would know that everything will end to you, no matter how long you might live. The slow and tedious ways of earth would become unbearable. You would welcome the end, meanwhile living languidly in a world no longer to your liking. No one can change that fact, certainly not I. That is in the hand of God only, Adam.

"So, no matter what, you would hate me for curing you. You would hate everybody on earth, including yourself. You could no longer be an excellent physician, for the very thought of just ministering to others, all of whom are sooner or later doomed, would pall on you. It would not be curing you; it would be killing all of what is the real Adam. Though you may not fully comprehend the consequence to the evolutionary plan of the worlds, the second consequence is just as dire, and surely you comprehend that, Dr. Adam."

Launie came close, caressed his hair and kissed him full on the lips.

"That is for your understanding, Adam, and confirmation that in the end we all meet. Even Saturn must go on," she said, with a tenderness that was reward in itself.

SON OF THE SUN: The Secret Of The Saucers

As she drew her head back Adam saw that Lyra had risen and was standing before him. She bent down and added her kiss, smiling warmly.

"Never let it be said, Adam, that I was not alert and attentive during this fine meeting."

"Imagine," Launie said in a low voice. "A peer kissing you after me, and where my own lips had touched you. That is real democracy, is it not?"

"Yes, Launie, it is. It is also the result of true spiritual awareness and of intellectual maturity."

Lyra suggested it was time for some refreshment and for more casual conversation. Launie and she quickly got the table ready in the dining area, and all were summoned to be seated. In the course of the conversation, which touched upon various subjects, mostly on the lighter side, Adam raised a question, directing it at Orion.

"Our earth has experienced great earthquakes since our known history. Is it always to have such shuddering and destructive spasms?"

"Your earth, Adam," Orion replied, "is not fully set in spherical stability. It is still in the process of formation into a more perfect sphere, being drawn toward its own center by the force of gravity. Since its orbit around your sun is elliptical and not circular, the sun's gravity varies and prolongs the process of earth's attaining spherical stability. However, it is gradually settling into a more compact sphere, becoming rounder, much as a snowball is molded by hand. This settling is what causes some mountains to be pushed upward.

"As the curvature of the earth attains a stronger arc form, there is less pressure exerted on the core, and the inner heat of the earth will cool accordingly. In turn, the cooling causes a thicker crust to form on the inside of the existing crust of the earth. Thus, in the future the earth will be a completely solid sphere. No more hot springs or volcanoes will erupt. No more earthquakes will occur," Orion assured him.

"You begin to see," Lyra added, "that all things adjust themselves in about the same timing? No civilization is given more to struggle against than it can conquer. True, things become more complex, conflicts among men become much greater, and even nature seems to take on new proportions when some of its forces have been understood and conquered. That is all part of evolution." She paused, waiting for a word from Adam. He obliged her promptly.

"Then, Lyra, would it be not wise for man to just sit back and wait for these things to adjust themselves, rather than to fight them?"

"It would be plausible, but not wise," she replied. "Also, there is man's insatiable curiosity to contend with. Many men sit back and let things just go as they will, but many do not. Even this arrangement is part of the original Plan. Furthermore, if man just sat back, he would merely have the first problem all the time, never surmounting that one, and that major one would sooner or later wipe him

SON OF THE SUN: The Secret Of The Saucers

from the face of the earth. Remember, Adam, that cancer, just for one example, is such a problem. To many people that one problem is more grave than atomic energy in the form of explosives."

"May I add my own affirmation to that," Adam said, "by merely indicating my comprehension? In short, then, action is the only rule and, in the final analysis, learning the only true virtue."

"Not quite, Adam," Lyra rejoined. "The love of learning is the only virtue. Everyone learns something, but not everyone is endowed with the pure love of learning," she finished, smiling.

Launie looked at her peeress, and received these simple words with sheer admiration.

"Since we have time on our hands," said Adam, "there are a few questions I would like to ask just for the record. I have recently read the book, 'The Secret of the Saucers,' and I find my own experiences bearing it out. Some things do not seem to correlate, however.

"For instance, Orfeo says in his book that he had the sense of being on an asteroid. Yet I find myself in a huge space ship in the atmosphere of Venus, and his description defines the same things I am seeing here. How is that?"

"That one is for me," spoke up Neptune. "It was I who almost entirely arranged and conducted our part of the communication with him, as you noted in the book.

"With that experience, Adam, you will find much actual detail. However, some of the most profound exchanges between Orfeo and myself were allegorical and symbolical, so that their essence could be applied to many situations just as passkeys apply to many locks.

"For instance, an asteroid is a piece of a broken planet. Lucifer, the name given to that former planet, denotes evil, and of course, evil in any degree is but a product of ignorance.

"Thus, Lucifer the planet had once attained material symmetry, but it was gained in a cold, hard way, not in the least graced by the living warmth of spiritual truths. Thus it destroyed itself. This story has been handed down for countless millenia, and will go in the future throughout the cosmos.

"Thus, who are the Luciferians, and who are the non- Luciferians? Only their deeds and results will tell. On earth each one has it within him to be either one, so the analogy or allegory is maintained perfectly. Earth can retrogress by sluggish ignorance and apathy, or it can destroy itself by arrogant materialism. The only other course is beauty and perfection in total. That day, for either of these ends, is far off as yet, and what will be must come about by the free choice of the people.

"Due to Orfeo's ignorance at the time, although he saw much that you see now, he was unaware as yet as to where he was or what it all meant. Eventually, it did dawn upon him, and our giving to you the actual experience (in the physical body) still represents no interference with earth's evolution. He was made to see part of

Andromeda on Venus. He was, because of his share of ignorance, half Luciferian and half not. But his pure love of learning has elevated him upward, and that makes him one who does not wish to belong to that long-established hierarchy of Lucifer, so he does not today. Being such a good example of an 'inbetween' is one of the reasons for his experiences. He was a materialist, true enough, but his love of learning brought him into the Cosmic Splendor, or the Light, and our contact with him was made permissible.

"Many on earth have speculated," Neptune continued, "as to whether there is such a thing as intelligent life in forms different from the human. Well, if there is we have found no traces of it. Many of your intelligent fellowmen know that it could not be by nearly mathematical ascertainment. For instance, if you plant an apple seed you get an apple. Some will say this is not so, because if you plant a peach stone you do not get an apple and they let it go at that, reasoning no farther. Willfully, they would lead the ignorant to think that they themselves believe so when they are in reality deliberately falsifying, knowing within themselves that the same law holds for both seeds and for all seeds.

"Thus any seed that can produce the brain of a monkey will in turn lose its properties upon gestation, true; but the brain of the monkey follows predestined laws that make it form a monkey. A brain capable of intelligence follows a natural course which makes it produce the implements of intelligence such as the thumb, the hand, and so on. The human machine is therefore the most efficient mechanism in the universe, so far as we can calculate. From there, only a higher Intelligence arises. Truly, then, we must surely be created in the image of the Father."

"Neptune, are the ignorant and the malevolent made also in the image of the Father?" Adam asked him eagerly.

"The Fatherhead is Infinite. It has a Triune Personality, and you are considering only the two of Him; in fact, hardly more than one. Remember, Adam, Positive and Negative, Action and Reaction? These exist even in the Ultimate One. The word 'and' is His third aspect, and completes the Triune Being. Whereas mortals know life only at the third manifestation, or as the result of the Positive and Negative, the Father knows all three forms of Life simultaneously. This phenomenon is reserved solely for the Father," Neptune said, speaking the last words slowly that they might filter to the souls of all those present, as well as to his own.

They made such an impression on Adam that it prompted him to ask another question.

"Neptune, do I return to earth? In brief, where do I stand? I feel that you have at last interfered with our evolution, for I am sure no one on earth has thought in the direction of those last statements of yours heretofore."

"Not so, Adam. Quite a few people on earth have come upon this awareness. You will meet one of them when you return to earth. Did our ship not pick you up from Twenty-nine Palms? Did you not read 'The Secret of the Saucers' just recently?

SON OF THE SUN: The Secret Of The Saucers

The author of that book is one of them, and he has been staying in Twentynine Palms of late. You will meet and speak with him soon after your return, and you will see that he has come upon such an awareness, even before you mention it to him."

Adam smiled in rapt admiration, then asked, "Since it was under your guidance that Orfeo heard five words of your language and remembered them, is there a language that will finally be chosen by the people of earth from among its many?"

"Not from any one existing language," replied Neptune. "But they will frame a perfect one from three of them. The English for vastness, the Spanish for phonetic beauty, and the Italian for specific spelling. They who will fuse these three, with their three characteristic elements retained intact, will give the earth its great language. As you have already guessed, it is our language. Of course, you know we augment our word language with that of mathematics, and by means of these two you could converse with any intelligent life in the universe. You see, Adam, we come from these unities in the beginning, and to them we must return."

"I see it so clearly," Adam said, in half reverie. "I think a good name for such a language would be 'Sonado' ".

"Wonderful!" erupted Launie with glee. "You get the idea very rapidly, Adam. And remember, an earthman came upon the name by his own efforts; it was not from us. Speak to me fluently in Sonado, and Leo would relinquish his love for me, gladly making you a gift of me."

"I think Leo has an ironbound claim on thee," Adam responded, half in regret and half in jest. "It will be many years, Launie, before any of my people shall speak to yours in Sonado."

Orion sat more erect in his chair, inspired to a beaming smile. Gently he said to Adam, "Bon sonado, but e tem a mas."

Adam looked to Launie for an explanation. She shrugged her shoulders and said she did not know what it meant, but Saturn understood and enlightened Adam.

"What Orion said is simply, 'Well said, but it is time to eat' ". Adam marvelled, not only at Orion's hasty creation, but at the facility with which Saturn quickly interpreted the sentence. He had to admit to himself there was a complete ease in the sentence, there was phonetic pleasantness, and it must be easy to spell, for he found himself remembering it completely. Rising from his chair, he said to the company, "Bon sonado, but e tem a mas."

* * * *

Thus Adam was permitted to see the innermost philosophy of these people. It was simple, but utterly profound. At first he found it difficult to understand why in the physics section he was given much of what really was religion, and in the religious session he received what might be called higher physics. The difficulty did not clear up, for by now Adam found it impossible to separate one from the other. Now he knew that no one truly probes a thing deeply until that thing be-

SON OF THE SUN: The Secret Of The Saucers

comes nothingness, yet everything. It is so with the hydrogen atom. It is equally so with man himself.

When the intellect and the intuition reach the point where no mortal can provide any light or reply, then the light and the reply is provided by hierarchies more enlightened in the Divine Estate. Indeed, then, man has heard the Word of God; but not from God directly. Man has uttered the Word of God, and utters it eternally; but man is merely the image, the third harmonic of God. In that one-third man has often felt he was the total image, for sometimes the one-third seems to reach into the infinity of matter and thought. Yet the other two-thirds, equally infinite, being the material estates and domains of action and reaction, are totally unknown to man.

Suddenly, almost terrifyingly, Adam hit the ultimate thought, from which he shrank back at once. Was there anything imaginable that God could not do?

The answer came back to him almost in the same instant. Yes, there is. God cannot make an exact and absolute equal to Himself, for in such a case a conflict would result in which the eternity of Creation itself would be at stake, and in this conflict Creation would dissolve, because all Creation is in constant ferment, every minute particle of which registers with God, and has purpose.

Adam knew now with absolute finality that he must not be healed by any being except one of his own earth brothers, for it was part of the purpose, and a place and period in that cosmic fermentation, that he be healed only by the efforts of himself or his family of earth.

This, then, is what is commonly known among more enlightened earthmen as the Plan, the Purpose. Every hair on our heads is counted; a sparrow does not fall that the Father does not know of it. How long before intelligent man sees this truth?

As they dined in silence, Saturn was in attunement with Adam's every thought. Other than ordering their particular meals, few words had been spoken by anyone in the group. It is a code that when any being is contemplating the Ultimate, no other entity shall commune with or interfere with that being's adoration, for in the eyes of the Ultimate, the last is equal in His love with the foremost. The most vicious creature imaginable required as much birth pain of God as did the highest Archangel, if not more so, though that creature must, within eternity's time, rise to sit in Love with that Angel.

A learned man basks in his reflections. A wise man glories in all that happens before his eyes. An ascended one knows that to gain favor and grace forever in the eyes of the Creator, he must drench himself with the love of pure learning, and the love of pure learning encompasses that which has occurred, that which is yet to occur. The rapture of that high estate cannot be contained within a mono-entity, but must be shared and consummated between that entity divided, as man and woman, and the third essence, the third harmonic, results in further creation, their children. Thus, the allegory of Adam and Eve supersedes all other knowledge. By the same token, an absolute knowledge of the hydrogen atom would open for man the way to the very Highest.

Thus Adam learned, on board Andromeda.

Chapter 12
THE EASE OF FORGETTING

The small group dined in harmonious silence. Other groups sat around at various tables, pleasantly conversing and eating. Adam noticed that it was the same Cafe Venus which Launie had named the night before. It seemed a long time since he had been here, and the glamor must have worn off, because in some way it was less attractive than on the previous occasion. Not even the company of these highest of peers on Andromeda nor the presence of Launie herself appeared able to restore the cosmic glitter of it, which was so recent yet so long ago.

Only Saturn, who was in rapport with Adam in thought and spirit, was able to remove the cold chill that otherwise would have settled about them as they lingered over dessert. Once more, there was music softly beginning to peal from seemingly everywhere. It was an overture which Adam nearly recollected but could not quite recognize. Then it burst into its full melody, an orchestration the equal of which he had never heard on earth.

There was no doubt as to what the melody was. It was "La Vien Rose."

So enthralling was the music that the entire establishment thawed from its chill and turned into the most delightful place in which Adam could imagine himself. At that moment she came to the table. There was no doubt in Adam's mind that she was one of the peers. Certainly she was far from being one of the retarded ones.

Even the expression of Saturn mellowed as he looked into her eyes and received the message she handed him, fused on a plastic type paper. He looked at the missive, looked back into her eyes, and merely nodded his head. The entire exchange was in silent pantomine, but Adam could feel that something very critical was transpiring. By the looks on the faces of his group he felt sure it all concerned him. Launie looked at the lovely peeress who had seemingly intruded on the group, but for once she did not smile.

Saturn once more examined the written information, looked up into her eyes, and asked, "And this is your absolute decision, Aleva? In the event you did not return, there would be nothing that you, and you only, felt would have been taken with you and lost to us forever?"

SON OF THE SUN: The Secret Of The Saucers

"No, Saturn," she responded. "Nothing would be left behind me that would be so unfinished another could not finish it. I am fully ready for either the beginning or the end."

Launie dropped her head into her arms on the table and sobbed somewhat convulsively. Adam would have rushed to comfort her, but he knew not what was going on and something within him held him back, to listen further and receive perhaps the solution to what was being hinted, or was about to transpire. Also, he felt that Launie had no need of comfort from an amateur such as he, and once more he felt his inferior stature in the presence of these people.

In his dejected state this exquisite woman, Aleva, stood looking into Adam's eyes with such self-sure poise that he could not help but feel he had always known her, if only by some common chord she struck within him. She was warm, understanding, somewhat aggressive, feminine; and so wel-comely overcoming that even Launie gradually faded in Adam's "undying" esteem. Yet he knew in this moment that he could love Launie in a way he could not love this one. Launie could meet Adam on his own level some day, but how could Aleva come down to absorb the manly love, limited though it might be, that Adam was capable of? No, indeed. She was more aloof in that regard than Lyra.

By now Adam looked tired and worn. Launie could see that as she raised her head from her folded arms. She arose and went hurrying off, returning once more with a tall glass of nectar which she proffered to Adam. He took two sips and set the glass back on the table. He grimaced a little, even though it was delicious. Somehow it tasted different from all the other potions of nectar he had drunk. Launie told him it was a little different. It was more potent, and would calm his system for a much longer period of time than the other mixtures had done in the past. For at least eighty hours it would enhance his whole being and he would have no need of further help physically. And, she assured him, when its effect wore off completely, his memories of these days would be deposited deep into his subconscious, to be recalled only as a dream, far off, half real and half not. Only the essence of his recollections would tell if they were real or not. With that assurance to Adam she bit her lips hard, and wept like a child.

Launie cried so hard Adam joined her by intuitive response. As their eyes were dimmed by bittersweet tears, Adam could see everyone but Launie leave the table and go out of the room.

Only Launie was left with him, but it was not the Launie he had known these few days. She had changed in appearance and in aspect, he noted, as his eyes cleared up from their tears. He had known an unreachable Launie, a devastating Launie. Now, before him and close to him was a more real Launie.

Her apparel had become a sea-blue color fringed with white, so that she became a fleecy cerulean picture. She was like a young maid of earth on a Sunday morn going to church, or floating through a meadow of daisies and sumac, ivy and dandelion and butterflies. Her unbelievable beauty had mellowed to a more real and credible warmth. She was truly flesh and blood. She breathed air and she exhaled perfume. At last she was a woman, and Adam felt like a man. Launie had fallen and Adam had risen. He now loved her more than any word or philosophy could save him from. Not only would he claim her from Leo, but he would challenge the gods if need be, to claim her, and he said so to her, for he held her by the elbows, and said:

"Dora; my Dora. You have waited, and I have wasted so much time. So, I was a doctor, and not a bad one. But I let my greatest patient fall back into limbo. I am yet a doctor, Dora, and better yet, a physician. Love has made me a true physician, and this degree is not written on paper but in the records of the Ether. In my awareness of that, I say to you and hereby vow that henceforth I will be, so far as I am able to be, all that you ever expected of me. I do all things with you in my mind, and I bitterly regret any slight which I have shown you.

"You, Dora, have been me and I have been you. We both have wandered afar but we have returned to each other, never again to part. The horizon is yours, and it is also mine. The past is you to me, and it is I to you. I now rest for all time, knowing you cannot go so far that you cannot hear my voice. For all voices shall to your ears be but milestones leading you back to me. It must be so, for it is so with me."

As they sat alone at the table, Launie listened to Adam and her tears flowed steadily. She bit her lips, for indeed, Launie had taken on the appearance of Dora.

"You see, Adam?" she sobbed. "My people chose me to be your host and guide here, because I resembled Dora more than any of the others on Andromeda. A slight change in me, and you see only her.

"Yes, you were a good man and a good physician. But you slighted love, and though you were highly desirable on earth, you remained unreachable to the one who loved you.. She has not been married to any other man. You were attracted to her, but you let your profession come first. She waited day after day and month after month, until she no longer knew why. A face and a voice kept haunting her, and the face and the voice kept saying, 'Wait for me. I am far from you, but I will come to you.' So, she still waits.

"Yes, Adam, it is Dora, whom you know from away back. You are now ill and doomed, but she has been ill very long, and she now knows that she is doomed also. Will she know only lonely days and bitter suffering? Will she pass on in that bleak aloneness that is unbearable? She could stand all that, as many women must, but she owes a few debts, and she cannot bear to think she may pass on with those debts over her head. When you go back to earth, Adam, rush to her, lift her up financially and hold her in your arms. She is Launie, Adam, and Launie is Dora, If you will not do for her what you can, you would not do so for me. I must have your answer, Adam, not by intuition, but by your words."

SON OF THE SUN: The Secret Of The Saucers

"Launie," Adam managed to whisper. "I saw you as Dora, and for the first time loved you as only love could understand. I cannot wait to return to her. She has been neglected and frustrated, true enough. But it was not intentional on my part, and I have received the reward that such selfishness earns. Somehow, I feel that she also slighted some essence, which if not slighted would have made her mine and I her own long ago. But it does not matter now. What matters is that she wants me more than anything else, and I feel the same way toward her. She is free to claim me, as I am free to claim her. It is all in good order. Where is the power that would keep me from Dora? I ask you, Launie, where is such a power that would dare keep me from her?"

"There is no power that would dare so," Launie replied, her eyes still wet. "But do you not already forget Launie and what she said to you so recently, yet so long ago? It was recent in time, Adam, but long ago in your memory. Do you not re-member asking me how it would be possible for you ever to forget me? And this moment I might ask of you, how will it be possible for you ever to remember me? You are already impatient to see more of Aleva; and hopelessly impatient to see Dora. I ask you, Adam, not how will you forget, but will you sometimes remember Launie?"

Adam looked at his bracelet, which had his name, number, and symbol en-graved upon it, and which could not be removed except by severing his hand from his arm.

"No, Adam," said Launie, anticipating his thought. "Such are not for the souls of the enlightened ones. That bracelet will serve you only should you become stranded in space within the cosmos. It is not a memoir. It will be dissolved from your wrist the moment you have gone back to earth to stay, and so will I dissolve from your memory. Whatever you remember of me will be like a dream that you can thrust aside. So a pupil does with the teacher, but the teacher finds it hard to thrust aside the memories of the pupils. You have been my teacher and I yours, so we can drop each other in the activities of the future, in activating what we have learned from each other. Thus, Adam, forgetting is easy. Remembering is the dif-ficult part."

"Well said, Launie," Adam countered. "I still am enslaved to you. But what is that undertone of music, and why does the room get brighter? I have learned that every new overture is but the dawn of a new event. I would embrace you as my own, but what is this new something that sweeps over everything about us? I feel I must look into it, and you must be with me. Come, let us go out, for it is Androm-eda itself that changes."

So saying, Adam took Launie by hand and hurried to the outside of the Cafe Venus with her.

The world of Andromeda was not the same. Adam looked above him, then to the horizon all around him. There were no longer dark clouds and lightning, but white and fleecy clouds and blue azure. This sky was highlighted by a huge bright spot from which there was heat emanating, like a desert when the sun blazes. He looked askance at Launie.

"Yes, Adam," she informed him. "Andromeda has surfaced over the main body of clouds which envelop Venus. That bright spot you see is the sun. It is large only because you are closer to the sun than you would be on earth. The heat you feel is that of the sun. We are foreign to it by birth, Adam, but you are the son of the sun. Yet, Alpha Centauri is the same to us as the sun is to you. We may understand it better than you do, but it is still your source and sustenance of life. All earth people are sons of the sun, which is in turn the son of the Father. The very beginning is traced back to the words, 'Let there be Light; and there was Light.' That light sustains all that lives under it. It is the beginning and the end. You are truly a son of the sun.

"Do you remember seeing three ships dip into the ocean of Jupiter? You marvelled at that, thinking it was a high accomplishment. It may be to you and your people, but to us it is elementary. All of us would and could go into Jupiter's red ocean. Some of our most daring and inquisitive men have gone right into the sun, and have come out again. It is still hazardous and very much problematical, for the core of the sun is ultimate heat and force and no material can stand up under its horrendous radiation. As for our women, a mere handful have dared it. It is the very source of ultimate heat, and even we blanch at the prospect of approaching the sun.

"Only our finest crafts can make the dip and return, and only our peers have the kind of courage and skill required to do so. The critical moment inside the star is more than most people could bear. The closest I have been to it is at the orbit of Mercury."

Adam seemed transfixed as he listened to Launie and looked at the bright spot the sun made on Andromeda's ceiling. He felt within his every fiber that something Launie was trying to say involved him. Even the traffic in the air was at a minimum, as though all of Andromeda awaited in a suspense equal to his own. Adroitly, Launie continued to speak.

"When Aleva came to our table and spoke with Saturn, she brought written data from Antares that all was in order for her trip. Saturn gave his approval. Yes, she has fully decided to go into the sun, but only if it means something to some branch of learning. We would have nothing to learn from her trip which would add to our records. It would not be an exploration for our sake, but it would be for yours."

She paused, allowing the impact of her suggestion to sink into Adam's consciousness. It was hardly necessary, for he had absorbed the idea as she spoke. He gave his answer deliberately.

"I accept the offer, Launie, with my gratitude," he simply replied.

SON OF THE SUN: The Secret Of The Saucers

"Oh, no, Adam," she replied. "You have the haste of the reckless. Your decision while you are still with us would not be valid. The nectar influences you, our environment molds your mind, Aleva is exciting to you. You have not long to live, so what would it matter? None of these reasons are valid with us. You must decide soberly, of sane mind, and from your home planet. You must remember that you have happy months awaiting you with Dora, and happiness awaits her because of your returning to her with love. You must decide with absolute resolve that the exploration is paramount in your desire," she advised him.

"I understand, Launie," Adam said. "The way I feel at this moment I pray that my decision as Adam, the earthman, will bring me into such an ultimate experience. Meantime, do I have more to see on your good ship Andromeda? I never tire of it."

"None, Adam; none that would add to your knowledge or be more interesting to you than what you have already seen. Whatever else remains is beyond your ken. We would be hurting you to show more without explaining it fully, and explaining would be interference. Let us go back to my house, but first take this capsule and swallow it."

He complied with her request, and soon they were back in Launie's cottage. She took off her lovely jacket, placed it on the back of a chair, then turned to face Adam again. She was once more Launie, the original Launie. Yet she so much resembled Dora!

"Did I not tell you," she said, softly, enchantingly, "that I would be easy to forget? But only in your vision of another, in a vision of where you belong . . . with Dora. Your trip back home will be occluded from you in restful sleep. You have nothing more to see in space for the time being, and you need the rest. Besides, you must forget and regard your recent experience as just a long dream. The capsule I just gave you shall bring sleep to you, Adam."

Adam heard her voice as if it came from far away, and through a hazy mist. He hurried for the divan to sleep. So sleepy was he that her thanks and farewell words did not register with him.

* * *

Adam awoke back in his rented cabin, to the light of the morning sun. The only thing different this morning was that the sun felt closer to him, warmer to his thoughts, intelligent in its perpetual being, and hotter than any man had ever conceived it could be. He had, it seemed to him, experienced a dream that was realistic, and the sun was part of that dream; the last part.

While dressing and grooming he could think of nothing but the dream. It was odd how the effect of it seemed to expand his awareness, giving him knowledge of things in a vastness that he had never been conscious of before. Even the sun seemed to submit to his knowledge of it, as if it silently said, "Yes, Adam, what you now feel I am, that I am." It was odd, he mused, how you can spend a lifetime

SON OF THE SUN: The Secret Of The Saucers

seeking knowledge and learning, and in one instant or in one night feel it suddenly mature into more knowledge than you had ever sought. Oh, well, he reflected, that's life and that's maturing. And what a dream this sudden flowering of awareness brought with it!

He went out to his car, to go into town for breakfast. It was a little more difficult to start than usual. The battery must be getting sluggish. A thin film of dust covered the windshield and all the windows. That was odd, because it was crystal clear just last night. Oh, well, a dash of water would fix that.

The town was really quiet for a Wednesday morning. It was rather strange. You never can tell about these dreamy desert communities; they behave oddly, doing as they please, when they please. A community could be as psychologically variable as an individual. Sitting at the counter in a cafe, he remarked to the waitress how strange he felt, how peculiar the town seemed for a Wednesday morning.

"Wednesday?" she asked in astonishment. "Are you kidding? This is Sunday morning. Brother, where were you last night? Well, what will it be, hot cakes and tea?"

"No. No, not this morning. Make it hot cakes and coffee," he replied.

"Oh, coffee this morning, eh? You were out, weren't you? Say, we haven't seen you for a few days. What's the matter, mad at us?" she kidded.

"I couldn't be mad at anybody, the way I feel. But I am sure mad at myself, and for no reason, except maybe because it's Sunday."

"Shall I put your favorite music on the machine?" she asked, hoping to shake him from his mood.

"Yes; yes, indeed. Here is the money. I insist you use it."

Adam felt strange. Cold electricity seemed to shoot through him, and goose pimples wanted to rise from his skin. He felt good as the waitress selected the number from the music box. Then the goose pimples were no longer undecided; they burst out fully all over. The number "Siboney" burst out from the music box, and the waitress remarked how these machines were always making errors. Adam felt even more concerned about it. He did not remember Siboney being among the records in the machine. They must have brought in some new ones since he last ate here. Why did it haunt him so? Oh, so what! he reflected. He had more important things to muse over than a music record.

He dreamed of Dora. Yes, Dora. It may have been a dream, but he knew Dora and he felt sure she was in the straits his dream had told him of. Anyhow, he would be going back to Seattle in a couple of days, and would rush to her. He wanted so much to see her.

Throughout the rest of the day, which did prove to be Sunday and not Wednesday, Adam wrestled with many new thoughts. Dream or no dream, something about the desert demanded his being here. Yet, he wanted to take off for Seattle to be at Dora's side, if not for her sake then for his own. He now needed her more than she

SON OF THE SUN: The Secret Of The Saucers

ever needed him; and all because of a long dream.

But that bright sun in the sky. It was not the sun he had known for thirty-eight years, yet it was the very same sun, the same sun Dora saw, that Dora felt through the hazy atmosphere of Seattle. Surely she was more subject to the sun than she was to Adam. She was a product of the sun, as every-one else was on earth. Whatever she needed of Adam he could send her. Yes, he could send it. So he made out a check for one thousand dollars and sent it to a close friend who could easily and quickly locate Dora. That would relieve her of any financial worries. He mailed it, and felt wonderful about it. He was now free. Free to do what he pleased and should do. There was some unfinished business to be done here in the desert, but what it was he could not put his finger on. He just felt he must stay a while longer, then he would fly to Dora as fast as his car could go.

All this day, Sunday, a day of rest, Adam was doing things that would seem insane to him any other time. Yet he was busy, settling his earthly affairs, for in one way or another be would not be long for this world. As if to prove it to himself, he put his finger on the little lump under his ear. The lump had changed. It was soft and barely discernible to the touch. Was everything going mad, or was it he? Did he have a dream last night, or was it a dream? Why had the car windows gathered dust? Why was it Sunday instead of Wednesday?

He had a dream "last night." It seemed so realistic, insisting on thrusting itself into his wakeful memory. The gist of the dream seemed to ask of him, "Would you go into the sun, Adam, with only a problematical chance of coming out again?" He looked up at the sun, and its bright rays made him sneeze. That was nothing in comparison to what it could really do to him. In his consciousness he could sense that a beautiful and ascended woman would offer her very body and life to the sun, and surely many women would. Why not he? After all, he had only seven more months to live. Instant atomizing by the sun would be far better than the slow torture of his ailment, and if he should come out, oh, if he should come out again, what words he could leave for his fellow-men! Only Dora stood in his way, and he had mailed enough money to relieve her of her earthly worries. Would that not be enough to bring happiness to her heart and reassure her that

Adam still reserved a place for her in his deepest thoughts? Yes, he thought, that is settled. He would go into the sun, with fervent zest.

But what silly thoughts! Why should he be thinking such immature things? He would stay in Twentynine Palms a few more days, and that was all. Then he could go to Dora. Yes, Dora.

Would she look like the woman he had just dreamed about? Then there was another. Yes, she called herself Launie. —But that was all just a dream.

Or was it? Adam kept trying to probe within his mind. All through the long Sunday he reflected, until the day was ended by the setting golden sun, which had set the same way for millions of years. When the stars appeared and it was fully night,

SON OF THE SUN: The Secret Of The Saucers

Adam felt strange in town. The town merely went about its usual ways, but they were now entirely strange and foreign to him. These were the slow, step-by-step ways of evolution, and Adam felt himself thousands of years ahead of that pace. It would take the whole world, of which Twenty-nine Palms was such a small part, many years to unfold into the knowledge and awareness he now felt. He did not belong here. He belonged back in the comforting solitude of his cabin.

* * *

A lone car made its way on the desert road to an isolated cabin. It carried its driver from the life of the town to the loneliness that only the desert can bestow. A loneliness it is, so absolute there is only one way beyond it, and that is the road back to life. As Paul once said, to be reborn there must first be a separation. Adam was separating himself from all earthly things he knew, but he was hitching his wagon to a star, the star of ultimate finality in the physical world. Though it had been hid behind the earth, the star was his very own, his life. It was his beginning, and it was his end. The star was his own sun.

He stepped out of the cabin and looked up at the canopy of stars which were but radiant suns, by the billions, and by the billions, planets revolved around them to be nourished by their heat, light, and sustenance. Earth was no more and no less than one of these, each in a formative stage, some far behind near the beginning, some far ahead near the horizontal end. Earth, he thought, must be somewhere between these two extremes.

None of their populace, he further mused, can call himself accomplished until he can go into the very source of life and emerge again; that is, go into the sun and come out. Then, and then only, could the civilizations say they understood matter and spirit. It would be the ultimate and crowning glory of exploration.

If, he reasoned, we could get closer and closer to the sun, we could eventually approach its surface, and then bore deeper and deeper into its body to a point somewhere near the absolute core.

Why not?

Man probes his earth, the space which cradles his earth; he probes his own physical self, and his spiritual essence. He gets answers only by small bits at a time, always proportional to the time and effort he gives his probing. True faith is rewarded by intangible answers. Physical investigation is rewarded by physical response. So it is.

Indeed, not only would I venture to go into the sun, he mused, but I would give my life, this one life, this one awareness, to only begin the journey into it.

SON OF THE SUN: The Secret Of The Saucers

Chapter 13
INTO THE SUN AND OUT AGAIN

Ah, look at that star far above, he said to himself. It has decided to move and roam about the heavens. It is not a meteorite, nor is it an airplane. It is curving and becoming somewhat larger. Do I not recall seeing something like that not too long ago; in fact, very recently? What is all this confusion in my mind, anyhow? Why is it that the essence of these thoughts remains paramount in my mind, and what should be important has turned to mere slow, plodding motion on earth? That star has really become bigger now. It is not only curving, but spiraling downward, right above me.

Just look. It has gone completely out, like a phantom. Was it real in the first place? Am I trying to comprehend the incomprehensible?

Is it my sense of doom that calls forth my intuitive wisdom? But why should the wind begin to blow? Does it know my thoughts and respond to them? The leaves fly away from near that tree. Is it a whirlwind? There is a glow there. Now there is a ghostly sphere. It reminds me of the ship, the ship that "she" mentioned. "She?" I believe in my dream it was "Launie."

But Adam was not dreaming. The ship emerged into full view, a perfect sphere. A dark area appeared in it, and from this a ramp seemed to extend down to the ground, from which a lovely lady walked, or waltzed.

"Adam, we know you have fully decided of your own free will, but tell me as confirmation to yourself, do you still wish to go into the sun, and probably out again?"

Now he knew her for sure. It was Aleva, the Aleva of his realistic "dream." At last he was her own, and she was his; but only if he agreed to go into the sun. He must answer her.

"Yes, in all humility, I wish to go into the sun whether I come out again or not; it does not matter to me, nor will it to anyone else," Adam replied, walking as though spellbound toward her and to the half-phantom craft.

"Then come," she said, "and know that you are entering a ship so well constructed it all but breathes and thinks. You have been re-orienting yourself on earth, Adam," she said, as he entered the craft, "and you have decided freely. It was not a dream you had, but a real experience. It should be no problem for you to remember me, Aleva. I am the third woman in your extraterrestial experiences. There will be no more. There is no need of more. If we emerge from the sun, you know that the fourth woman, Dora, your true earth love, awaits you and needs you, as you need her. Are you still ready and willing?"

"Yes, Aleva. I am ready, willing and able. My will would fly into the sun. All you do is provide the means," Adam said, then hastily apologized.

"I am sorry, Aleva. You also provide the support, for I would not go without you."

"Nor I without you," she assured him. "Your people have a habit of shortening names! Vega gave you your pseudonym of Adam, so by your own custom, why do you not merely call me, for short, 'Eve' "?

Adam and Eve. Into the sun, the sustaining light of Creation, God's candle that was Light when called for. All by his own decision and desire, though arrived at slowly and painfully like pulling a rib from his side, Adam had determined to experience the ultimate in adventures.

Thoughtfully, they entered the craft. They went to their respective seats as the thin ramp was drawn back to its slot, and the door slid shut behind them. On one side of Eve's seat was a small box with buttons, the only means of control for this superb craft. Otherwise, it was not much more than a round, hollow shell, the only flat part being the floor. Yet the outside appearance of the ship was entirely and perfectly spherical, so the floor had to be thick and solid, and joined to the craft completely.

This little craft was dazzlingly active at its hull. It was far more perfect than the one Adam now recalled vividly, the one which had taken him to Venus with Vega at the helm. This was one of those perfectly built ships designed to explore the depths of stars.

Eve turned her smiling eyes to Adam and asked him, "Are we all ready?"

"I am ready. Go as though I were not here with you."

She touched a button. There was no response except a slight push by the seat against his body. The soft light within the ship went out altogether, then returned. Eve explained they had in that short time traversed the magnetic ionosphere of the earth. Already they were a thousand miles above, or away from the earth, though only a couple of minutes had passed. Adam felt alert, and asked questions of her as they came to his mind.

"What is our velocity now, Eve?"

"Two hundred thousand miles per hour," she answered casually.

It was incredible, even though Adam had flown before in one of their ships at fantastic speeds. He knew that every atom of the ship and his body were propelled equally in the same direction at the same instant, but it still remained a problem too great for his reasoning powers.

Eve then turned a main dial which lighted up dimly, to show it was turned on. Turning to Adam, who sat close beside her, she said, "We are on full automatic control now. I need do nothing else to guide the ship. I could not anyhow, at the velocity we are going. We are already a few thousand miles from earth, and accelerating hundreds of miles by the second. Now we shall make the entire hull around us transparent, Adam. Look!"

No sooner had she said it than the ship became as transparent as if the hull did not exist. Space was filled with stars as light filled the interior of the craft. They looked behind them to see the magnificent earth falling back, and the sun coming into view as they swerved on a turn in space.

The sun! At last Adam saw the sun from the purity of space, though it was shaded safely by the ship's now partially opaque hull. Gracefully, the craft veered and assumed a course straighter, straighter, and then directly toward the sun.

Adam jumped a little at the sudden realization that the craft was really headed for the sun. Though it was still more than ninety million miles distant it seemed only hours away, and he instinctively turned to Eve for a word of reassurance. Sensing his feelings, she softly and disarmingly assured him with, "Remember you decided to go, and you would not want it different. The worst that could happen is sudden oblivion, and whatever follows that. Anything else would be much harder on you, so do not think of the negative side, but ponder the positive. You can change your mind at any time before we cross the orbit of Mercury, and after that you will challenge the sun, its glory and its inferno, with every essence of your being, which is equal to the essence of our most enlightened peer."

Adam's concern for his safety melted. Something she said had seized his interest. "Why the orbit of Mercury, Eve? What happens after that?"

"Beyond the orbit of Mercury all radio contact begins to fade away; even the best of apparatus cannot pierce the turbulence of the sun's environment. Likewise, human spirits become entities unto themselves, the lowly reach out to their vital zenith to meet on equal basis the very high ones. The sun melts all matter within itself to a nondescript form, for in its core there is no hydrogen atom and no uranium atom, nor any other atom. All are fused into ultimate heat and light. That is where we are approaching together. If anything happens, we become one in subatomic vapor. But then, do we not become total light?"

Adam listened intently. He became resolved at once, not to be courageous, but to maintain a state in which he would be devoid of any concern for his own survival.

"What is our velocity now?" he asked.

"Ten million miles per hour," she responded.

"Give her the gas. Step her up, Eve. I went this fast before. It was easy." Adam laughed, as thrilled as a boy; yet he knew full well he was experiencing the incredible. Eve smiled so broadly it was nearly a laugh. And the stars around them dimmed slowly as the sun became brighter.

The hull gradually became darker, and now the sun looked as it would look through smoked glass. The push against his back by the seat assured Adam that the ship was still accelerating swiftly. This was the superb little craft, the very best of Alpha Centaurian production. They made none better, big or small. This would be the first time it would dip into the sun. Dip into the sun indeed! thought Adam. It had no name. He turned to Eve and said, "I have not yet named this ship and it has suddenly come to me. Since it dips into the sun, may I name it the Little Dipper?"

"The Little Dipper it shall be," Eve echoed gaily. "You should know it is made of 30 layers of plastic-crystal material. The first five layers reflect back all light, and most thermal heat. Other layers are positive-charged and negative-charged, and each is insulated from the other by nonconducting sheets. Thus, you see, any radiation is converted into positive or negative energy by the skins after the rays have been rendered unstable by the magnetic field that surrounds our Little Dipper. But you already know of these things, and that the Little Dipper is the finest of ships."

"What is our speed now?"

"Twenty million miles per hour," she replied, somewhat somberly. "Notice how they have opaqued the hull to almost darkness?"

"They? Who are they?" he asked.

"The crew in the monitor ship, Adam. They are vectoring us in true course, and taking every precaution for our safety. That ship, though much larger than ours, has also been in the sun, so why not call it the Big Dipper?" she suggested.

"That will be its name if I have anything to say about it," said Adam. "Look! We can see nothing outside any longer."

As though the ship itself had heard him, the interior be-came dimly lighted by the sparkle of the crystal hull. Eve explained why this was. "Our monitors are controlling the molecules of the Little Dipper's hull," she said, "merely to test it. It is responding perfectly, otherwise they would halt our progress and cancel the trip.

"As I have said," she continued, "beyond the orbit of Mercury they can no longer help us, leaving the control entirely to its automatic system. They will keep testing up to the orbit of Mercury, and from then on these few dials and buttons alone will tell us how we are doing."

"We have been on our voyage an hour, Eve. What is our velocity now?" he asked her.

"Wait, Adam; wait until you hear music. Then you will know our speed. You can look through a section of the hull and see our monitor ship. They will clear a window to our right," Eve told him.

SON OF THE SUN: The Secret Of The Saucers

The window appeared almost at once, and some distance away Adam saw an elegant cigar-shaped craft, the same one he had seen in Andromeda, the one which had escorted him to Venus. Then a huge sphere, bright and massive, slid behind them and out of sight. Adam thrilled to the sight.

"What was that, Eve?"

"That was Venus. Did you see how fast it slipped behind? There, there comes the music. We have attained fifty million miles per hour, Adam. Oh, glory! From this velocity we begin soon to slow down."

Fifty million miles per hour, Adam reflected. He kept very still, thinking he would prevent any disturbance to the Little Dipper. One smallest error, one miscalculation of anything in the system of the little craft, and they would be atomized into thin smoke.

He was not alarmed, however. The music was not only enthralling; it was familiar. He had heard it before. Ah, yes! Not long ago on Venus itself had he not been with someone, a beauty called Launie, whose face now smiled vividly in his memory? What a delightful memory! What an exquisite moment to see her in his vision, with another lovely woman beside him. Eve seemed to know what he was thinking. Her countenance took on a beauty that enveloped Adam's emotions almost divinely. Such music, such a woman! Such an astronomical velocity: fifty million miles per hour!

Eve halted his racing thoughts with her voice. "Look toward the floor of the ship, Adam. It is now transparent."

He looked and saw tiny darts of lightning like St. Elmo's Fire shoot out from the ship. They became larger and brighter by the moment. Eve explained before he could ask about them.

"Yes, Adam; that is the discharge you read about in Orfeo's story. Our ship is now coasting and uses no energy. We are approaching the sun and its radiation is becoming more intense, so the Little Dipper merely discharges it all back into space. Now look above at our monitor ship. It will slow down by a few million miles per hour."

Almost as she said it the monitor ship went out of sight. My God, Adam thought, now all other life but mine and Eve's is east of the sun.

Adam and Eve in the Little Dipper, actually racing into the sun!

"We are decelerating rapidly, Adam, but we shall still enter the sun at more than a million miles per hour. We will need the inertial force as well as our magnetic propulsion, whatever is available to us in the sun, in order to penetrate deeply into it. Otherwise we would merely be belched back and away from it. When you hear a ping it will indicate we have traversed the orbit of Mercury. The monitor ship will await us when we emerge, if we emerge, from the sun. That Big Dipper has been in the sun also, as I told you."

There were a few seconds of silence. Then, amidst the notes of the music, a reverberating "ping" sounded. Adam and Eve looked at each other, nodding a little. They knew that not even the most remote and dead planet was closer to the sun than they were now.

The lightning discharge from the ship's bottom was furious, the streaks reaching away from the Little Dipper many yards into space.

Suddenly the entire hull became opaque and nothing outside could be seen.

"We must be entirely protected now," Eve said. "In fact, the hull of our craft will become more opaque as we approach the sun. Look, even now the sun makes its outline in front of us. It penetrates the hull. Oh, Adam, this is the moment. I am, after all, only a woman; I must lean on you spiritually. Hold your courage, and know that from now on you have no mortal peer in the cosmos. Know that in God's plan and in God's eyes you are my strength. Now," she said, pushing a button gently, "our seats are on swivel so we may turn in all directions, for in the sun we have no control over the Little Dipper. It may be spun like a top, but we will remain erect."

As she spoke, catapulting Adam into a new estate, the music became distorted. Suddenly it became a mere jumble, then a constant humming static. The radio waves were a torrent of noise, steady and angry. Adam took all these developments without loss of poise. Adam the primitive now felt himself Adam the master.

Yes, now he was aware of the fact that all other mates and partners were east of the sun, and soon he and Eve would be one, fused by its fire into perfect love, into perfect oneness.

Only in the bowels of the sun can man and woman be merged into soulmates, which nothing can rend asunder. West of the sun is all manner of aspiring evolution. West of the sun is the fusion of perfection, known only by the highest beings, swarming majestically around the Fatherhead. Yes, now he knew. He knew not from what he had fallen, but he knew to what he must aspire.

As he thought these things, Adam's face became the countenance of a god, and sitting beside him, snuggling closer and closer, was truly a goddess. Fear? Apprehension? What were these? He no longer knew such immature emotions.

The interior of the ship began to flicker, like sheet lightning. It grew more rapid. The hum which was once music became mixed with a faint roar. The disc of the sun now engraved itself fully across the entire front of the Little Dipper. Yes, they were approaching the sun. If he could look at it he would see it fill all the space in front of him: It was no longer a disc, big or small, but an endless, bubbling ocean of seething energy.

The flickering lightning became rapid vibration. Adam knew that the Little Dipper was adjusting itself to the intense energy. The first six layers of its hull were perfect light and heat reflectors, giving all back from whence it came. Other layers took care of kinetic energy and photonic bombardments, converting these into electrical form and discharging them. The discharges around the

SON OF THE SUN: The Secret Of The Saucers

Little Dipper now reached out more than a mile. Adam was as much in love with this superb ship as he had ever been with anything or anyone. He felt that matter was becoming spirit in the Little Dipper, but somehow all his feeling of this kind of love was sublimated to Eve. He loved her in a vastness far beyond his control. Truly he was fused in oneness with her.

The roar became louder.

"We have just penetrated the sun's corona, Adam," Eve told him, her self-control having quieted her emotions somewhat. As the ship's molecular structure adjusted to the intensity of the radiation, the flickering inside became so rapid it seemed almost too fast to be seen with the eye. At the same time, the craft was slowing down rapidly. All at once there was no more flickering, and they felt a slight jolt. The roaring became like that heard at the foot of Niagara Falls.

They had penetrated the surface of the sun and already were miles within its mass. The ship hummed in its meeting with the sun's resistance. The Little Dipper could withstand the enormous friction, but the fire of the sun was another matter. They were swallowed up in an inferno that would make the hottest steel furnace frigid in comparison. Eve reached down by her side and brought out two pairs of dark glasses, attached to platinum-like wires.

"Put these on, Adam," she directed, handing him one of the pairs. "Soon the intensity of the sun's interior will penetrate the ship, and our eyes cannot stand it. These will shield you from the light. They are grounded with wires so converted energy will be drained away."

It was none too soon. The glasses, jet black in color, were put on at the moment the light began to penetrate the Little Dipper. They were now submerged deep into the very body of the sun. Adam forgot there was such a place as earth, or that there were any beings other than Eve and himself. To be here with her was more than an experience. Without her it would be an intolerable inferno, with her it was the taste of Paradise. He was tasting love untarnished, love inviolable.

All around them was something without form, one essence extracted from both, the state of limbo and the state of Paradise. The best and the worst became one mass of light. Eve gave to Adam the precipitated essence of loving life. Now he knew why no man could make such a trip without a mate.

The Little Dipper came to a terrifying, grinding stop. The roar was deafening, the heat almost unbearable. Adam and Eve perspired freely. He looked to her for some explanation, but she was prostrate, her head resting on his shoulder. He was suddenly alone.

Adam could have screamed out for mercy, but the roar would have drowned his voice even to his own ears. Yet something amid all this, perhaps audible or perhaps just his own ultimate energy, seemed to be saying, "Fear not, for I am with you."

The ship throbbed and crackled as if it would soon be crushed, then he noticed the hull was revolving. Eve had told him it might spin, though true to her assurance, their seats did not. It sounded as if the ship had already been crushed, and he imagined he could feel the heat and the sides closing in upon him.

Oh, why had he ever brought himself here? Who created all this infinite fury? Why doesn't Eve awaken? Why . . . why . . . "Fear not, Adam, for I am with you."

How could such words be coming intact into this smashing holocaust? Even radio waves no longer existed here. He wanted out! Eve breathed a sigh, which he felt but did not hear. She was mercifully oblivious to the infinite furnace around them.

Thank God, she was in deep slumber, and the maelstrom was not getting any worse. Adam felt a push on his body. What was it? The force of the sun's core was now pushing the ship away. It could go no deeper and, entirely subject to the force of the sun, was being ejected backward. Backward. Backward, thank God! Adam could hardly wait.

Like an abating storm the surrounding fury repeated its effects, this time in reverse. Another few seconds and the Little Dipper would once more be master of the situation. What a ship! What a majestic product of man, of the Universe, Adam began to reflect. Once more he was a human being, capable of thinking. Yes, he was sure they were on their way out. "They?" He and Eve? Was he conscious again of her presence? Her beautiful head still rested on his shoulder. The fury around him was no longer terrifying, for he was certain that the ship was rapidly being forced outward. Ah, even in this sweltering heat, life was once more indescribably wonderful! Eve would soon awaken, to be enchantingly at his side. The motion backward accelerated almost violently. Minutes went by and the indescribable cascade became understandable turbulence again. Gradually the ship's hull began to stop spinning.

There were some grinding, jolting sensations, through which the state of just being was like a rebirth. The automatic controls had begun to assert themselves once more.

Eve moved her head and sighed convulsively. She opened her eyes, and Adam's delight knew no bounds. They were safe. They had made it. Now they had no more than the mere fury of the sun's lesser madness and turbulence to deal with, but the Little Dipper was more than equal to this area. In silence Adam and Eve looked at each other, loving in a oneness that was indivisible.

The heat abated, and they no longer perspired. The roar of a million Niagaras remained like a constant challenge to their nervous systems and made conversation impossible, but the worst was definitely over. They had rocketed into the sun at a thousand times the speed of a fast bullet, and were now being ejected by a force within the sun which accelerated the Little Dipper to the same dizzy velocity, much like a volcano spews out molten rock and metal.

Adam and Eve kept on looking into each other's eyes, enraptured with the awareness that each was the only living companion the other had in this ultimate of physical experiences. Then, at a velocity almost equal to that of a solar prominence, they were flung out into the coronal halo of Old Sol.

Once more the Little Dipper was operating in the orientation of its own automatic controls, and the maelstrom of sound and fury around them died out like a flash storm in the summer.

Conversation was again possible. As they looked searchingly at one another, Adam was the first to speak.

"You knew what such a trip could be like, Eve, and you volunteered to go into it with me? Was it a form of madness, or your desire?" he asked.

"I would do it over and over again, Adam, if it served to teach or to unfold someone, but never just for the adventure of it," Eve answered him.

"I learned the vast distance between you Alpha Centaurians and myself in the scale of cosmic evolution, yet you have shown me that within myself is something that overtakes you as a woman. I could not have known what endurance I had except in that ultimate test within the star, my sun. I ascended because you descended, yet it was not ascension or descension in their literal sense but a bringing out of the man and the woman. Thank you, Eve. Thanks a million times over."

"You have learned, Adam. But I am still a woman, and we are still in the fusing glow of your sun. My emotions, usually calm and oriented, are swirling. Let me ask you," she said, seriously, "if you were given the choice to be with any of the women who have awakened you into that kind of love for the remainder of your life, which would you select? Remember, there is lovely Vega, devastating Launie, and me. Any one of us, to spend the rest of your living days with you."

As she finished saying this, she drew herself up in her chair, removed her glasses and moved about subtly, so all her physical beauty was accentuated and merged hauntingly with her spiritual fineness.

Adam removed his own glasses. He looked at Eve in complete absorption. Her exotic presence lent perfume to the air he breathed. He reached into his soul to garner its message. Then he answered her, thoughtfully, "I would select Dora."

"Why?" she asked, as though seeking a new wisdom.

"Because she also is a woman. I find that I love her, and I have so much to teach her, she has so much to teach me. Also, she needs me and I need her. She is of my own earth, and the matter that composes her also composes me. We are formative spirits on each other's level, physically equal. I would have nothing to say to your women; only to listen. I have much to say to Dora, who will listen and rejoice to my presence and my words. You and yours have the love of pure learning. We have yet to develop that on our earth.

"Eve," he continued, speaking slowly, "I loved you in the sun as I can barely remember now, nor repeat again outside of it. I love you so much at this moment that I could leave you and not miss you, knowing you also have loved me equally.

SON OF THE SUN: The Secret Of The Saucers

It is strange but true. I have learned."

"Yes, you have learned," she replied, "and I also have learned. I have learned what it is for a peeress of the Alpha Centaurians to feel somewhat inferior to an earthman. It is an experience which I can best describe in one word, 'delicious.' However, our slowest men, any one of them, would have been just a little more than your equal in the sun."

At that moment the nondescript humming of the radio system in the craft became jumbled static. Then the familiar resonant "ping" sounded.

"Adam!" exclaimed Eve. "We have just crossed the orbit of Mercury again. Oh, glory to life and living! Listen, listen. The noise becomes music again. Do you recognize the selection? It is from your own earth."

Indeed he recognized it, in spite of its splendor of arrangement. Of course he knew it! It was "La Vien Rose."

The Little Dipper was again ruler of her own destiny. She zoomed on, "east of the sun," and the hull became transparent. Off to the left and slightly above, the monitor ship seemed to remain motionless, yet both crafts were darting at millions of miles per hour, speeding homeward. One's home base being the atmosphere of Venus, the other one headed to bring an earthman to his home planet. The music swelled throughout the interior of the Little Dipper.

"Eve," Adam bolted, "how far were we into the sun?"

"Fifty thousand miles," she replied. "We could not go deeper."

"Fine!" Adam shot back. "Now, then, if any light ray is ultimate heat and the core of the sun is merely a mass of light, what is the measure of that heat in Centigrade or Fahrenheit degrees?"

Calmly, Eve answered him. "It is measured in this way. The wave length multiplied by the frequency, multiplied by the mass in photons, multiplied by the speed of light." That was all Eve would say.

Adam comprehended her at once. He had imagined it was that. It was a computation well within the functions of the quantum theory and the theory of relativity combined. Furthermore, it was so basic, so primary, so fundamental, that from that point on any good mathematician could give earth-men what the Centaurians had.

But why go into such things in the splendor of the space around him, the stars suspended like spheres, the Big Dipper escorting the Little Dipper homeward, and Eve beauteously beside him?

She touched a button and a section of the Little Dipper's hull converted into television. The interior of the Big Dipper ship was fully seen in three-dimensional scope. Among the crew was one who looked concerned, yet reverently thankful. His eyes moved from Eve to Adam constantly.

"He is Enados," Eve said to Adam, as she looked at the image in arrested rapture. "He is my mate, and the leader of the crew of the Big Dipper. But for them, we could not have made the trip we just completed. See how happy they are that we have emerged safely? Are they not like children? Their knowledge makes them appreciative of everything, thus they rise from childhood, and learn and learn. When they have learned enough, as children they become, but with knowledge. A child knows by natural intuition, and learning merely confirms his intuition. Has this not already been taught to your people by the illumined ones and by the scientific ones as well? But your people must learn to put it into practice. It is the only lasting truth. Yes, Adam, that is why you chose Dora. Because through her you once more become the physician you were, physician to her body and physician to her spirit. You will find awaiting you all that is yours."

The music stopped and there was a momentary silence. Eve looked up toward the Big Dipper ship. Then, turning to Adam, she said, "Watch. They will put on a demonstration for you."

There was music again and life came into motion all around them, with the thrilling background an abyss of star-studded wonderment.

Adam and Eve laughed. They laughed like children as the Big Dipper veered leftward and began to perform. She weaved from side to side at millions of miles per hour, and rolled over and around, like a colt in the grass. She zoomed up and zoomed back down. She changed colors gracefully to the tune of music. Now flashes of lightning darted from her hull, now she became a mass of flaming glory, color merging into color. Adam felt sure she was burning herself up and would be expended in a burst of light, but she merely expanded her darting streaks of lightning and billowed out the colorful flame which enveloped her. The Big Dipper had become like a living artist, performing her graceful antics in the void of interstellar space. It was done as she traveled close to fifty million miles per hour. Every maneuver, every twist and turn, had consumed hundreds of miles, though the occupants of the Big Dipper experienced no more than slight sensation of movement.

Jokingly, Adam said to Eve, "Now I can say that I have seen a 'flying saucer.' And won't my own people look askance when I tell them! 'Yes, Adam has finally snapped,' they will say."

"No, Adam," she consoled him. "You will not know that feeling. You have not much time on earth. The one you shall tell it to will wince a little, but he will recognize the validity of what you say. It will be he who will gladly take on the consequent reactions."

She gave Adam a little time to digest what she had said, then she took a small box from the side of her seat and gave it to him.

"Here are some pellets. They make a nectar when put in water. Use them only as needed, and use them wisely. You will get no more of them."

He took them and placed them in his pocket. Then, turning to Eve, he asked her simply, "Tell me, if Enados is the true Centaurian name of your mate, how would we say it on earth?''

"Well, on earth the equivalent would simply be Adam."

He nodded his head in musing comprehension. "Bon sonado, bon sonado," he said.

"Look, Adam! Look! There it is, and there it goes," exclaimed Eve. "That was Venus!"

Tears came into his eyes as the sight and name of Venus recalled vivid memories. He clearly recalled all that had happened there, and he could see her so plainly, elusive, captivating, childlike, yet so understanding. Enchanting, yet careful to become relegated to the forgotten. He smiled broadly as the tears streamed down his cheeks. Launie. Was she real? Launie. Did she still think of him? Could he recapture Launie in the person of Dora? Yes, and more than that, he could hold Dora, kiss her, and make her his very own. Could he forget Eve? Surely he could. Dora and he would be Adam and Eve.

Once more he looked up toward the Big Dipper. It had assumed its motionless semblance again, escorting the Little Dipper. It was like a cruiser escorting a small launch.

Then, one of the larger spheres suspended there in space became larger and larger. A nearby orb also grew. They were the earth and the moon, being rapidly approached by the Little Dipper.

"Here, Adam," Eve said, handing him a capsule. "Take this."

He complied with her request and sat back again in confidence. She had tears in her eyes, for she, a peeress, had found she was not first place in the choice of a primitive earth-man. From her world Adam would still select Launie.

When he had swallowed the capsule she asked him what number he wanted to hear. "I would hear again Siboney," he said.

Eve looked up toward the mother ship, the Big Dipper, and the strains of Siboney filled the Little Dipper, the magnificent little craft that had challenged the sun.

The capsule took effect at once and Adam was sleepy. Before him in the hull of the ship, the music of Siboney produced a beauty who danced to it. As consciousness slowly left Adam, he watched her move to the familiar rhythms. As lovely as ever, as poignant on film as she was in person, Launie danced on, her exotic face and eyes angelically lulling Adam into blissful sleep.

Chapter 14
ADAM SAYS GOODBYE

Adam woke into just another desert morning, the sun already shining its brilliance upon the earth. He was alone in his little rented cabin. He felt as though he had awakened from a living dream which now insisted on being continued into his conscious state. All through the day it drenched his consciousness, as water drenches cloth.

It was a day named Friday in a month called December, but to Adam it was just part of earth's rotation basking in the face of the sun. There should be order and perfection, like symmetrical and desirable weather conditions, but the presence of high mountains upset this possibility. People should be aware of the grandeur in which they were immersed and which swirled majestically about them. But they were far more aware of the little things that faced them, like making the next hour of time productive of another dollar.

Amid the perfect order of the cosmos, Adam saw the riotous state which ignorance had nurtured. Mountains caused storms, and mountains of ignorance caused havoc between his earth brothers. In the blindness of such ignorance, people even took each other's lives; yes, took lives that required so much of the Creator to put into being. He had to divest himself of such enlightened vistas for all around him the best of earth was as yet a wilderness, and his best of friends could turn at any moment into crucifying maniacs.

    * * *

Came the sunset. As it slowly went beneath the horizon, he was left alone once more in the lonely exile of earth's wilderness. He was hungry, but it was not only for food. He wanted something to eat, true enough, but he also longed for companionship that would understand him, someone to whom he could pour out his soul before he should depart for Seattle to claim his own. Gentle Dora, his love, was not as yet prepared to receive the story he had to tell.

Tiny's Cafe, in the heart of Twentynine Palms, seemed to call out to him for this evening's meal. Big and kindly Tiny, moving about in his cafe, would be the best person for Adam to be near this evening.

That is how Adam came to be sitting alone on a Friday evening at a table with three glasses beside him. That is how he knew I would come in, for he had put his hand into his pocket and had found the pellets of solidified nectar. So, he knew he did not dream, because the pellets performed like miraculous things.

Thus I learned why Adam and I had met. There was now nothing left of his story. It was nearly dawn again, and this would be Monday morning, but I was surely not going to work. I resigned myself to a day of relaxed comfort, and asked Adam to stay until sunrise. We would talk casually and iron out some things in the story. Adam agreed, and we turned on the radio to receive any relaxation it had to offer in these wee hours of the day. I brewed some fresh coffee.

"Well, Orfeo," Adam sighed, "there you have it as it happened. Now I should make out a check," he added, taking a small check book from his pocket. "Let me see; what was it I said you could have? I think it was ten thousand dollars, wasn't it?"

"Yes," I replied. "But wait until I swallow hard, Adam, and digest that huge number for awhile. I am a poor mathematician and such hard realities as figures stagger me, but the call of that much money is irresistible music, not a problem in addition."

"Don't worry, Orfeo. I have sent Dora what she needs, as you know by now. I can well afford that amount for you and, would never miss it. The main thing now is, do you wish to accept it?"

I walked over to him, leaving the coffee percolating. "No, Adam; I do not wish to accept it under your terms."

"But I have not stated any hard terms, Orfeo. Just some conditions, such as writing the story I told you, and believing it. Is that too harsh a bargain?" he asked me.

"If I am to carry it out, Adam, it is not harsh, but let us say that it is difficult. If I did not carry it out, my conscience would slowly wilt me inside. Whichever I do, the money would stifle me. But," I pursued, "let me ask you something. Did you accept Saturn's offer to cure you when you knew he could, and when he extended the gift of such a cure to you?"

"You are a scholar and a philosopher, Orfeo," he slowly answered. "No, I did not accept it and I would not now accept it. Nature has a Divine plan whose vastness is far greater than any riches, and far more meaningful than my limited self. Were I to have accepted his offer, I would be alive but not living, and in a few years I would have to face once again the prospect of going, this time in fear. I do not want fear."

"Well," I replied, "I feel the same toward your offer. Give your small riches where they belong. I have my riches. These three nights cannot be purchased with money. Your story is in my hands. If I cannot write it, I have lost nothing. If I am ever up to writing it, the satisfaction and comfort it can bring me will far exceed what you offer and it will be with a clear conscience that I get what I get. I must face my wife, my sons, my friends, and the world, Adam, and I want to face them for what I am. You have revealed to me a mine of endless wealth. I do not want to lock the doors to it with a mere ten thousand dollars. I would give that

SON OF THE SUN: The Secret Of The Saucers

much just to see Launie dance in the glass once more. I really would."

We drank our coffee in silence. Adam was in wistful memories at the mention of her name but he remained quiet. The dawn was now bright morning, with a full sun in the east.

"Just look at that clear sun, Adam," I said, breaking the long silence. "I'll bet Earl saw nothing like that in Seattle. He should be back any minute. He was due back yesterday, in fact."

Adam looked into space. "Yes, Seattle," he said. "I must go back to Seattle. Dora is in cloudy skies. I shall brighten them like the sun for her, and she for me. Ah, yes. You may not believe my story, Orfeo, but you can believe Dora is in Seattle, and that's where I should be. I can hardly wait to go to her. I wonder, do you think she will be as happy as I think she will?"

"No," I answered him. "I believe she will be much happier than you think she will. If not, she will be the loser, not you. One thing you must bear in mind is that no matter how she takes it and no matter how you feel when you see her, no two people on earth have ever experienced any more poignant affection and love than Dora and you will be experiencing in that moment. Take her in your arms, Adam, and let come what may. Stay with her until she cries for joy. Then you will really know what it is to be one instead of two. Did not your hosts tell you of her straits, and how she longs to see you just once more?"

"Yes, indeed, Orfeo. But I am in the process of waking from another world as yet, and I cannot recall at this moment if it was all real or if it was a prolonged dream," he demurred.

"Adam," I said. "Do you not feel relieved in having told me your so-called dream? Was it not weighing upon you until you should tell someone who would understand? Do you not now feel pleasantly divested of a heavy burden? Well, I am sure you feel all these things. When the nectar fully wears off and when you feel secure in having deposited this story with me you will come face to face with the reality of it all. With many who have visions and dreams which make their life much more meaningful, we find that the vision or dream is but the conscious embodiment of many facts which had been forgotten until the vision wrested them from the buried storehouse of the subconscious. The vision and the dream then fade, going back into the vault whence they came. It is such a phase that you are in now.

"You can rest assured," I continued, "that I will put your story down in some form, and that I will tell the essentials of it as best I can. But to write it as a story just as you told me, Adam, that is a task for one with talent. You see, I am not a professional writer."

Adam came to life, and in gentle reprimand said, "Don't ever say that again, Orfeo! You have a complex. Get rid of, it this very instant!" For a moment he looked into my eyes with understanding, but also with stern authority. Then he added:

SON OF THE SUN: The Secret Of The Saucers

"We have enough professional writers. They are doing more to retrogress the world than to help it progress. Only a handful can be thanked for constructive and progressive works, and remember your simplicity, your freshness in the field of writing will lend my story more strength and beauty than the professional touch ever could. Truth, remember, from the mouths of babes? Libraries are filled with high-sounding philosophies. What have they accomplished so far? Where does any philosophy lead except back to the pure intuition of childlike souls? If it does not lead back to that, then it is false. It may sound big, but after awhile it curdles the soul and is automatically rejected. Furthermore, who but you would listen to my story at this time, let alone write it?"

"Adam, it will be as you say. I will write it when I feel capable. But tell me," I added in puzzlement, "why are you so concerned about a world in which you will no longer be? I know you are aware of this, and you are no longer afraid, but why such an intense concern? I should like to write all the facts, including that, if and when I do."

"I do not know why," he said, half to himself. "But as a physician I know and have seen quite a few men and women attain a noble stature when they became resigned to fate. They did not seem to look into the end, but rather into a beginning. This was so whether they were church members or atheists. They became more concerned with the destiny of earth than they had ever been before. The wisdom of the doomed is such that it cannot be told or written. Of that I am sure. But you ask me why? I ask you the same. Why?

"You will find, Orfeo," he continued, "that man has learned quite a bit in regard to the questions, What, Where, When, How, but to that one question, 'Why?', there is not yet a glimmer of a reply. Some day, perhaps ages from now, we shall have answered the first four questions. Indeed, they are the only ones man probes. When they have been unveiled, the biggest question of all,

'Why?', will stand before us as broad as infinity.

"No, I am no more doomed than anyone else. We live on and on in birth and rebirth. We must keep spiraling upward or remain in the dark. Nature itself demands our upward climb, and if we cannot attribute intelligence to Nature, then it must be an innate urge guided by a Supreme Intelligent Power. Heaven is inherent within earth. It is hidden behind many veils. We have hardly begun to remove one of them as yet," he said, receding into calm reverie. Then he added slowly, as if speaking to an unseen being, "I wonder how many veils the Alpha Centaurians have removed."

The rising sun lighted up the desert. For the third time Adam and I beheld the coming dawn as the desert began to glow through our windows. With the reality of rock and sand all around us, Adam found himself not only at the end of his story but at the beginning of his own awakening between two worlds. One was under his feet, in the air all around him, the other sunken like the ended night into the quicksands of elusive memory. Which was more real? Which world was more important? These questions were going to be with him as long as he lived, be it seven months or seven centuries.

The world in which he lived now was a pageantry of evolution never ceasing. The other world was similar, but its form of evolution seemed to be less complex and given to deeper searchings. Yes, the other world was something for earth men to aspire to. Adam, having spent seven short days in a small view of it, was no longer adapted to his normal function on earth. How could he go back to his profession? The glory of the future pervaded his whole being like a Divine essence and he wanted to savor of it every moment. He could see the potential for his own earth, but it would take much time and billions of people to bring this spacial globe into alignment with such beauty. But it did not seem impossible. The faith within him had converted Adam the mortal, into Adam the angel.

* * *

Perhaps untold time awaits earth's reaching the perfect state, but what is time to the Eternal One? Only the state of nearperfection will bring man face to face with the greatest and final question, "Why?" with some promise of at last knowing the answer.

It became 9:00 o'clock far sooner than it normally should have, for I was unconscious to the passing of time. Adam had to say goodbye. I watched him drive off toward town, a mile and a half to the south. The realization that he was leaving for good shocked me into wanting to call him back. Suddenly I had so much more to say to him, or rather to ask of him. There was an emptiness within me that had no bounds as I watched his car go on down the road, climb the hill, then disappear forever down the other side. He had never told me where his cabin was and it would have done little good if he had, because Adam's car was ready for its journey to Seattle. I knew I would never see him again. Even so, I felt alive with a story that not only filled me with a new kind of awareness, but was big enough to be told to the four corners of the world. My life had somehow been doubled in scope.

I kept looking at the top of the hill over which Adam's car had just faded from view, and I could only think to myself these words:

So long, Adam! Happiness to you, Dora! Yes, Dora, happiness to you! Adam and you will find the dawn of happiness at a milestone where so many others find an end to theirs. I saw a thread of truth in the fabric of existence, a thread which weaves quietly but strongly into the entire pattern, where those who turn the page of life pass the thread and the torch into the hands of others. This thread shall eventually become the whole fabric and the torch shall become like the sun.

Indeed, one person alone, with the true vision, could redeem a whole world though only the vision and a few seconds merged together. Because Adam was, the earth shall be; that is, it shall become what it can be, as the attained ones of another world watch and wait.

SON OF THE SUN